AF361492

REMAKING EUROPEAN POLITICAL ECONOMIES

European Union Studies

European Union Studies features the latest research on topics in European integration in the widest sense, including Europe's role as a regional and international actor. This interdisciplinary series publishes the research of Canadian and international scholars and aims at attracting scholars working in various disciplines such as economics, history, law, political science, and sociology. The series is made possible in part by a generous grant from the European Commission.

The first series of its kind in Canada, and one of only a few in North America, *European Union Studies* is unique in looking at the EU "from the outside," making sense not only of European integration but also of the role of the European Union as an international actor.

GENERAL EDITORS:

Randall Hansen
Professor of Political Science
Munk School of Global Affairs & Public Policy
University of Toronto

Amy Verdun
Professor of Political Science
Founding Director, European Studies Program
University of Victoria

For a list of books published in the series, see page 279.

DENNIS ZAGERMANN

Remaking European Political Economies

Financial Assistance in the Euro Crisis

UNIVERSITY OF TORONTO PRESS
Toronto Buffalo London

© University of Toronto Press 2024
Toronto Buffalo London
utorontopress.com
Printed in Canada

ISBN 978-1-4875-4903-9 (cloth)   ISBN 978-1-4875-5228-2 (EPUB)
                                  ISBN 978-1-4875-5063-9 (PDF)

European Union Studies

Library and Archives Canada Cataloguing in Publication

Title: Remaking European political economies : financial assistance in the Euro crisis /
    Dennis Zagermann.
Names: Zagermann, Dennis, author.
Series: European Union studies.
Description: Series statement: European Union studies | Includes bibliographical
    references and index.
Identifiers: Canadiana (print) 20230502156 | Canadiana (ebook) 20230502237 |
    ISBN 9781487549039 (cloth) | ISBN 9781487552282 (EPUB) | ISBN 9781487550639 (PDF)
Subjects: LCSH: Economic assistance, European – Greece – Case studies. |
    LCSH: Economic assistance, European – Ireland – Case studies. | LCSH: European
    Stability Mechanism – Case studies. | LCSH: Economic and Monetary Union –
    Case studies. | LCSH: Greece – Economic policy – Case studies. | LCSH: Ireland –
    Economic policy – Case studies. | LCSH: Financial crises – Greece – Case studies. |
    LCSH: Financial crises – Ireland – Case studies. | LCGFT: Case studies.
Classification: LCC HC240.25.G8 Z34 2024 | DDC 338.91/40495 – dc23

Cover design: Hannah Gaskamp
Cover image: artGALINI/Shutterstock.com

University of Toronto Press acknowledges the financial support of the Government of
Canada, the Canada Council for the Arts, and the Ontario Arts Council, an agency of
the Government of Ontario, for its publishing activities.

Yo [Julia], I did it![1]

Contents

Tables and Figures

Tables

Figures

Acknowledgments

I started studying political science in 2008, a few weeks after Lehman Brothers went bankrupt. The global financial crisis and the subsequent euro crisis accompanied me during my entire studies. Trying to understand the crisis-related political and economic developments was of key interest to me as a student. I first had the idea to research the euro crisis and its effects on the political economies of euro area members most affected by the crisis in 2013/14. This book is the product of that research focus. Writing a book takes a lot of time, of course. Over this long period of time, I was very fortunate to have my work supported and discussed by several people.

I would like to express my sincere and eternal gratitude to Ulrike Liebert. Thank you for your continuous support of my research, for your patience, motivation, and immense knowledge. Your guidance helped me during this long time of research and writing the book. I could not have imagined having a better advisor and mentor. Thank you, Ulrike.

I would like to thank Amy Verdun for her support of this project. Thank you, Amy, for your guidance and highly appreciated support. Without your renowned expertise in European political economy research, your highly knowledgeable input, and constructive criticism, this book would not have been possible. Your interest in my research gave me the confidence to finish this project. Thank you, Amy.

Throughout the years, several colleagues engaged with my work and shared valuable and much-appreciated insights. I would like to thank my fellow participants at the CEuS research seminar, in particular Stefan Wallaschek, Esther Somfalvy, Anders Hentschel, and Angelika Schenk, my former CEuS colleagues Janna Wolff, Tatjana Evas, Anne Jenichen, Henrike Müller, and Katrin Dorow, as well as my EUROSEM colleagues Valerie D'Erman, Daniel Schulz-Bianco, and Paul Schure.

I am deeply grateful for the editorial team at University of Toronto Press. I was very lucky that Daniel Quinlan took on my book proposal and advised me during the publication process. He and two anonymous reviewers provided me with much-appreciated and highly constructive feedback. I am thankful for their critical engagement with the manuscript and the very useful comments on improving the book. I would also thank Perrin Lindelauf for his excellent copy-editing during the publication process and Carol Ross for her language editing at earlier stages.

Julia and I first met during the early stages of my time as a PhD candidate. Thank you for your enormous love and support during all these years, during the good and bad times, for being there when I was unsure about my research, for sharing my accomplishments with me, for supporting me when I had to work late, on the weekends, or had to travel for research, and for being the best partner that I could think of.

I am grateful for the support of my family. Coming from a working-class background certainly comes with its own difficulties in academia. Nonetheless, my family always encouraged me to pursue this route and supported me when I needed them. Thank you, Mama, Papa, and Lisa.

During the work on this project, my friends certainly saw very little of me. Thank you, Ole, Zoran, Sandra, Benny, Sabrina, Stefan, and Suki for your friendship. Thank you, Christina, for making trips to the library less lonely and certainly more fun when I moved back to Hamburg, and for becoming a very good friend. I do not take it for granted and see myself as very lucky to have all of you in my life.

This work was supported in part by a Jean Monnet Network entitled "The Politics of the European Semester: EU Coordination and Domestic Political Institutions (EUROSEM)" Agreement number: 600110-EPP-1-2018-1-CA-EPPJMO-NETWORK (Grant agreement nr 2018-1359), with the support of the Erasmus+ programme of the European Union.

Abbreviations

AIB	Anglo Irish Bank
ALMP	Active Labour Market Policy
AMECO	Annual Macro-Economic Database of the European Commission's Directorate General for Economic and Financial Affairs
ANEL	Independent Greeks – National Patriotic Alliance
CME	Coordinated Market Economy
COFOG	Classification of Function of Government
CPE	Comparative Political Economy
DG Finance	Directorate General for Economic and Financial Affairs
DI	Discursive Institutionalism
DV	Dependent Variable
EC	European Commission
ECB	European Central Bank
ECON	EP's Committee on Economic and Monetary Affairs
EDP	Excessive Deficit Procedure
EFSF	European Financial Stability Facility
EFSM	European Financial Stabilisation Mechanism
EGSEE	General National Collective Agreement
EIB	European Investment Bank
EMC	Economic Management Council
EMF	European Monetary Fund
EMU	Economic and Monetary Union
EP	European Parliament
EPL	Employment Protection Legislation
ERO	Employment Regulation Order
ESF	European Stability Fund
ESM	European Stability Mechanism
EU	European Union

EWG	Eurogroup Working Group
FDI	Foreign Direct Investment
GDP	Gross Domestic Product
GLF	Greek Loan Facility
GMI	Guaranteed Minimum Income Scheme
GSEE	General Confederation of Greek Workers
HCAP	Hellenic Corporation of Assets and Participations
HI	Historical Institutionalism
HRADF	Hellenic Republic Asset Development Fund
IAPR	Independent Authority for Public Revenue
Ibec	Irish Business and Employers Confederation
ICTU	Irish Congess of Trade Unions
ICTWSS	Institutional Characteristics of Trade Unions, Wage Setting, State Intervention and Social Pacts
IFAC	Irish Fiscal Advisory Council
ILO	International Labour Organisation
IMF	International Monetary Fund
ISME	Irish Small and Medium Enterprises
JA	Jobseeker's Allowance
JB	Jobseeker's Benefits
JLC	Joint Labour Committee
LABREF	Labour Market Reform Database of the European Commission
LME	Liberal Market Economy
LTU	Long-Term Unemployment
MEP	Member of the European Parliament
MFTA	Medium-Term Financial Assistance
MME	Mixed-Market Economy
MoU	Memorandum of Understanding
MTFS	Medium-Term Fiscal Strategy
ND	New Democracy
OECD	Organisation for Economic Co-operation and Development
OMED	Organisation for Mediation and Arbitration
PASOK	Panhellenic Socialist Movement
PBO	Parliamentary Budget Office
REA	Registered Employment Agreement
RI	Rational Choice Institutionalism
RRF	Recovery and Resilience Facility
SEO	Sectoral Employment Order
SEV	Hellenic Federation of Enterprises
SGP	Stability and Growth Pact

SOE	State-Owned Enterprise
SRF	Single Resolution Fund
SSI	Social Security Income
SYRIZA	Coalition of the Radical Left – Progressive Alliance
TFEU	Treaty on the Functioning of the European Union
TSCG	Treaty on Stability, Coordination and Governance in the Economic and Monetary Union
VoC	Varieties of Capitalism

REMAKING EUROPEAN POLITICAL ECONOMIES

Chapter One

Introduction

In 2019 the European Union celebrated *EURO at 20*, the twentieth anniversary of the euro as an accounting currency in combination with fixed exchange rates. Introducing a single currency was the final stage of building an Economic and Monetary Union (EMU) that was set out in the Delors Report of 1989 (Committee for the Study of Economic and Monetary Union 1989). Three years later, on 1 January 2002, the euro was introduced as a physical currency and replaced national currencies. From its beginning with eleven initial members in 1999, the euro area increased to nineteen members in 2019. Today, over 345 million European citizens share the euro as their single currency. Hence, EMU and the euro could very well be described as a success story.

However, *EURO at 20* also coincided with the tenth anniversary of the Greek government announcing severe fiscal difficulties in October 2009. Marking the starting point of what became the euro crisis, the Greek announcement gave an early insight into the existential political, economic, and institutional crises that EMU would experience in the following years. The euro crisis moved to the forefront when the global financial crisis of 2007–8 began to have severe fiscal effects on three of EMU's peripheral members (Tooze 2018, 322): Greece, Ireland, and Portugal developed unsustainable deficits as a result. Greece certainly was in a difficult fiscal situation as it entered the crisis and was exposed to foreign investors in sovereign debt markets. It also had a long-running history of socio-economic dysfunctionalities. Even though Greece was not as strongly affected by the banking crisis as other countries, the global economic development further increased unsustainable public and private deficits in the country and ultimately disclosed its economy's structural problems (Tooze 2018, 323). Ireland, by contrast, was exposed to the crisis early on, as its construction sector started to freeze up rapidly in 2007 with secondary effects on its banking sector and public finances. A guarantee of 440 billion euro for the Irish banking sector, announced on 30 September 2008, put additional fiscal burden on the government (Tooze 2018, 322).

The strained fiscal positions of the European periphery quickly transformed into a fast-paced struggle to secure the single currency (Tooze 2018, 322). The European Council and the Eurogroup, the two central intergovernmental EMU decision-making bodies, met almost every month with even more frequent critical communication between summits. These meetings in Brussels often went on all night to find solutions that would reduce pressure from financial markets on sovereign debt. Press conferences were frequently timed so as to present summit results before stock market exchanges opened their doors in order to regain the trust of financial markets and reduce interest rates on sovereign bonds. However, by 2012, European politics had become almost paralyzed by ever-increased yields on government bonds. Exit strategies from EMU became a realistic danger during this period. The possible risk of breaking up the euro area was frequently discussed in political and academic debates, as the Streeck/Habermas controversy illustrated (Habermas 2013; Streeck 2013b, 2013c).

A central strategy to cope with the euro crisis was the development of financial assistance programs for countries in severe fiscal stress. With no institutional architecture behind it, the first program was granted on an ad hoc basis, administered by the European Commission and the European Central Bank (ECB) in cooperation with the International Monetary Fund (IMF). These three institutions, quickly known as the Troika, became driving forces in drawing up and putting through policy conditionality programs associated with financial assistance. Furthermore, the euro area established institutions in order to organize financial assistance, to provide additional oversight for the adjustment process, and to engage in the transfer of tranches. The European Stability Mechanism (ESM), the latest developmental stage of these institutions, is a case in point for exploring the crisis management regime: on an intergovernmental basis it provides temporary financial assistance while requiring the receiving governments to implement macroeconomic adjustment programs. The programs are supervised by non-majoritarian, supranational institutions with little parliamentary influence (Verdun 2015).

In this financial assistance architecture, the ESM is not simply a treasury institution. While the IMF, the ECB, and the European Commission certainly have strong ownership of and agency in the financial assistance procedures, the ESM progressively increased its role in supervising programs and developing competences of its own while respecting the mandate of the European Commission. What is more, it is the only regional counterweight to the IMF that is fully functioning and has developed viable expertise (Ban 2020, 81). The reforms required by European financial assistance programs are supposed to lead to stable budgets and competitive national economies. Financial assistance programs during the euro crisis came with wide-ranging reform requirements for state budgets, labour markets, health care, product markets, and pension systems. The ESM, in cooperation with other institutions, has the ability to influence core economic institutions of member states in fiscal need.

Its potential capacity to influence political economies touches on a key question of comparative political economic research: Will European political economies converge over time due to external factors? This book therefore explores whether the ESM, as the permanent financing institution for financial assistance programs, has enabled political economic convergence of EMU members in fiscal need during the euro crisis. This research objective can be broken down further into the following questions: (1) How were political economic varieties within EMU affected by the establishment of the ESM? (2) What is the role played by ideas of political economic development in the single currency to explain convergence? (3) What was the impact of path dependence to explain persisting divergence between European economies receiving financial assistance programs?

The following sections will give this objective more substance by reviewing the current state of research, outlining the gap in the literature, and discussing the structure of the book. Section 1.1 focuses on why the euro area materialized and highlights broader political and economic developments. Section 1.2 provides a review of varieties of capitalism (VoC) literature concerned with converging and diverging tendencies in EMU. Section 1.3 reviews the current state of research on the establishment and role of the European Stability Mechanism. Section 1.4 provides a short interim conclusion on the state of research, identifies the gap in the literature this book aims at filling, and provides readers with an overview of the book.

1.1 Euro Area Crisis and EMU Governance

The euro crisis is a widely researched political and economic phenomenon. Research about the euro crisis particularly focuses on three aspects: first, the reasons for the outbreak of the crisis; second, policy paradigms for crisis management; and finally, reforms in EMU governance as a reaction to the crisis. In the initial years of the euro crisis, political economic research focused strongly on how and why the crisis had materialized. Two explanatory hypotheses can be identified: a fiscal hypothesis that focuses on fiscal profligacy or a competitiveness hypothesis that underlines the importance of macroeconomic imbalances (Johnston 2016, 12–21; see also Nölke 2016, 142).

The "fiscal position" (Johnston 2016, 12), as put forward by several scholars (e.g., Buiter and Rahbari 2010; Franz et al. 2010; Illing 2013; P. Lane 2012; Sinn 2014, 38–81), initially gained a lot of support as it matched the public assessment of the Greek crisis in 2009 and 2010[1] (Johnston 2016, 12) and fit well with the ordoliberal German economic discourse (Dullien and Guérot 2012). In this line of thought, the euro crisis developed primarily as a consequence of fiscal profligacy of Southern European countries in general. Greece was considered to be the prime example. Increased yields on sovereign bonds were thus seen as a consequence of higher risks for sovereign default (e.g. Franz et al. 2010, 102; see also Johnston 2016, 12-21 for an overview). According to this strand of research, EMU was considered to be in need of stronger fiscal surveillance mechanisms to prevent ever-increasing sovereign debt. The fiscal hypothesis stressed the necessity of structural adjustments primarily for countries with fiscal as well as current account deficits – despite social and political costs – and did not acknowledge that macroeconomic imbalances in EMU could also result from unequal developments in countries with current account surpluses.

Countering the fiscal hypothesis, several scholars highlighted that sovereign debt does not sufficiently explain why the euro crisis came about (Blyth 2013, 5–7). While Greece might have been an example of fiscal profligacy and socio-economic dysfunctionalities to a certain degree, this was not the case for other countries affected by the crisis (Johnston 2016, 12–13). In contrast to fiscal mismanagement, the "competitiveness position" (Johnston 2016, 15) underlines diverging socio-economic fundamentals as the explaining factor for the euro crisis (Johnston 2016, 15–16). Based on a descriptive socio-economic data analysis, Illing, Jauch, and Zabel argued that the euro crisis developed because of reversed capital flows after the global financial crisis and reduced competitiveness levels of the economies in the European periphery (Illing, Jauch, and Zabel 2012). Their research highlighted that reduced levels of competitiveness did not necessarily come from a lack of wage moderation. Rather, they resulted because of higher capital inflows in line with the Balassa–Samuelson effect and increased levels of productivity (Illing, Jauch, and Zabel 2012, 158).

Johnston prominently put a strong focus on diverging labour markets as the key explanatory factor for the euro crisis (Johnston 2016). According to Johnston's analysis, wage developments in sheltered sectors in Southern Europe produced higher inflation than in Northern Europe and resulted in competitiveness divergences. In turn, this led to large current account imbalances in EMU. Johnston highlighted that "EMU's current crisis […] is a direct consequence of structural flaws in the governance of labour markets that are present in EMU's institutional design" (Johnston 2016, 5). Johnston showed that EMU favoured member states with comparative advantages of corporatist labour market institutions, which allowed them to effectively moderate wages and keep inflation low (Johnston 2016, 42, 46–53; see also Johnston and Hancké 2009). Her analysis is shared by a larger number of economists and political scientists alike (e.g., Bofinger 2015; De Grauwe 2012; Hassel 2014; Lapavitsas and Flassbeck 2013; Lapavitsas and Kouvélakis 2012). Authors such as Peter A. Hall have underlined that, instead of fiscal profligacy, "many of the dilemmas stem from basic differences in the political economies of northern and southern Europe" (Hall 2014, 1226; see also Hancké 2013a; Iversen, Soskice, and Hope 2016; Iversen and Soskice 2018).

Wage developments thus played an important part in the development of the euro crisis. However, as Müller, Schulten, and Zuckerstätter (2016) argued, wage moderation alone does not automatically increase price competitiveness. Reducing competitiveness to price differentials limits our analytical scope and disregards other important variables. Instead, non-price competitiveness factors should be included in the analysis as well (Müller, Schulten, and Zuckerstätter 2016).

Related to how the single currency's crisis developed, political economic research has also put a lot of emphasis on the political and economic ideas that shaped crisis management. Brunnermeier, James, and Landau (2016) have identified a fundamental dispute between German ordoliberal and French interventionist traditions that became increasingly more relevant during the euro crisis. In their analysis, the Deauville meeting in October 2010 was central in this ideational conflict, as the German chancellor was able to put through most of her ordoliberal positions, demanding structural, pro-cyclical adjustments in countries with severe deficits while forestalling European fiscal instruments (Brunnermeier, James, and Landau 2016, 17–42).

This ordoliberal direction of the crisis management was not without contradiction. Rather, as several scholars have highlighted, the beginning of the global financial crisis saw European governments opting for anticyclical stimulus packages that were associated with Keynesian economic ideas (Blyth 2013, 54–6; see also Tooze 2018). However, the Greek announcement of 2009 changed the scenery and led to a paradigm shift (Blyth 2013, 59–64; see also Tooze 2018). Starting in 2010, members of the single currency began putting forward pro-cyclical adjustment packages, which were further institutionalized through financial assistance programs. As Galanos and Poufinas have illustrated, financial assistance programs in the euro area largely resemble structural adjustment programs employed by the IMF in the 1990s (Galanos and Poufinas 2018, 2; see also Greer 2014; Perez and Matsaganis 2018). According to several scholars, the paradigm put forward at this stage of the crisis was only revised to small degrees during the entire period, despite diverging economic experiences throughout the crisis (European Parliament 2014; Hall 2014). Some variation between the program countries has however become empirically visible (Hardiman et al. 2017). A change in policy preferences also arose during the outbreak of the COVID-19 crisis. Instead of focusing on immediate debt reduction, most European governments have opted for strong debt-financed stimulus packages. At the time of writing, the debt criteria of the Stability and Growth Pact are a key issue of the fiscal policy debate at the European level.

While a lot of research has been conducted on the influence of the programs on the member states' political economies, the role of national governments within the programs has been less researched. Moury et al. (2021) have shown that, despite existing implicit and explicit constraints, national governments were able to put forward policies and resist parts of the agenda of external actors. According to Moury et al., national governments were able to influence the policy agenda throughout the MoU process. The program countries' governments were, however, able to influence the policy agenda to different degrees (Moury et al. 2021, 146–63).

Competitiveness, debt ratios, and balanced budgets were key focus points of the euro crisis management. As Stützle has traced, balanced budgets were a central guiding principle on the path towards EMU starting in the 1970s. Their relevance and institutionalization were further advanced during the euro crisis (Stützle 2013). In line with the guiding principle of balanced budgets, lower levels of social protection and flexicurity programs were endorsed during this period – primarily for countries with financial assistance programs but also for other EMU members (Busch et al. 2012; Hermann 2014, 2017).

Some authors have argued that, based on these developments, political economies that rely on economic governance through markets can be regarded as role models for the policy conditionality attached to European financial assistance (e.g., Nölke 2016, 152). Erik Jones attributed this tendency to the persistence of the Brussels-Frankfurt Consensus, which, according to him, seeks to commit EMU members to fiscal discipline, low inflation, competitiveness, and an emphasis on market liberalization (Jones 2013, 146–51). These principles had shaped the

EU since the Maastricht Treaty and were still a dominant paradigm for EMU during this period (Regan 2017; Stützle 2013). As Peter A. Hall has argued, this market-based economic governance paradigm effectively expected EMU members to converge to models similar to itself (Hall 2014, 1225).

More recent research identifies smaller changes towards social investments (e.g., Crespy and Schmidt 2017). As D'Erman et al. (2019) have shown, EMU's political economies receive different kinds of recommendations in the European Semester (D'Erman et al. 2019, 202–5). Another study (D'Erman et al. 2022) revealed that recommendations are met by social partner dynamics that make implementation less easy. In this line of thought, Jones argues that small steps towards a new, more flexible economic paradigm are becoming visible (Jones 2013, 145). The European reaction to the COVID-19 pandemic, particularly NextGenerationEU (see 8.2), shows stronger steps in this direction at the time of writing.

Critical research inspired by Poulantzas, regulation theory, and neo-Gramscian approaches to European political economy analyse EMU's financial assistance architecture as part of a new crisis in constitutionalism in EMU and further advancements of neoliberal economic policies by dominant societal blocs (Bieling 2011, 2013; Bieling and Buhr 2015; Bieling and Guntrum 2019; Stützle 2013). Neo-Gramscian case studies, however, do not include the ESM and its predecessors as a key variable explaining socio-economic change (Chasoglou 2015; I. Kompsopoulos 2016; J. Kompsopoulos 2018; Lux and Kompsopoulos 2019).

The changing nature of economic paradigms has also been highlighted by scholars in terms of European economic governance. Verdun and Enderlein argued that a lot of the debate during EMU's initial years focused on its sustainability, as the single currency was lacking centralized governance mechanisms (Enderlein and Verdun 2009, 491). The purposely incomplete EMU framework, as Verdun analysed, "provided only weak coordination of fiscal policy and no obvious mechanism to facilitate macroeconomic adjustment within the member states" (Verdun 2013, 30; see also Jones, Keleman, and Meunier 2016, 1011; Tooze 2018, 98). Economic policies were not set at the EU level because of EMU's asymmetric governance framework (Enderlein and Verdun 2009, 498–9; see also Verdun 1996). Prior to the euro crisis, Schäfer described EMU governance as an institutional setting with a predominantly non-binding nature (Schäfer 2005). As Moses has shown, based on a comparative case study of Ireland, Iceland, Latvia, and Hungary, the monetary union in Europe has come with stronger ties on national policymaking (Moses 2017).

While the blame for the crisis was mostly put on deficit countries, it became clear that the single currency did not have instruments to cope with asymmetric fiscal and economic crises. EMU therefore underwent wide-ranging institutional redesigns through which the euro area has implemented several new instruments and rules. These range from new fiscal and economic governance mechanisms such as the European Semester, the Fiscal Compact, as well as intergovernmental financial capacities, such as the European Financial Stability Facility (EFSF) and ESM (Verdun 2015). The way EMU has gained more influence over national economies is a central research topic in post-crisis EMU research. The extent of its influence and its general direction, however, are up for debate. Authors such as Majone have portrayed EMU as a policy area with little parliamentarian influence (Majone 2014). Other authors, such as Genschel and Jachtenfuchs, have argued EMU to be a polity that has gained significant influence on core state powers, such as fiscal policy or public administration (Genschel and Jachtenfuchs 2015a, 2015b, 2018; see also Schelkle 2015). The new governance repertoire included in EMU has been described as contested (Jabko 2015) but is increasingly becoming more stable.

Verdun argued that, despite extensive reforms, EMU remains asymmetric (Verdun 2018, 4). Outside of the financial assistance programs, most socio-economic coordination takes place in the European Semester, which is described in the literature as an innovative form of European economic governance (Verdun 2018, 5; Verdun and Zeitlin 2018; Zeitlin and Vanhercke 2018) that informally gave the Commission more power over national policymaking processes. Compliance, however, varies across countries (Verdun 2018).

The strongest direct influence on socio-economic policy can be attributed to financial assistance programs. Several studies have focused on the influence of such programs on the countries' political economies in general (Blyth 2013; European Parliament 2014; Greer 2014; Hardiman et al. 2017; Kennedy 2018; Perez and Matsaganis 2018), with a country-specific focus (Brazys and Regan 2017; Dimoulas and Fouskas 2017; Donovan 2016; Featherstone 2011; Featherstone and Papadimitriou 2012, 2017; Gkasis 2018; Regan 2014; Roche, O'Connell, and Prothero 2017a), or with a focus on specific policy fields, such as labour markets (Hermann 2014, 2017; Kennedy 2016; Murphy and Mercille 2019; O'Connell 2017; Theodoropoulou 2015, 2018), fiscal policy (Armstrong 2013; Gabor and Ban 2012; Schlosser 2019), or the public sector (Hardiman and MacCarthaigh 2017; MacCarthaigh and Hardiman 2019; Spanou 2018, 2020).

1.2 Varieties of Capitalism: Trajectories of European Socio-economic Models

A second important strand of research focuses on differences between European economies as well as political economic trajectories of EMU. Varieties of Capitalism (VoC), as a central approach in this field of research, has generally assumed that institutional features of political economies remain stable despite exogenous factors (Hall and Soskice 2001). Some researchers have argued that there are indeed few signs of political economic convergence, despite broader changes in political economies (Schmidt 2002; Amable 2003; Crouch 2005; Beramendi et al. 2015). Other authors have critically argued that divergence in the euro area might even increase, as political and economic adjustments come with high costs (Sadeh 2006). In contrast, convergence theorists have long argued that political economies would converge into a market-based model of capitalism because of strong exogenous factors (Baccaro and Howell 2011, 2017a, 2017b; C. Lane 2006; Strange 1996). In the case of EMU, some scholars argue for a simultaneous development of divergence and convergence as a consequence of EMU incentives, Europeanization mechanisms, and strong national feedback loops (Schmidt 2002; Lütz 2004).

Empirical studies have put forward heterogenous results on converging or diverging trends in EMU. However, a majority of publications argues that, despite common trends, differences between EMU members remain visible (Hall 2007, 2012, 2014, 2018; Hassel 2014; Johnston 2016; Johnston, Hancké, and Pant 2014; Johnston and Regan 2016, 2018; Molina and Rhodes 2007; Regan 2014). As Andrea Herrmann (2005) argued, European wage-bargaining systems developed in different directions since the euro was adopted. While EMU certainly put similar adjustment pressures on national socio-economic institutions, it did not lead to similar results. Some countries have adjusted their wage-setting mechanisms to focus on coordination and higher centralization. Other countries have reacted to adjustment pressures from EMU with decentralization strategies. Herrmann's findings suggest that working to keep competitive advantages can provide an explanation for divergent adjustment strategies by EMU member states (Herrmann 2005, 307). However, Herrmann's analysis was carried out prior to the euro area crisis and not too long after the euro was adopted.

Hendrik Enderlein has argued that entering EMU put specific adjustment pressures on its member states and their ability to address economic conditions (Enderlein 2004). Due to the integration of monetary policy at the European Central Bank, additional adjustment pressure was put on fiscal and labour market policy. Drawing on several case studies, Enderlein found that a majority of EMU members reformed their fiscal and labour market policies with a focus on higher centralization in order to regain national governance capacities (Enderlein 2004, 189–94, see also Enderlein 2006).

As Uwe Becker has shown, not only were political economies in EMU comparatively stable between 1998 and 2008, they also developed heterogenous levels of competitiveness and diverse adjustment capacities. Becker concluded that countries with strong corporatist institutions were able to adjust to EMU, while Mediterranean countries lost competitiveness and were less able to cope with the change (Becker 2014; see also Becker 2009).

Not only was convergence of economic institutional settings expected by some scholars, countries were also expected to converge in terms of economic growth, current accounts, inflation, and employment numbers (Young and Semmler 2011, 10; see also Bearce 2009). However, based on descriptive socio-economic data, Bearce summarized that, prior to the euro crisis, EMU members showed higher standard derivation rates in terms of government consumption, inflation, and unemployment than non-EMU countries (Bearce 2009). Bearce's findings were supported by other publications on VoC and EMU (Hancké 2013a; Hall 2012, 2014, 2018; Hall and Gingerich 2004).

Other authors, most prominently Kathleen Thelen, have argued that liberalization is a common trend in all European political economies (Thelen 2012, 2014). According to Thelen, countries are adjusting in different ways to exogenous pressures, but all of them include some form of liberalization. She concludes that reconfigurations of more egalitarian forms of capitalism are necessary if their welfare systems are to be sustained. Drawing on empirical results from case studies on institutional changes in industrial relations, vocational training, and labour market policy, Thelen argues for a stronger analysis of the political coalitions and shifts in the political landscapes on which political economies are based, in order to understand their current trajectories of socio-economic adjustment (Thelen 2014, 193–207; 2012). Likewise, Bieling and Buhr argue that there is a common trend of deregulation and flexibilization in EMU labour markets as a result of the euro crisis. They underline that deregulation processes are heterogeneous and lead to different forms of liberalization (Bieling and Buhr 2015, 333–8).

Based on a study of labour market adjustments in Europe shortly after the sub-prime crisis, Lallement has argued that labour market reforms generally followed the trajectory of each country's variety of capitalism. Liberal, coordinated, and mixed-market economies, three ideal types of VoC, generally adjusted their labour markets according to their comparative institutional advantages (Lallement 2011). According to Lallement, their distinct differences remain viable, despite severe economic pressure due to the crisis and EMU adjustment pressures (Lallement 2011, 639). However, the adjustment periods after the global financial crisis were short and changes within the VoC models cannot be ruled out for the future (Lallement 2011, 639).

Contrary to this initial assessment by Lallement, Theodoropoulou (2018) was able to illustrate in an edited volume that there was a common trend in European labour markets as a consequence of the euro crisis. Welfare readjustments and flexicurity approaches were the most common developments. Countries that engaged in welfare reforms mainly focused on including activation policies in their labour market regimes and reduced levels of social protection. Other countries directly retrenched their welfare systems. The key driver, in almost all cases, has been fiscal pressure and budgetary restraints (Theodoropoulou 2018).

Based on similar assumptions, Nölke concluded that EMU provides economic advantages for coordinated market economies, "given their superior ability for wage moderation and their lower propensity to engage in financialization, overheating and real exchange overvaluation" (Nölke 2016, 156). Liberal market economies are able to adjust to EMU pressures due to their flexibility and lower reliance on the state for aggregate demand. However, as Nölke underlines, EMU potentially puts mixed-market economies into a precarious situation (Nölke 2016, 156; see also Hall 2018, 16). According to Schweiger, EMU's focus on market competition on the one side, and fiscal policy constraints on the other, "encouraged European economies with a pronounced state culture to transform themselves towards the liberal model" (Schweiger 2014, 13).

In addition to change in European political economies, scholars debate whether putting together different socio-economic models in a single currency regime contributed to the development of the euro crisis. Central to this strand of research are publications that focus on growth models. Governments are assumed to engage in different economic strategies, which are distinguished in two ideal types: export-led and demand-led growth. Export-led growth strategies focus on remaining competitive on international markets for goods and services. They emphasize wage moderation, producing high value-added goods, or capital-intensive rather than labour-intensive production (Hall 2012, 358). Demand-led growth strategies focus on "macroeconomic expansion and a tolerance for asset booms" (Hall 2012, 359), higher wage inflation, and periodic exchange rate devaluation (Hall 2012, 359).

The growth model perspective was further pursued by Baccaro and Pontusson with a focus on a post-Keynesian, predominantly Kaleckian economic approach (Baccaro and Pontusson 2016). Accounts of economic growth strategies can be found in the growing body of studies concerned with socio-economic differences in the single currency (Hassel and Palier 2021; Amable et al. 2019; Hall 2014, 2018; Johnston and Regan 2016, 2018; Mitsopoulos 2016; Perez and Matsaganis 2018).

Some authors, however, argue that the growth model perspective is not necessarily new to VoC, having already been engaged by certain scholars. In addition, some argue that the post-Keynesian analytical approach might not be the most sufficient to analyse current developments in EMU (e.g., Hope and Soskice 2016). However, the growth model perspective has gained a lot of traction in political economic research. In terms of EMU, as Johnston and Regan have argued, diverging growth models produced unsustainable tensions among EMU members due to deficits and surpluses in external accounts. This has wide-ranging effects on EMU as both growth models, according to Johnston and Regan, are at risk of becoming incompatible within the same currency area (Johnston and Regan 2016, 2018; see also Hall 2018, 15).

1.3 European Stability Mechanism

Lastly, the European Stability Mechanism itself and its role in European financial assistance form a third central field of research to which this book contributes. The ESM and its institutional predecessors have been addressed by political science scholars to a smaller degree, as research on EMU development has focused more on the roles of the IMF (e.g., Clift 2018, 2020; Lütz and Kranke 2014), the ECB (e.g., De Grauwe and Ji 2015; Lüggert 2019; Zagermann 2019), a possible decline of the European Commission's role (e.g., Majone 2014; Kassim et al. 2013) as a result of an increased influence of intergovernmental European institutions (e.g., Puetter 2012; Abels 2018a, 2018b, 2019), the general feasibility of austerity strategies in general (e.g., Blyth 2013) or within different political and institutional settings (e.g., Walter 2016), as well as new governance mechanisms, such as the European Semester (Verdun and Zeitlin 2018; Zeitlin and Vanhercke 2018).

Some scholars, such as Verdun (2015), Salines, Glöckler, and Truchlewski (2012), Gocaj and Meunier (2013), or Schlosser (2019), have conducted research on the establishment of EMU's financial assistance architecture, of which the ESM is an integral part. In their research, Gocaj and Meunier (2013) draw on historical institutionalism to analyse how the establishment of the EFSF and the subsequent ESM created strong path dependencies for the EU's crisis management. The beginning of the euro crisis in 2009/2010, they argued, can be identified as a critical juncture. The initial decision to grant Greece financial assistance with the help of the Greek Loan Facility (GLF, see chapter 4) and the decision to establish the temporary, intergovernmental EFSF had a strong impact on future policy choices (Gocaj and Meunier 2013, 240). According to Gocaj and Meunier, the ESM is the result of path dependence established with the EFSF, despite heterogenous results (Gocaj/Meunier 2013, 248–50).

Analysing the ESM's establishment process from a historical institutionalist perspective, Verdun concludes that the incomplete, asymmetric institutional design of EMU shaped the institutional response to the crisis. An institutional response to the crisis was necessary, as EMU lacked instruments to cope with a crisis of such nature. What is more, the EFSF as well as the ESM certainly were shaped by previously existing institutional settings and structures within EMU (Verdun 2015).

In that line of thought, Salines, Glöckler, and Truchlewski (2012, 666) argue that, although the crisis facing EMU is existential in nature, the institutional reactions to the crisis, such as the establishment of the temporary EFSF and the permanent ESM, are shaped by EMU's institutional setting and are best analysed as forms of layering and redirection (Salines, Glöckler, and Truchlewski 2012, 666). Rather than developing a fiscal or political union, EMU has developed mutual assurance mechanisms such as the ESM (Salines, Glöckler, and Truchlewski 2012, 667). Likewise, the EFSF and later the ESM were not created as institutional innovations. Rather, they layered the initial ad hoc Greek Loan Facility and were redirected after their initial establishment. Redirection, according to Salines, Glöckler, and Truchlewski (675–7), is a common form of adjustment in EMU as a reaction to the crisis.

A second strand of ESM-related research has focused on the European Stability Mechanism's engagement with national parliaments. Höing analysed why national parliaments are included in ESM operations to different levels (Höing 2015, v). Höing presents a typology of parliamentary participation in ESM affairs that distinguishes between parliaments with quasi-veto powers, parliaments with a consultative or political role, parliaments with information rights, and parliaments with no formal role in ESM operations (Höing 2015, 221–2). According to Höing, national parliaments gain stronger participation rights in ESM operations if their countries are in a good economic situations and the parliaments already have formal powers in EU affairs (Höing 2015, vi, 223–4). Moschella has analysed that the heterogenous involvement of national parliaments in European financial assistance in general and the ESM in particular has led to more radical positions of some creditors, Germany in particular, and strengthened divisions among members instead of reducing them (Moschella 2017). Drawing on a qualitative document analysis, semi-structured expert interviews, and participatory observation of parliamentary involvement in the third financial assistance program for Greece, Kreilinger argues that parliamentary involvement differs in terms of its timing and setting of participation (Kreilinger 2019, 149–52).

The role of the ESM in European financial assistance and EMU governance has been discussed by only a few scholars. A central publication, though, is Pierre Schlosser's book, *Europe's New Fiscal Union* (2019). In his analysis, Schlosser argues that the "institutionalisation of central fiscal powers at Europe's centre" (Schlosser 2019, 4) took place as a consequence of the euro crisis (Schlosser 2019, 4). While EMU has not developed a state-like fiscal authority, its centralized fiscal powers are visible in four central spheres: (1) enhanced fiscal surveillance mechanisms, (2) a fiscal capacity, (3) a lender of last resort capacity, and (4) a banking resolution regime (Schlosser 2019, 4–5). Schlosser argues that the ESM and its institutional predecessors should be analysed as "an informal Eurogroup instrument" (Schlosser 2019, 95), which led to a redirection of the Eurogroup "into the executive arm of the Economic and Monetary Union" (Schlosser 2019, 95). The ESM and its institutional predecessors thus play an integral part in the financial assistance architecture. They enhance intergovernmental settings like the Eurogroup at the expense of community institutions like the European Commission, which, according to Schlosser, have become considerably less influential (Schlosser 2019, 95).

Shawn Donnelly (2018) provides additional analytical insights into the ESM's role in EMU. According to Donnelly, the establishment of the ESM shows how German interests in particular were at play during central decisions of the euro crisis. He argues that the role of the EFSF and the ESM can be analysed as being a means to "uphold interdependence on German terms [...] and to augment German leverage over others in making and enforcing demands on others through the Eurogroup" (Donnelly 2018, 88). From a realist institutionalist perspective, the ESM underlines that national governments have more power over the financial assistance architecture than European institutions do. The ESM, according to Donnelly's analysis, has increased bargaining power particularly for the German government (Donnelly 2018, 106) and hence has an important role in further changes to EMU, mostly in line with German interests (Donnelly 2018, 179–92).

Ban and Seabroke put forward a study on the ESM's accountability structure for Transparency International, which highlighted a lack of transparency in the central decision-making bodies of the ESM (Ban and Seabroke 2017). According to Ban and Seabroke, three countries have de facto veto power in ESM decisions. It is, however, unclear how this influences policy conditionality in ESM programs, due to the lack of transparency (Ban and Seabroke 2017). Howarth and Spendzharova's (2020) analysis revealed that the ESM's inadequate accountability structures are a result of its institutional design and its "dual institutional embeddedness" (Howarth and Spendzharova 2020, 213) as an intergovernmental institution outside of EU law that is included in EMU governance.

Other authors include the ESM in their analysis, albeit only as an instrument to combat the crisis or as one of several institutions to illustrate the complexity of the euro crisis. Abels (2018a, 2018b, 2019) focuses on the central position of the Eurogroup in post-crisis economic governance. Here, the ESM is a key aspect of the strengthened position of the Eurogroup in EMU governance. However, Abels does not engage with internal decision-making processes of the ESM, nor with its specific role in economic governance or the financial assistance programs (Abels 2018a, 2018b, 2019). Henning goes into some detail on the ESM's institutional development but focuses on the complex and tangled governance structures of the euro crisis, of which the ESM is one part of his analysis (Henning 2017).

1.4 Outlook and Structure of the Book

The preceding sections emphasize how the euro crisis is a central research topic in political science. The literature provides us with a detailed analysis of the reasons for the euro crisis, as well as examinations of the central approaches and guiding policy paradigms that were used to extricate EMU from that crisis. However, as this review also highlighted, the current state of research certainly has gaps which this book will address. First, the ESM and its predecessors have been subject to little research, as the focus has mainly been on other institutions or newly created governance mechanisms in EMU. Hence, an empirical assessment of the development of the ESM and its role within European financial assistance is still missing. Second, while European financial assistance programs have been extensively researched, as has been the question of the compatibility of different varieties of capitalism in the same currency area, the programs' influence on central economic coordination mechanisms – and thus the possibility of institutional change in EMU's VoCs – has not been addressed to the same extent.

To fill these research gaps, the book will proceed as follows. Chapter 2 discusses the theoretical framework of this analysis. Drawing on VoC theory and new institutionalism, the book will identify differences in socio-economic institutional settings among euro area member states and hypothesize dynamics of institutional change based on the financial assistance programs.

Chapter 3 provides the reader with the research design of the book. A comparative political economic analysis proves to be a very promising approach: based on two case studies, the project provides a comprehensive analysis of institutional changes in the economies of euro area members under fiscal stress. In addition, the chapter discusses the different empirical sources on which the case studies are based: socio-economic data, qualitative texts, and semi-structured interviews.

Chapter 4 provides an analysis of the European Stability Mechanism and its role in economic and financial governance during the euro crisis. The analysis starts with an overview of policy debates to integrate fiscal policy at the European level from the early 1970s until the stage-setting Delors Report of 1989. Second, the chapter discusses how the European financial assistance architecture was built, from initial ad hoc solutions to the permanent European Stability Mechanism. Third, the chapter analyses the ESM's decision-making processes. Last, European financial assistance programs in general, as well as the division of labour among the different institutions included in the process, will be discussed.

Chapter 5 analyses the case of Greece, which is particularly interesting as Greece was a culminating point for the outbreak of the euro crisis in 2009. The chapter will analyse the economic institutional setting of Greece prior to the euro crisis, highlight how Greece developed an existential economic crisis, and provide an analysis on institutional changes in Greece's fiscal and labour market policy due to its financial assistance programs.

Chapter 6 provides an analysis of the Irish case. Ireland, long known as the poster child of European economic integration, was perceived to be an unlikely candidate for such an existential economic shock. The chapter will therefore go into detail on the fundamentals of the Irish economy, tracing how the Irish crisis developed and analysing how Ireland's fiscal and labour market policy was affected by the financial assistance program.

Chapter 7 gives a synopsis of the analysed financial assistance programs. In this chapter, a comparison of political economic trajectories of the programs and their influences on the varieties of capitalism in Greece and Ireland is put forward. Furthermore, the influences on the program, including the role played by related institutions in general and by the European Stability Mechanism in particular, are assessed.

Chapter 8 will provide the reader with a closer assessment of developments concerning the ESM after Greece exited from its third financial assistance program. The chapter will assess the ESM reform process, which culminated in an amending agreement to the ESM Treaty in 2021, and will give an outlook on the ESM's potential role in combating socio-economic crisis in light of developments that occurred during the COVID-19 pandemic.

Chapter 9 provides a summary of the answers to the research questions, thereby concluding the book. In addition, it provides an overview of the contributions of this book to the state of research, highlights its limitations, and offers an outlook on future research projects.

Chapter Two

EMU and the Dynamics of Institutional Change

This chapter provides the theoretical framework and central theoretical assumptions the book draws on. It is developed in three parts: first, the framework uses VoC theory to assess different ideal types of capitalism in EMU. Second, the framework highlights different paths of economic adjustment that EMU's varieties of capitalism can be expected to pursue in times of severe exogenous pressure. Some VoCs, as the framework underlines, are less likely to pursue adjustment strategies fitting best with their comparative institutional advantages due to persisting economic and institutional constraints of EMU. Third, including new institutionalist approaches, the framework will theorize that the European Stability Mechanism, as symbolic representation of the European financial assistance architecture, amplifies such constraints and leads to a specific form of economic adjustment in fiscal crises. A key assumption of the framework therefore is that the path of adjustment taken by European financial assistance programs favours marked-based governance regimes over state-based coordination and thus encourages institutional change particularly in mixed-market economies.

Choosing a comparative institutionalist analytical lens, on the basis of VoC theory and new institutionalism, enables the book to appreciate different paths of political economic developments and their respective institutional foundations (Clift 2014, 101). The observation of similar paths of economic adjustments focusing on reducing deficits and liberalizing labour markets, despite experiencing different crises within heterogenous institutional settings, serves as the starting point for the analysis.

Comparative Political Economy (CPE), as Hall and Soskice argue, "revolves around the conceptual frameworks used to understand institutional variation across nations" (Hall and Soskice 2001, 1). CPE scholars are generally interested in explaining (economic) institutional change, especially in line with globalization and liberalization processes (Hall and Thelen 2008, 7–8). The book thus adds to both lines of theoretical thinking by explaining institutional changes in economic settings within the euro area.

Applying a VoC approach instead of focusing on general trends of neoliberalism provides several advantages to the analysis. First, by focusing on different ideal types of capitalism with different predominant forms of economic coordination (see 2.1), a VoC approach offers the possibility to analyse the initial situation of different groups of political economies in the euro area at the start of the euro crisis. As will be discussed below, EMU includes a variety of political economies with diverse institutional economic settings. As the euro crisis developed, they experienced the crisis differently based on their institutional foundations and comparative (dis)advantages. Second, unlike an approach that focuses on broader trends of neoliberalism in European capitalism, applying VoC enables us to explain heterogenous adjustment strategies that resulted from differences in institutional settings. Last, applying a VoC approach in the context of the institutional constraints of EMU and policy conditionality for financial assistance enables us to analyse why some adjustment strategies that would stabilize their respective comparative institutional advantages are no longer feasible for EMU member states. Unlike an approach that would focus on neoliberal trajectories only, applying a VoC lens gives us the analytic tools to highlight why some political economies, in light of severe exogenous shocks and institutional constraints, are able to maintain their comparative institutional advantages. It also allows us to understand why other political economies, under the same constraints, develop adjustment strategies that accentuate forms of economic coordination that are not congruent with their comparative institutional advantages.

For this, the chapter proceeds in four steps. First, by outlining the Varieties of Capitalism approach applied in this book (see 2.1). Second, by illustrating existing adjustment pressures within EMU (see 2.2). Third, by putting forward new institutionalist perspectives on institutional change (see 2.3). Last, by explaining the hypotheses that are derived from the framework (see 2.4).

2.1 Varieties of Capitalism

Institutional settings of political economies, as well as their adaption to new economic contexts, have been at the centre of CPE research for as long as it has existed as a field of research. The Varieties of Capitalism approach, first developed by Hall and Soskice (2001) and then advanced by Vivian A. Schmidt (2002) and others (e.g., Amable 2003), offers theoretical insights to assess the differences of socio-economic models in the single currency and prospects of institutional change within EMU without following a deterministic analysis of a general liberalization. VoC theory follows the dual convergence thesis (Hay 2004, 235–8), which highlights that, despite macro trends such as globalization, distinct socio-economic differences between political economies are clearly visible and should be expected to be resilient.

The central distinction between varieties of capitalism is their predominant form of economic coordination. VoC theory, as used for the analysis of this book, assumes three forms of economic coordination: market-based coordination, non-market coordination (Hall and Soskice 2001, 8; Clift 2014, 202; Lallement 2011, 628), and state-based coordination (Schmidt 2002, 2007, 2009; Molina and Rhodes 2007). The predominant mode of coordination of political economies corresponds with the institutional setting and its support for market, non-market, or state-based forms of economic behaviour (Hall and Soskice 2001; Schmidt 2002).

The single currency thus includes different political economies. Their economic institutional settings condition governmental and business activity, as well as their comparative advantages against other economies (Hall 2014, 1223; Regan 2013, 2; see also Schmidt 2002). VoC highlights the importance of such institutional settings in contemporary capitalism: institutions are key factors in shaping the positions of central political economic actors, such as governments, firms, or trade unions, and influence their interaction (Thelen 2010, 42). National institutional settings are, as Bruff argues, "the basis for different 'types', 'models' or 'varieties' of capitalism [...]. They play a critical role in the evolution of national capitalisms, too, be it successful adjustment to new economic realities or failure to adapt through inertia" (Bruff 2011, 483).

Political economies can be divided into different spheres, such as corporate governance, industrial relations, finance, and social protection, as well as education and training (Hall and Soskice 2001, Schmidt 2002). All sectors are equally important for the predominant form of economic coordination, as it is not the structural characteristic of a single institution that explains the socio-economic model. Rather, VoC theory allows us to understand how economic institutions and spheres are interlinked and in combination create distinct socio-economic models (Regan 2013, 2; 2017, 917; see also Schmidt 2002, 112).

Varieties of Capitalism therefore are characterized by high ratios of institutional complementaries, which have similar forms of economic coordination throughout the different spheres of a political economy

(Hall and Soskice 2001, 17–21; see also Hancké, Rhodes, and Thatcher 2007, 10–13). This allows forms of coordination in one subsystem of the economy to enhance the results in other spheres as well (Hall and Thelen 2008, 8). Furthermore, these institutionalized forms of economic coordination are expected to be resilient if exposed to exogenous factors. VoC assumes powerful feedback loops at play, which support the resilience of differences in economic coordination between political economies (Thelen 2010, 42). The way political economies are institutionally structured also conditions the policies that governments can be expected to choose and support (Hall and Thelen 2008, 8; Regan 2013, 2; 2015, 3, see also Thelen 2014, xix–xx; Thelen 2009, 472; Hall and Soskice 2001; Schmidt 2002). Therefore, VoC theory allows us to highlight diversity among the euro area's political economies and enables us to categorize possible changes in their economic coordination (Lallement 2011, 628).

The typology for EMU's varieties of capitalism presented here is derived from the original VoC approach by Hall and Soskice (Hall and Soskice 2001) and includes modifications by Vivian A. Schmidt's account on European capitalism (Schmidt 2002, 2007, 2009), Molina and Rhodes (2007), and, more recently, Hancké (2013b) and Johnston with different co-authors (Johnston 2016; Johnston, Hancké, and Pant 2014; Johnston and Regan 2016).

According to their contributions, we can assume three ideal types of capitalism in EMU (e.g., Schmidt 2002, 107–47, 303–9). The typology provides the categories of liberal market economies (LME), coordinated market economies (CME), and mixed-market economies (MME). MMEs were only marginally discussed by Hall and Soskice (Hall and Soskice 2001, 21). However, as Schmidt (2002) and Molina and Rhodes (2007) have highlighted, MMEs have a specific mode of economic coordination.[1] Based on a typology of Schmidt (2002, 113, see table 2.1), central features of the varieties presented here are (1) business relations, (2) government relations, (3) labour relations (see table 2.1).[2]

Schmidt has shown that, instead of thinking of MMEs as hybrids between CMEs and LMEs, they are a distinct ideal-type (Schmidt 2002, 111). What is more, she has shown how, in light of globalization and European integration, differences between the three models remain visible (Schmidt 2002, 111–12).

In 2002, growth regimes were not yet as prominent in comparative political economic research. However, based on current research (see 1.2), one could argue that LMEs and CMEs are predominantly export-led, whereas MMEs can be described as predominantly demand-led.

Table 2.1. Ideal-typical characteristics of the models of capitalism (Schmidt 2002)

	Market capitalism (US, UK)	Managed capitalism (Ger, NL, Swed)	State capitalism (Fr, It)
Business relations	Market-driven	Non-market managed	State-organized
Inter-firm relations	Individualistic, competitive	Mutually reinforcing, network-based	State-mediated, organized
Industry– finance	Distant	Close	State-mediated
Investment	Short-term view	Long-term view	Medium-term view
Government relations	Arm's length	Negotiated	State-directed
State character	"Liberal" arbiter	"Enabling" facilitator	"Interventionist" leader
Fiscal policy	Restrained	Redistributive	Interventionist
Currency	Hard; low inflation	Hard; low inflation	Soft; high inflation
Labour relations	Adversarial	Cooperative	Adversarial
Wage bargaining	Market-reliant	Coordinated	State-controlled
Government role	Bystander	Coequal or bystander	State-imposed

Source: Schmidt (2002, 113)

2.1.1 Coordinated Market Economies

One of the ideal types of varieties of capitalism are coordinated market economies. Their distinct socio-economic model relies heavily on non-market economic coordination among social partners and market participants. This allows CMEs to develop export-led growth models based on higher levels of wage coordination, sector-coordinated vocational training, and research coordination among private firms (Hall 2014, 1226). CMEs' socio-economic model has a clear incentive for stable fiscal policies and supply-side labour market reforms (Regan 2017, 971).

CMEs' business relations focus on non-market coordination. Inter-firm relationships are mutually enforcing and based on relational or incomplete contracts (Hall and Soskice 2001, 8; Schmidt 2002, 114). Business associations play an important role for the distribution of information and the emergence of corporate strategies. Firms, in general, act strategically with each other (Hall and Soskice 2001, 8; Schmidt 2002, 114). Typically, business relies more on traditional banks than on financial market investors, which allows business to engage in long-term strategies. In ideal-type CMEs, banks have access to detailed information and do not rely on quarterly reports. Thus, they focus more on company values and market share gains of their investment. Reliability is a key aspect for business in CMEs (Schmidt 2002, 114; Hall and Soskice 2001, 19–23).

Government relations in CMEs emphasize negotiations between market participants and the government (Schmidt 2002, 114). The state holds a more central role, acts in support of business activity, and thus enables social partners in their coordinative efforts (Schmidt 2002, 114; 2009; Lallement 2011, 636–7). In ideal-type CMEs, industrial relations are highly cooperative and can be described as corporatist. While the state enables wage bargaining, it does not actively intervene in the process. Collective agreements result from coordinated decision-making between business associations and trade unions (Schmidt 2002, 114). However, the state does engage in coordinating broad consensus about economic coordination. Therefore, according to Schmidt, economic adjustment is "led by firms and jointly negotiated cooperatively between business, labor, and the state" (Schmidt 2009, 522).

2.1.2 Liberal Market Economies

A second key ideal type of modern varieties of capitalism are liberal market economies. This distinct socio-economic model relies heavily on market-based economic governance and has a clear incentive for stable fiscal policies and supply-side labour market reforms.

Business relationships in LMEs are driven strongly by market competition as inter-firm relationships lack strong cooperative networks. Rather than cooperatively working in business associations, businesses are competitive and their relationships are based on individual contracts (Schmidt 2002, 112). Strong antitrust regulations ensure that inter-firm relationships do not undermine competition (Hall and Soskice 2001, 30–1). Licensing is an important tool for inter-firm relations as well, as market mechanisms are frequently used to set industry standards (Hall and Soskice 2001, 31). Relations between businesses and financial institutions are distant in liberal market economies. Business is highly reliant on equity markets and venture capital. Hence, firms are very attentive to their balance sheets and quarterly profits (Schmidt 2002, 112; Hall and Soskice 2001, 27; Lallement 2011, 636).

Government relations with business and labour are best defined as at arm's length. The state is limited to setting the economic legal framework and ensuring competitive coordination. Hence, the government is highly relevant as an agent of market preservation, but it is less able to influence economic adjustment (Schmidt 2002, 112–13; 2009, 521; Hall and Soskice 2001, 31). Public expenditure is typically restrained; LMEs therefore have limited levels of redistribution. Social security entails only very limited, basic support to vulnerable individuals (Lallement 2011, 636). Labour relations underwrite LMEs' centrality of market-based coordination: wage bargaining is highly decentralized and fragmented, and wages are mostly set individually between employers and employees. The influence of trade unions is marginal and often limited to a small number of sectors (Schmidt 2002, 113). Firms are not obliged to establish representative bodies for employees. Hence, management-labour relations are often adversarial (Schmidt 2002, 113; Hall and Soskice 2001, 30).

2.1.3 Mixed-Market Economies

Countries in Southern Europe are commonly described as mixed-market economies (MMEs). Their distinct socio-economic model focuses on state-based economic coordination and relies on expansionary fiscal policies as well as demand-side labour market reforms (Regan 2017, 973).

Business relations in mixed-market economies are typically organized by the state. Cooperation between firms is mediated by governments and state agencies. If mediation by the state is lacking, inter-firm relations are highly competitive and market based (Schmidt 2002, 115–16). As a consequence of their lack of autonomous coordination, firms often address the state to veto economic developments or demand financial compensation by the state (Molina and Rhodes 2007, 227). Industry-finance relations depend on the government as well. Instead of banks or venture capital, firms rely on the state as a "compensator of last resort" (Molina and Rhodes 2007, 227). Due to high levels of state regulation and direct state intervention, MMEs entail very little competitive pressures for private firms in terms of finance. Hence, financing often takes a medium-term perspective (Molina and Rhodes 2007, 226; Schmidt 2002, 116).

Government relations in MMEs tend to be hierarchical. The state aims at influencing business via economic planning, industrial regulation, and business endeavours of state-owned enterprises (Schmidt 2002, 116). At the same time, regular state intervention supports economic models in MMEs that focus on financial compensation through the state in times of crisis instead of firms adjusting to new economic situations (Hassel 2014, 9; Schmidt 2002, 116). The state acts as a gatekeeper and often picks winners and losers by intervening in economic processes instead of arbitrating between economic actors (Molina and Rhodes 2007, 227; Schmidt 2002, 116; 2009, 552). Industrial relations are characterized by fragmented trade unions and employers with limited capacity to organize wage bargaining (Regan 2017, 971). The state compensates for lack of coordination between employers and employees. Governments often use social pacts to set standards for the national political economic development (Molina and Rhodes 2007, 234; Hassel 2014, 27–9). Labour-management relations are typically adversarial (Schmidt 2002, 116).

2.2 Adjustment Pressures in Times of Crisis

The following sections provide theoretical insights on why economic crises affect the varieties of European capitalism differently and why, due to institutional and financial constraints of EMU (see 2.2.1), political economies with a higher reliance on state-based coordination should be expected to adjust in a more fundamental way (see 2.2.2). Here, the European Stability Mechanism and its predecessors come into play, as they constitute new additions to economic crisis management procedures in EMU and can be assumed to intensify adjustment processes in times of severe crisis.

Economic crises have severe effects on political economies. In general, the perception of economic crisis arises when the GDP of a political economy decreases. The consequences of GDP reductions are higher unemployment rates, decreased tax revenue, higher spending for social welfare, and political tensions. Therefore, we can assume governments to put policy programs in place which aim at stabilizing the economy. While governments might differ in their macroeconomic perspective (Keynesian vs. neoclassical economics) and thus in the effects their programs have on socio-economic development as well as distributional conflicts, they can generally be assumed to focus on securing economic growth.

What also differs in times of economic crisis are the reasons for economic recessions. Generally, there are three possible reasons for economic crises within political economies: (1) they can develop as a result of exogenous shocks; (2) as a result of endogenous developments within a political economy; or (3) due to a combination of both factors (Nölke 2016, 143). These different reasons for the emergence of political economic crises matter because they potentially lead to different forms of adjustment.

2.2.1 Institutional Constraints on Economic Adjustment in EMU

In times of economic crisis, VoC ideal types should be expected to adjust according to their own political and institutional logic (Schmidt 2002; Hall and Soskice 2001). While political economies do experience institutional change over time (e.g., Schmidt 2002), the broad differences between the varieties should be expected to be resilient (Hall and Soskice 2001). Moreover, VoCs should not be assumed to copy economic coordination mechanisms of other socio-economic models (Regan 2017, 979). That would lead to different results as a consequence of their different institutional capacities. Institutional and political constraints of EMU, however, make some adjustments less feasible than others.

Because of the single currency's institutional design, euro area members have limited policy discretion to adjust to economic crises (Offe 2013, 67–8; 2016, 50–70). Countries in crisis cannot adjust interest and exchange rates in EMU, as both policy fields have been integrated at the European level. The single currency includes fixed exchange rates and thus does not give its members the opportunity to individually adjust their exchange rates. At the same time, interest rates within EMU are set by the politically independent European Central Bank for the entire euro area. Expansionary fiscal policy has, for the longest time, not been feasible in EMU as a result of its fiscal framework and a higher awareness of sovereign debt in European politics (Regan 2015, 970; Höpner 2013, 294). Fiscal policy has de jure – and, slightly less strictly, de facto – been strongly regulated by Europe's monetary integration. As Hancké argues, "[p]ut differently, if countries within EMU face asymmetric shocks, fiscal, monetary, and exchange rate policies are no longer among the weapons of their disposal" (Hancké 2013b, 9).

As table 2.2 illustrates, this pushes the adjustment predominantly to internal devaluation policies (see also Höpner 2013, 294; Regan 2017, 970). A fifth option would be an exit from the single currency, which is, for political, institutional, and economic reasons, a highly unrealistic scenario (Offe 2016, 71–80). Offe describes this phenomenon as the euro trap (Offe 2016).

As a result, EMU members' key policy instruments at hand are internal devaluation, reductions of fiscal spending, and structural reforms of their labour markets (Regan 2017, 971; Höpner 2013, 294; see also Buti and Carnot 2012; Armingeon and Baccaro 2012).

The European Stability Mechanism and its institutional predecessors, as new institutional additions to the Economic and Monetary Union,[3] can be theorized as deepening the constraints on adjustment strategies. While the ESM allows member states of the euro area to avoid sovereign default by granting financial support, the programs appear to one-sidedly focus on internal devaluation instead of taking the political and economic differences of the respective program countries into account (Regan 2017, 979). With this focus on economic adjustment through internal devaluation, as will be illustrated below, the ESM poses distinct pressure on MMEs for institutional adjustment.

Table 2.2. Economic adjustment strategies

	Monetary	Fiscal
Internal	Interest rates	Expansionary fiscal policy
External	Exchange rates	Restrictive fiscal policy

Source: author's compilation based on Höpner (2013) and Regan (2017)

2.2.2 Economic Adjustment Pressures of EMU's Varieties of Capitalism

According to VoC theory, we should see economic adjustments to economic crises that support predominant forms of economic coordination and comparative institutional advantages of the respective political economies. As I have argued above, the VoCs of the euro area have limited policy space available at times of severe economic crisis (see 2.2.1). This, as I will argue below, leads to distinct problems for mixed-market economies.

Adjustment processes are mediated by several factors, as Schmidt (2002, 62) has illustrated. Drawing on VoC theory, we can assume that economic vulnerability and political institutional capacity have significant effects on the adjustment processes of some political economies. The limited policy space available in EMU can be expected to constitute comparatively less adjustment pressure for coordinated market economies. As argued above (2.1.1), in CMEs, business and industrial relationships are largely based on non-market cooperation. While an economic crisis should pose a distinct threat to some sectors of the economy, the close relationships between firms and finance should provide firms with financial flexibility, as the investment culture is focused on long-term investments (see table 2.1). CMEs' greater reliability of cooperative firm and labour interrelations allows governments to seek common solutions in times of crisis (Schmidt 2002, 134). While firms, governments, and organized labour have difficulties responding quickly to new socio-economic environments due to long-term planning strategies, their supportive business networks and cross-shareholding structures enable firms to cope with economic recessions (Schmidt 2002, 134–6).

During economic recessions, the state is able to offer leadership without fiscally exposing itself to unsustainable levels (Schmidt 2002, 134). Rather, as a consequence of coordinated action between firms and labour, CMEs can internally adjust to economic crises without changing their predominant forms of coordination. We should expect a small shift towards market-based coordination in their labour market regimes. Overall, however, CMEs' institutional settings and forms of economic coordination should be expected to be resilient, even considering their limited policy discretion (see 2.2.1) due to coordinated action of business, labour, and the government.

In line with VoC theory, liberal market economies should also be expected to experience only smaller degrees of institutional change. As a result of their high reliance on market-based coordination, firms can be expected to adjust rapidly as they do not focus on coordinative efforts in inter-firm relationships. While unsustainable business models will most likely go out of business due to short-term financial strategies, the focus on radical innovation can be expected to lead to a quick adjustment to the new socio-economic environment (see 2.1.2; also Schmidt 2002, 131–2). High labour market flexibility, individual contracts between employers and employees, decentralized wage bargaining, and less influence by trade unions support fast internal socio-economic adjustments (Schmidt 2002, 131). Hence, in times of severe economic crisis, few institutional changes to their socio-economic models should be expected.

In LMEs, the limited role of the state in coordinating the economy in itself does not constitute a specific, EMU-related adjustment pressure. Severe economic crises, however, could potentially lead to a slightly stronger role of governments. Governments in LMEs have to react to economic recessions and possible bankruptcies of firms in important sectors in order to reduce risks from economic instabilities in times of economic crisis (Schmidt 2002, 132). At the same time, their emphasis on labour flexibility can be assumed to lead to a loss of skill-based knowledge, which leaves LMEs more vulnerable to competition from lower-waged and lower-skilled countries (Schmidt 2002, 133). The government can thus be assumed to be more active in times of crisis than before the crisis, in order to stabilize business structures.

Mixed-market economies are the VoC ideal type that is most exposed to adjustment pressures from economic shocks in combination with limited policy options in EMU. As described above, MMEs rely heavily on state-based coordination and fiscal compensation policies (see 2.1.3). In times of economic recessions *and* institutional constraints, the strong reliance on the state potentially becomes problematic. State-based MMEs, unlike market-based LMEs and non-market-based CMEs, should therefore be expected to experience distinct trouble in adjusting to the new socio-economic contexts. If, as table 2.2 highlights, monetary forms of adjustment are obsolete because of fixed exchange rates and centralized interest rates, this puts the pressure of adjusting to crisis dynamics predominantly on fiscal policy. Here, the state is constrained in terms of deficit spending, which is more central to MMEs than to CMEs or LMEs.

In times of severe economic crisis, states with MMEs can be expected to experience strong fiscal and political pressure as a consequence of institutional and political constraints (see 2.2.1). In political economies with economic coordination less reliant on the state, as is the case in LMEs or, to a lesser degree, in CMEs, this should not necessarily lead to severe adjustments to their economic model. In state-based political economies, however, the state potentially loses its capacity to fulfil important coordinative tasks, such as the organization of business relations, the mediation of industry-finance relations, or the capacity to control bargaining processes (see 2.1.3). Furthermore, the state is less able to act as a compensator of last resort.

The lack of coordinative capacities, along with limited policy options, leads to the assumption that the distinct economic institutional setting of MMEs is more prone to adjustment pressures in EMU in times of severe crisis. The route of adjustment can therefore be expected to focus on market-based coordination. While business and industrial relations in MMEs within EMU were not necessarily market based before the crisis, business and labour may not engage in non-market coordination with MME state governments. Instead, as argued above, outside of state-based coordination, their relations are adversarial (see 2.1.3 and table 2.1). It is therefore unlikely that they are able to achieve CME-like coordinative institutions, once state-based coordination comes under severe pressure. Having theorized possible directions of change for the varieties of European capitalism, the theoretical perspective on *how* institutional change in EMU's varieties of capitalism can be expected to develop is of equal importance.

2.3 The ESM's Potential Role in Institutional Change

As argued above, the single currency's institutional setting poses distinct policy limitations for the varieties of European capitalism in times of severe economic and fiscal crises. The European Stability Mechanism and its institutional predecessors, which have been added to the institutional setting of EMU as a central response to the euro crisis, offer the possibility to avoid sovereign default, albeit at the cost of reinforcing the limited policy range available in EMU (see above). At the same time, the programs offered by the ESM and its institutional predecessors, conducted in close cooperation and with a division of competences with the European Commission, the European Central Bank, and the International Monetary Fund, have been criticized for being one-size-fits-all solutions, which do not consider the differences in economic institutional settings of the euro area (Regan 2017, 984) and for being strikingly similar to the liberalizing structural adjustment programs of the 1980s and 1990s (Greer 2014).

Drawing on new institutionalism will allow this book to conceptualize *how* institutional changes are influenced by the European Stability Mechanism, as well as the limitations of such changes. The chapter will therefore discuss incentive structures (rational choice institutionalism), historical-cultural dynamics (historical institutionalism), and discursive processes (discursive institutionalism) as possible factors of change facilitated by the ESM (in collaboration with other institutions).

2.3.1 Rational Choice Institutionalism

Rational choice institutionalism (RI) was one of the first interpretations of new institutionalism. Prominently put forward by scholars such as Douglass C. North (1990), RI emphasizes the role of institutions as an exogenous constraint on the game between rational actors (Shepsle 2006, 23). RI scholars argue that "institutions are the rules of the games in a society or, more formally, are the humanly devised constraints that shape human interaction" (North 1990, 3). RI theorists assume political actors to be highly rational beings that pursue their political interests according to a "logic of calculation" (Schmidt 2010, 2), which takes place in institutional settings (Schmidt 2010, 2). These institutions, or "rules of the games" (North 1990, 3), are perceived by RI as structures of incentives (Schmidt 2010, 2). To put it another way, RI theorists focus on how the interests and preferences of political agents are influenced by institutional incentives. Historical context is not considered as an essential incentive structure (Thelen 1999, 376).

RI posits three essential theoretical assumptions: (1) political agents have fixed preferences and behave strategically to maximize the attainment of their interests; (2) politics is primarily seen as collective action dilemmas; and (3) institutions structure strategic interactions, as they affect "the range and sequence of alternatives on the choice-agenda or by providing information and enforcement mechanisms that reduce uncertainty" (Hall and Taylor 1996, 944–5; see also Schmidt 2010, 4–6; Steinmo 2008, 126). Taking these theoretical assumptions into consideration, RI theory sees institutional change as caused predominantly through exogenous shocks. As RI assumes fixed preferences of political agents and relatively stable institutions, the rules of the game should not be assumed to change from within (Schmidt 2010, 5; Thelen 1999,

381). Rather, RI theorists see equilibria established by interests and institutional settings.

From a RI perspective, the establishment of the ESM can be theorized to lead to institutional change in the single currency's VoCs as a consequence of changed incentive structures. First, economic crises lead to disequilibria in the game among political agents. They must adjust to a new socio-economic context, which changes the status quo of their strategies to put forward their interests: politics has to react to a crisis in the economic sphere. Second, the establishment of the European Stability Mechanism (and its predecessors) changes the institutional setting of the euro area and thus the incentive structure for European governments. Before the establishment of the ESM and its predecessors, governments were only able to refinance fiscal deficits on financial markets. In a scenario of lost market access due to unsustainable interest rates for government bonds (e.g., due to lack of trust from the financial sector), refinancing on financial markets is not a feasible option. In such situations, the ESM is able to grant financial assistance and prevent sovereign defaults. While the ESM does allow governments to seek financial assistance temporarily, it also puts forward wide-ranging economic adjustment programs in cooperation with the European Commission, the ECB, and, if requested, the IMF, programs that channel certain policies via incentive structures (Greer 2014). Third, the preferences of political agents should be kept in mind if we think about possible institutional change in line with RI theory. EMU does restrict the policy range of political agents and the financial assistance programs put forward through the ESM have been criticized for promoting very specific sets of policies (see 2.1 and 2.2). However, in scenarios of severe financial and economic crises within EMU, applying for financial support is now a possible approach. Therefore, as rational actors, political agents can be assumed to seek financial assistance and put through institutional change, as this scenario entails calculable risks.

2.3.2 Historical Institutionalism

Unlike RI, historical institutionalism (HI) claims that institutions do more than serve as incentive structures for political agents. Rather, they channel policymaking and structure political conflict. Interests and policy objectives are created within institutional contexts and cannot be separated from them (Thelen 1999, 375; Schmidt 2010, 3). HI sees political agents both as "norm-abiding rule-followers *and* self-interested rational actors" (Steinmo 2008, 126; emphasis by Steinmo). Political action, according to HI, is dependent on the individual and the historical context, as well as the formal rules of policymaking (Steinmo 2008, 126). Therefore, HI defines institutions "as the formal or informal procedures, routines, norms and conventions embedded in the organizational structure of the polity or political economy" (Hall and Taylor 1996, 938). Put differently, HI interprets institutions as legacies of historical processes (Hall and Taylor 1996, 938). As HI scholars emphasize the historical component of institutions and political action, they focus on the way institutional settings structure action and outcomes. HI thus seeks to understand how political processes are structured by the institutional setting in which they occur (Verdun 2015, 221)

It is not the historical development of institutional settings that is central for HI as such, but the "path dependencies and unintended consequences that result from such historical development" (Schmidt 2010, 10; see also Steinmo, Thelen, and Longstreth 1992; Hall and Taylor 1996, 938; Thelen 1999). Institutions and institutional change thus cannot be fully understood if they are seen outside of their societal and political context as they incorporate ideal and material political disputes of the past (Thelen 1999, 384). In this regard, HI sees politics and political strategies as affected by existing institutional structures and their history (Steinmo 2008, 125). In line with this argument, HI rejects the idea that the same operative forces lead to the same results in all institutional settings (Hall and Taylor 1996, 941). Institutional settings, according to HI theory, should be assumed to be less likely to change. Drawing on path dependence as their main logic of explanation, HI sees institutions not only as resilient over a long period of time but also as important for explaining political and societal developments (Hall and Taylor 1996, 941).

Changes to institutional settings, according to HI, are possible. HI assumes that institutions evolve in response to changing societal contexts. These changes are heavily structured by past trajectories (Thelen 1999, 387). To be more precise, changes thus most likely occur as a combination of critical junctures and path dependence, which incorporates "an initial shock followed by feedback loops, path dependency, and unintended consequences" (Gocaj and Meunier 2013, 240). Like RI, HI theory sees the main factor for institutional change in exogenous shocks. Critical junctures can be seen as a puncture of an ongoing political and institutional equilibrium (Thelen and Steinmo 1992). HI therefore illustrates processes of change as unconscious. Political agents, according to Schmidt, are "creating new practices as a result of 'bricolage' and destroying old ones as a result of 'drift'" (Schmidt 2010, 13; see also Thelen 2009; Streeck and Thelen 2005).

From an HI perspective, the ESM (and its institutional predecessors) can be theorized to lead to institutional change in the following ways: First, the economic crisis leads to a critical juncture in EMU member states, puncturing the equilibria established before the crisis. As the crisis unravels socio-economic structures within the member states, political agents must react. Second, the establishment of the European Stability Mechanism influences the institutional setting of EMU. As a permanent institution for financial assistance in times of crisis, the ESM adds a new political dimension to the single currency's governance and, in terms of its structural adjustment conditionality, follows the dominant path of socio-economic governance in EMU. Third, the implemented ESM programs lead to changes in the institutional structure of EMU members in question. However, policy legacies of the member states do not disappear. Rather, they channel policy debates surrounding the adjustment programs and, through feedback loops and path dependence, continue to matter. Therefore, through an HI lens, we can assume institutional change to occur to a certain degree in countries with ESM programs. This change is structured by existing policy legacies and path dependence, which prevents a full convergence.

2.3.3 Discursive Institutionalism

Discursive institutionalism (DI) is a comparatively new form of new institutionalism and can be seen as a concept of approaches that, according to Schmidt, put their focus on "the substantive content of ideas and the interactive processes by which ideas are conveyed and exchanged through discourse" (Schmidt 2010, 3). Ideas in DI are perceived on different levels. Analytically, ideas can be considered as policy ideas, policy paradigms, or even broader political philosophies (Schmidt 2010, 3).

The framing of DI as a form of new institutionalism underlines that it is not only concerned with ideas, but also with the institutional setting these ideas are discussed in (Schmidt 2010, 4). Unlike RI and HI, DI does not perceive institutions simply as constraint structures on political agents, whether as rational choice incentive structures or historical path dependencies. Rather, DI interprets institutions as structures which both constrain *and* enable. In this regard, they are constructs of meaning within "sentient (thinking and speaking) agents" (Schmidt 2010, 4). As explained by Schmidt, their ideational capacities explain how "they create and maintain institutions at the same time that their 'foreground discursive abilities' enable them to communicate critically about those institutions, to change (or maintain) them" (Schmidt 2010, 4; see also Schmidt 2008).

Ideas, like actors, are competing for political space and have influence on the policy agenda (Béland 2009; Béland and Waddan 2015; Schmidt 2008). Discursive institutionalism thus explains institutional change primarily through the influence of ideas and discursive interaction (Schmidt 2008). DI, unlike RI and HI, does not primarily attribute institutional change to exogenous shocks. Rather, discursive institutionalists primarily see institutional change as a result of endogenous processes through background and foreground discursive abilities and practices (Schmidt 2010, 5). In this line of argument, DI demonstrates how and when ideas in discourses empower political agents to overcome the constraints of interests and path dependence (Schmidt 2010, 4).

From a DI perspective, the ESM can be theorized to lead to institutional change in the following ways: First, the economic crisis leads to a political situation in which predominant ideas on political economic development come into question. Other sets of ideas on the way states and markets should be organized are competing with the ideas currently pursued by political and economic agents. Second, the establishment of the European Stability Mechanism adds a new dimension to the ideational processes around economic crises and economic development. This new ideational dimension in EMU competes with opposing ideas and thus changes how political agents in the member states, which are either asking for financial assistance through the ESM or are under immense fiscal stress, are thinking about the crisis. They thus implement institutional change, despite the constraints of interests or existing path dependencies.

2.4 Hypotheses

The following section derives hypotheses from the theoretical framework presented in the preceding sections. Based on the theoretical insights drawn from VoC theory on different modes of economic coordination in the euro area and EMU's institutional constraints on adjustment polices, we can derive that the European Stability Mechanism and its institutional predecessors add a new institutional layer to EMU's economic governance. As EMU renders several adjustment possibilities to asymmetric crises obsolete (see 2.2), the ESM effects political economic transformation processes of EMU's varieties of capitalism based on financial assistance programs. Some varieties of capitalism are affected more by structural adjustments included in financial assistance. Political economies that rely heavily on state-based economic coordination can be expected to be exposed to stronger transformative pressures. Based on VoC theory, this book pursues the following central working hypothesis in order to illustrate the different adjustment pressures for the varieties of capitalism in the euro area:

> The European Stability Mechanism (and its institutional predecessors), as a new institutional structure in the economic governance of the Economic and Monetary Union, leads to political economic transformation in EMU's member states that receive financial assistance and primarily exercises transformative pressure in political economies that rely heavily on state-based economic coordination.

Based on theoretical assumptions by new institutionalist approaches, we can assume that the European Stability Mechanism's influence on transformation processes in the euro area is structured by the socio-economic, historical, and ideational structures of the political economies that receive financial assistance. These structures, as implicated by new institutionalist approaches, influence the possibility and potential depth of institutional changes in countries that apply for financial assistance. They also explain the possible continuance of institutional settings in respective member states. To further operationalize the central working hypothesis in consideration of the theoretical insights drawn from new institutionalism on the logics and limits of institutional change, three hypotheses can be derived.

First, based on theoretical insights from rational choice institutionalism, we can assume that changed incentive structures play an important role in institutional changes. This role is based on the economic crisis in the euro area and the possibility of receiving financial assistance through the European Stability Mechanism (see 2.3.1). The first hypothesis will thus be the following:

> H1: Political agents of the member states will be influenced by the new incentive structures which the ESM provides and *will opt for institutional changes as a part of the ESM's conditionality principle in order to prevent sovereign defaults.*

Second, drawing on discursive institutionalism, we can assume that ideas about the way European states and markets should develop influence the projected forms of institutional change and lead to forms of political economic convergence (see 2.3.3). The second hypothesis will thus be the following:

> H2: Political economic convergence among member states results from the ideational mechanisms that are institutionalized by the ESM,

specifically ideas *about political economic development in the euro area which favour market-based coordination mechanisms.*

Last, drawing in historical institutionalism (see 2.3.2), institutional changes in European program countries all take place in specific historical, political, and institutional settings. These distinct political histories, institutional legacies, and path dependencies should be assumed to play an important role in forms of political economic transformation. The third hypothesis will thus be the following:

H3: The persistence of the variety of political economic regimes among member states results from institutional *path dependencies that constrain the fully fledged convergence of national political economies, despite the critical juncture of the fiscal crisis.*

Research Design

This chapter provides a discussion of the book's research design, including the methodology, data sources, operationalization, and case selection used for the empirical analysis. The book, as described above, focuses on analysing institutional change within the euro area's varieties of capitalism as a consequence of financial assistance programs carried out via the ESM and its institutional predecessors. In order to provide an in-depth empirical analysis of why and how the financial assistance programs attached to the ESM lead to institutional change, a comparative case study on EMU members receiving financial assistance programs will be conducted. Aside from the methodology and data, this chapter also provides readers with the central operationalizations for the analysis, which include the selection of the dependent and independent variables and central policy fields identified for the comparative case studies (see 3.1). In addition, the chapter provides the rationale behind the case selection, as well as the methodological approach and the data selected for the empirical analysis (see 3.2).

3.1 Operationalization

This book engages in a comparative political economic and institutionalist analysis to explore whether the European Stability Mechanism has a transformative influence on EMU's varieties of capitalism. In order to empirically assess such a transformative influence, the research design conceptualizes the socio-economic models as the dependent variable (DV). The financial assistance programs associated with the European Stability Mechanism and its institutional predecessors are operationalized as the central independent variable (IV), whose influence on the different national political economies will be tested empirically. Other independent variables could also play a role in institutional changes of European political economies. As such, economic recessions, changing government coalitions, and global economic trends are identified. However, this empirical analysis focuses on the influence of the ESM as the central independent variable because of its position within EMU's economic governance, its centrality for the euro crisis management, and the strict conditionality associated with its financial assistance programs. Thus, the research design will be y-centred because of its focus on transformative processes in the dependent variable (Gschwend and Schimmelfennig 2007, 21–4). While VoC theory underlines key features of socio-economic models in the euro area, the measurability of changes in EMU's varieties of capitalism has to be verified before the analysis.

The analysis of institutional changes to national political economic regimes (DV) focuses on the policy fields of fiscal policy and labour markets. Both policy fields have been at the centre of attention in terms of euro crisis management process, as they are central for state debt, economic governance, and economic competitiveness. At the same time, they are key features of the variety of economic coordination within the single currency (see 2.1; see also Hall 2014, 1223; Regan 2013, 2; Schmidt 2002).

First, labour markets are chosen for their central position within socio-economic differences in the euro area. As argued above, labour market regimes are important for socio-economic development and are a key feature of the different VoCs included the euro area. Second, labour markets play an important role within the structural adjustment processes initiated as a reaction the euro crisis (e.g., Schulten and Müller 2015). Furthermore, they are regulated on the European level by several instruments of the EU's economic governance (Van Gyes, Schulten, and Müller 2016, 12–15). Thus, labour markets have been chosen as a central part of the analysis in this book. Institutional changes in labour markets are operationalized by using central labour market indicators. In terms of labour market policy, the comparative case studies focus on institutional changes in the terms of trade agreements, levels of collective bargaining, employment protection legislation, unemployment support, wage developments, and representation of trade unions. The aim here is to evaluate whether and to what degree labour market institutions were transformed during the euro crisis.

Fiscal policy, especially in terms of fiscal state activity in economic realms, is the second central empirical feature of the analysis. Like labour markets, fiscal policy regimes are important for the differences in socio-economic models as they allow governments to be active in economic coordination or prevent such activity. At the same time, fiscal policy is the second central feature of current structural adjustment processes, as sovereign debt has become more politicized and European budgetary rules have intensified (Schlosser 2019). Thus, state activity in terms of fiscal policy has been chosen as the second central part to be analysed in this research project. The analysis of fiscal policy will be operationalized in terms of changes in budgetary revenue, taxation, as well as changes in government spending, especially in terms of state-based economic activity. The aim is to evaluate whether a transformation of fiscal state capacity has occurred, which has an effect on predominant forms of economic coordination.

While business relations are an important factor within the VoC framework (see 2.1), they are not included in the analytical part of this book for two reasons. First, business relations have, so far, not been as central to structural adjustment discussions in the euro area as other policy fields. While business relations might adapt to changes in labour market regimes and fiscal policy, the programs do not focus on the way businesses interact with each other to the same degree as they do on labour markets and fiscal policy. Second, unlike labour markets or state activity, business relationships are less formally regulated and thus play only a secondary role in political reform processes. There might indeed be distinct changes as a response to the crisis. However, regarding a possible influence of the European Stability Mechanism and its institutional predecessors, business relations are less focused on.

3.2 Methodology, Data, and Case Selection

Changes in a possible influence of the European Stability Mechanism on the euro area's varieties of capitalism are analysed in two steps. In order to answer the research question, I conduct a comparative case analysis by using a mixed-methods research design including socio-economic data, official documents, and semi-structured expert interviews.

3.2.1 Methodology

The book provides a mixed-methods comparative political economic study of two cases to analyse similarities in changes in the dependent variable (socio-economic models) as a consequence of the influence of the independent variable (financial assistance programs). As Lijphart has prominently argued, small-N analysis can be "more promising than the superficial statistical analysis of many cases" (Lijphart 1971, 685). The book thus provides two detailed studies on prominent cases of the euro crisis. For this comparative political economy study, time sequences play an important role, as socio-economic models have emerged over a long period of time, and possible changes will produce results that are visible over longer periods of time as well. Focusing on time sequences in empirical analysis is well known as process tracing (George and Bennett 2005; Beach and Pedersen 2013; Hall 2003, 2006).

Process tracing provides the central analytical tools to identify causal effects within temporal sequences, as the goal is to trace the causal mechanism that leads to a certain political outcome (George and Bennett 2005; Beach and Pedersen 2013; Hall 2003, 2006; see also Tilly 2001). It thus offers a fundamentally different methodological approach than statistical analysis (George and Bennett 2005, 13). With their central interaction of institutions, ideas, and interests, the structural adjustment programs associated with the ESM are complex phenomena. This kind of complexity can be analysed better using qualitative methods focusing on the precise political processes rather than large-N quantitative studies (Hall 2003). The analysis engages in mixed methods to combine quantitative and qualitative data (for an overview, see Kuckartz 2014) in order to analyse complex socio-economic developments in the dependent variable and thus be able to trace the political economic processes in the selected cases over the period of 2009 to 2018.

Such an approach has several advantages. First, a comparative political economy study based on process-tracing methodology and a combination of quantitative and qualitative data offers the possibility to take existing patterns of socio-economic developments seriously, as they are outcomes of historical process and, in general, are expected to persist (Rueschemeyer and Stevens 1997). Second, timing and sequencing are important factors in political economic research, as political decisions generate different outcomes depending on the time and context. This temporal dimension is best considered by small-N research designs, which take historical research into consideration (Rueschemeyer and Stevens 1997). Third, focusing on process tracing allows a comparative political economy study to identify key moments in which institutional change within the dependent variable is visible, and to identify key reasons for the change occurring (e.g., ideational processes, critical junctures, or rational choice calculations by political actors).

3.2.2 Data

The comparative case study uses quantitative and qualitative data to analyse institutional change in the dependent variable. The following subchapters provide an overview on databases used for the quantitative analysis of changes in labour markets and fiscal policy in the selected timespan (see 3.2.2.1). In addition, the subchapters discuss the text-based data used for analysing the financial assistance programs' policy focus and argumentation for certain policy reforms in the dependent variable (see 3.2.2.2). Last, they discuss the semi-structured interviews conducted for this research project, including the selection process of interview partners, access to the field, as well as development of the interview guide (see 3.2.2.3).

3.2.2.1 SOCIO-ECONOMIC DATA

First, in order to analyse institutional change in the dependent variable, the comparative case study draws on different sources of quantitative, socio-economic data that allow the book to illustrate and thus analyse changes in Greek and Irish labour markets and fiscal policy.

The quantitative analysis of labour market developments particularly uses the Institutional Characteristics of Trade Unions, Wage Setting, State Intervention and Social Pacts 6.0 database (ICTWSS), provided by Jelle Visser and the Amsterdam Institute for Advanced Labour Studies (Visser 2019b). The ICTWSS database includes central labour market data of fifty-five countries from 1960 to 2017. It includes 232 data variables[1] on collective bargaining, worker organization, and worker representation, which are key elements of political economies (Visser 2019a) and central to the research project. In addition, the research project draws on the European Commission's Labour Market Reform Database (LABREF), which includes quantitative data on labour market reforms in EU member states from 2000 to 2020 (European Commission 2022b). LABREF allows comparison of the quantity of labour market reforms in EU member states and distinguishes labour market reforms in ten categories.[2] In addition, the quantitative analysis of labour market developments draws on Labour Force Statistics by the Organisation for Economic Co-operation and Development (OECD) as well as quantitative data provided by the International Labour Organisation (ILO), Eurostat, and the Annual Macro-Economic Database of the European Commission's Directorate General for Economic and Financial Affairs (AMECO).

For the statistical analysis of fiscal policy developments, including the government's involvement in economic affairs, I have drawn on several statistical sources. Central to the empirical assessment of fiscal policy developments is Eurostat data on government revenue and expenditure, both in absolute terms as well as in relation to GDP. Furthermore, the analysis of fiscal policy includes Eurostat data on government expenditure by function (COFOG)[3] (Eurostat 2019), which allows tracing changes in the government's expenditure in several governmental sectors over time. Furthermore, drawing on the fiscal governance database prepared by the European Commission allows for an analysis of the inclusion of structural fiscal rules, such as those on expenditure and revenue, as well as debt and the budgetary process on different levels of government during the financial assistance programs (European Commission 2022a). In order to analyse the role of the government in economic affairs as a result of fiscal policy reforms, this book also draws on indicators of product market regulation[4] provided by the OECD (2018).

3.2.2.2 QUALITATIVE DOCUMENT ANALYSIS

Second, the analysis includes a qualitative document analysis of official documents associated with European financial assistance programs, including the memoranda of understanding, supplemental memoranda of understanding, quarterly reviews of the program process, as well as post-program surveillance reports. In total, forty-two documents have been selected (see appendixes 2 and 3 for a complete list of the documents analysed for this book). For the Greek case, twenty-one official documents related to the financial assistance programs were identified and included in the analysis (see appendix 2). Twenty-two official documents were used for the Irish case (see appendix 3).

In both cases, the documents were mostly published by the European Commission in line with the programs, putting forward the analysis of experts included in the financial assistance programs, their assessment of central developments in the Irish and Greek socio-economic models, and the policy conditionality attached to the programs. Including these documents in the analysis allows a careful examination of the institutions' perception of respective socio-economic problems and their solution proposals. It also allows for a discussion of changes in the institutions' perceptions and their policy focus over time.

The official documents are analysed using Maying's qualitative content analysis (Mayring 2010). The qualitative document analysis focuses on socio-economic models as well as on the policy fields of fiscal and labour market policies, for which coding categories were created deductively (see table 3.1).

Passages within the documents were coded based on anchor examples and coding rules. The qualitative document analysis was conducted with the support of MAXQDA. A quantitative analysis of the codings of all documents is presented in the respective chapters below.

Table 3.1. Coding scheme for qualitative document analysis

Socio-economic models	Labour markets	Fiscal policy

• Socio-economic Change
• Socio-economic persistence
	• Wage-setting mechanisms
	  o Liberalisation
	  o Sectoral coordination
	  o State-led
	• Employment protection legislation
	  o Retrenchment
	  o Social investment
	• Unemployment support and Activation
	  o Retrenchment
	  o Social investment
	• Public sector employment
	  o Reduction
	  o Preservation
	  o Increase
		• Fiscal governance
		  o Restrained
		  o Flexible
		• Fiscal policy direction
		  o Restrictive fiscal policy
		  o Expansionary fiscal policy
		• Government discretion in socio-economic issues
		  o Less
		  o More

Source: Author's compilation

3.2.2.3 SEMI-STRUCTURED INTERVIEWS

Last, the analysis draws on semi-structured interviews with experts. Using expert interviews requires a definition and selection of experts within the political process that is relevant to the focus of the research project. For this analysis, experts were defined as part of the political process of European financial assistance. Experts can be political actors or institutional representatives. They are distinguished between the following levels: (1) national governments (as the central level to implement financial assistance programs), (2) EU institutions (as the central level to negotiate on financial assistance programs), (3) parliaments (as the central level to control the political process associated with financial assistance programs, and (4) stakeholders (as the central level of actors affected by financial assistance programs).

The experts chosen for the analysis are thus able to give additional insights into key decisions, provide background information, or provide the research project with the perspective of central political organizations during the adjustment process. In this regard, as McLaughlin and Wright have argued, "[s]emi-structured interviews enable narratives to be formed about the perception of events and decisions relating to policy change among key informants and policymaking participants" (McLaughlin and Wright 2018, 8). Expert interviews are used in order to understand how European financial assistance programs are negotiated and implemented within the diverse political economies of the euro area. Expert interviews are able to give insights into subjective and strategic conditions of political processes concerning financial assistance by the ESM and its institutional predecessors. Furthermore, expert interviews allow for an empirical assessment of how political actors perceive their scope of action regarding reform processes associated with the ESM and its institutional predecessors.

In total, thirty-two semi-structured interviews were conducted over the timespan from February 2017 until August 2018. Of those thiry-two interviews, twenty-seven were included in this book (see appendix 1). The interviews were thirty to ninety minutes long; they were recorded and transcribed manually with the support of MAXQDA. Anonymity was guaranteed to all interview partners. Getting access to the field turned out to be more or less difficult depending on the institutions and experts approached for an interview. Whereas members of government departments, European institutions, and social partners were open to discussing the reform process, members of national parliaments often did not respond to interview requests.

The interviews were conducted by using a semi-structured interview guide to keep focus and not digress from the central research objective. The interview guide was created using the SPSS method proposed by Helfferich (2011).[5] The guide was used in a flexible way in order to be able to adapt to each interview situation and was primarily used to make sure all relevant topics were discussed. Furthermore, the guideline was not a strict sequence of questions. Rather, the sequence of questions depended on each interview partner. However, the guide was useful in ensuring the comparability of the expert interviews and in keeping the research objective in focus.

The analysis of the expert interviews was conducted using Mayring's qualitative content analysis (Mayring 2010) and was oriented on thematic units deducted from the theoretical framework.

3.2.3 Case Selection and Time Span

The global financial crisis and the subsequent euro crisis saw several countries develop serious balance-of-payments problems (table 3.1). Eight member states of the European Union received financial assistance programs. Five of them (Cyprus, Greece, Ireland, Portugal, and Spain) were members of the single currency and thus received financial assistance through the ESM and its institutional predecessors.

Of those five euro area members with financial assistance programs, Ireland and Greece were selected as cases for the comparative case

Table 3.2. List of economic adjustment programs

Country	Worth in billion euro	Time span
Cyprus	10	2013–16
Greece	280	2010–12, 2012–15, 2015–18
Hungary	20	2008–10
Ireland	85	2010–13
Latvia	2.9	2008–12
Portugal	26	2011–14
Romania	20	2009–11 (2011–13, 2013–15)
Spain	100	2012–14

Source: European Commission (n.d.), author's compilation; in total Romania was under three Balance of Payment programs from 2009 to 2015. However, the years 2011–13 and 2013–15 were treated as precautionary.

study.[6] Despite strong differences between both cases' political and economic institutional settings and diverse reasons for their severe crises, Ireland and Greece make for a fruitful case comparison for the objective of the book. The selection is based on four factors: First, they were the initial two euro area members to fall into balance-of-payments problems and thus apply for financial assistance. Their respective programs initiated the establishment of the financial assistance structure and thus shed light not only on the adjustment processes for financial assistance but also on the establishment of the institutional architecture behind the financial assistance. Both cases provide the strongest insights in how the financial assistance architecture has adjusted throughout the years.

Second, the countries' different political economic traditions allow us to analyse the effects of EMU's financial assistance architecture in separate socio-economic institutional settings. While Ireland can be considered as a real-type of liberal market economies, Greece is a prominent real-type MME case (see table 3.2). Both cases follow different historical paths of economic development, have different labour market institutions, and diverse state traditions in economic coordination. Nonetheless, their reform processes follow similar directions. Therefore, these cases provide instances for assessing whether political economic varieties in the euro area change in the hands of financial assistance programs, and why.

Third, both countries certainly faced different socio-economic crises that led to their respective financial assistance programs. Whereas Greece had had comparatively high debt ratios and structural economic problems for a long time, Ireland went into the crisis with a debt ratio well under the Maastricht criteria and a reputation for being a

Table 3.3. Varieties of capitalism real-types in the euro area

CME	MME	LME
Austria	Cyprus	Estonia
Belgium	France	Ireland
Finland	Greece	Latvia
Germany	Italy	Lithuania
Luxembourg	Portugal	
Malta	Slovakia	
Netherlands	Spain	
Slovenia		

Sources: Hall and Soskice (2001), Feldmann (2006), and Nölke and Vliegenthart (2009)

comparatively successful political economy. While Ireland was strongly affected by the global financial crisis in combination with a contraction of its overly large construction sector (see chapter 6), Greece's crisis developed from a combination of long-lasting economic problems in combination with the global financial crisis and fiscal problems (see chapter 5). Comparing both cases therefore allows us to analyse trajectories of economic reforms in light of different crisis developments.

Fourth, these cases are generally regarded as positive and negative examples of the euro debt crisis management. Ireland is portrayed as a "poster child for austerity"[7] (Mackintosh 2013), and the differences between the program countries have been of interest to several scholars (Greer 2014; Hermann 2014; Armingeon, Guthmann, and Weisstanner 2016; Hardiman et al. 2017). The cases selected for this study thus enable highlighting similarities and differences between two popular examples of European financial assistance.

The comparative case analysis focuses on the period from 2009 to 2018. Starting at the outbreak of the euro crisis in 2009 allows the book an in-depth analysis of the countries' paths to applications for financial assistance, the development of their structural adjustment programs, and the influence of the ESM programs on their socio-economic models. In 2018 the last country officially exited its financial assistance program. The book thus includes three central moments of financial assistance in EMU: First, the period after the collapse of Lehman Brothers and the outbreak of the global financial crisis, which also materialized in the European Union. Second, the period after the outbreak of the euro crisis, which led to the establishment of the ESM and its institutional predecessors. Third, the time span in which most countries exited their programs and entered the post-program period. By choosing the time span of 2009 to 2018, the book is able to provide an analysis on how socio-economic models were reformed in line with policy conditionality attached to the programs and whether socio-economic reforms were upheld after countries left their respective financial assistance programs. Furthermore, the specific time frame allows for an examination of the specific developments within the ESM and those related to it.

Chapter Four

The European Stability Mechanism

The European Stability Mechanism is the latest institutionalized form of the euro area's crisis management. As an intergovernmental organization based outside of EU law,[1] it provides financial assistance to euro area member states in severe fiscal stress, albeit with strict policy conditionality attached to it. The ESM and its institutional predecessors were therefore not only essential to cope with balance-of-payments problems in Greece, Ireland, Portugal, Spain, and Cyprus; the financial assistance also helped to deal with their exclusions from financial markets and thus prevented exit strategies from the single currency. Furthermore, policy conditionality attached to financial assistance gave the institutions involved with the programs, such as the ESM, a distinct role in the adjustment strategies followed by receiving countries.

Developing such a mechanism was thought to be unlikely shortly before the outbreak of the euro area crisis. After the European constitutional process failed in 2005 and the subsequent Lisbon Treaty was signed in 2007, EU experts assumed that the decade following the Lisbon Treaty would be a time without further creation of European institutions (Gocaj and Meunier 2013, 240). However, as the euro crisis materialized, several new governance instruments were added to European economic governance. In addition, already existing treaties, such as the Stability and Growth Pact (SGP), were reformed in order to give EMU more influence over member state budgets.

The European Stability Mechanism represents a central institutional innovation of the euro area's crisis management. Not only was it a central institution in the strategy of European heads of states and governments endeavouring to cope with the crisis, it also became a relevant institutional actor within the financial assistance programs and operates in a conflicted area around European intergovernmental arrangements (e.g., adjacent to the central role of the Eurogroup in its decision-making process) and close to community institutions (e.g., common operations with the European Commission).

The following chapter will go further into detail on how the ESM was developed, how its decision-making processes are structured, the composition of its governance bodies, its role in financial assistance programs, and its cooperation with other institutions involved in financial assistance. First, the chapter provides a short historical oversight of how the European integration process was concerned with financial assistance and convergence mechanisms in relation to a common European currency (see 4.1). Second, the chapter illustrates the establishment of the European Stability Mechanism during the euro crisis, including its different stages of institutionalization (see 4.2). Third, the chapter describes decision-making processes within the European Stability Mechanism and goes further into detail on how the ESM is linked to the European Commission and the Eurogroup, as well as the role parliaments play in ESM decision-making (see 4.3). Fourth, the chapter analyses how procedures concerning the European financial assistance programs work and gives an overview of the existing financial assistance programs (see 4.4). Last, the chapter will present a short interim conclusion on the ESM's development and its role within financial assistance (see 4.5).

4.1 European Integration, the Monetary Union, and Financial Assistance

Economic and fiscal integration are key issues of the European integration process and have been highly debated since the conclusion of the Treaty of Paris, which established the European Coal and Steel Community in 1951. A fundamental concern was financial assistance or financial transfers between the member states of the EU, which was also the case in terms of the Economic and Monetary Union. Economic governance, the role of fiscal policy, and the possibility of European financial instruments have therefore been of major concern of monetary integration discussions, starting in the 1970s and continuing until today. Monetary integration reflects debates on fiscal integration ranging from a Keynesian, demand-oriented perspective in the early 1970s to a monetarist, supply-oriented perspective in the 1990s.[2] Not only has the question of economic governance been a highly debated issue; the idea of a common European economic governance and common financial instruments found its way into the Werner Report of 1970, the Marjolin Report of 1975, the McDougall Report of 1977, and the Delors Report of 1989 (Verdun 2002, 56–92; 2013, 24; Mody 2018, 48–51, 54–7, 69–70; Schlosser 2019, 23–7).

Central in the early debate about a monetary union was the Werner Group. At the European Summit in The Hague in 1969, the heads of European states and governments decided to implement a working group,[3] which was supposed to present a plan for a European economic and monetary union. Pierre Werner, at that time Luxembourg's prime minister and minister of finance, served as the working group's chair (Mody 2018, 45). The Werner Group, as shown by Verdun (2002, 57), issued its first interim report in May of 1970, in which the group "dealt with the main aspects of establishing an EMU in three stages; that is, 1970/1 to 1972, 1972 to 1975; and 1976 or 1978 onwards" (Verdun 2002, 57). The interim report underlined European risk-sharing and solidarity as central aspects and argued for including social partners in EMU discussions (Verdun 2002, 57).

The Werner Report, presented on 8 October 1970, confronted the primary issue of common currencies: national governments lose a central macroeconomic adjustment mechanism by establishing a common monetary policy (Mody 2018, 45). Furthermore, the report argued for wide-ranging, harmonizing policy coordination at the supranational level in terms of budgetary, fiscal, regional, and structural policy (Werner Report 1970, 11; see also Schlosser 2019, 24). This included policies against structural asymmetries, as well as tax coordination, for example in the form of coordination of value added taxes. What is more, the Werner Report argued for a supranational Centre of Decision for Economic Policy (Werner Report 1970; see also Verdun 2013, 25) and argued explicitly for demand-oriented policy coordination at the European level (Höing 2016, 20).

The Werner Report argued in favour of centralized institutions, a larger community budget, and coordinated governance mechanisms (Schlosser 2019, 24). It did admit that a monetary union was likely to be an incomplete union, because movement of workers might not develop in a way that would even out asymmetrical developments (Werner Report 1970, 8). The Werner Report also argued that there might be severe political obstacles to providing strong fiscal safeguards to secure the single currency (Werner Report 1970, 12–13). However, the committee saw this as an opportunity: an incomplete monetary union might be able to produce political and economic tensions, which could lead member states to engage in "progressive development and political cooperation" (Werner Report 1970, 26) over time. As one potential end for this process, the Werner Report debated the European Parliament becoming the central decision-making body for European economic policy (Werner Report 1970, 13; see also Schlosser 2019, 24).

Whereas the Werner Report was largely arguing in favour of a common monetary union, Europeanized fiscal policy instruments, and, to some degree, financial assistance among member states, a second report written during the 1970s argued against a monetary union and common fiscal instruments. In the report of the study group entitled "Economic and Monetary Union 1980" (European Commission 1975), which is known as the Marjolin Report (Mody 2018, 55; Schlosser 2019, 25–6), the committee concluded that a single currency would necessitate strong community institutions. However, it also noted that EU member states were unwilling to subordinate their national interests under strong community institutions. Hence, a single currency (and much less so, financial assistance) would not be viable (European Commission 1975). Furthermore, the Marjolin Report was highly critical of the possibility of European policy coordination (Schlosser 2019, 25).

In 1974, the Commission installed a third working group of economists with the task of examining the role of public finances and European integration. The group was chaired by Donald MacDougall and presented the MacDougall Report (European Commission 1977) in 1977. The report focused primarily on possible necessities for European Community public finances if European integration were to be deepened in terms of economic and monetary policy (Verdun 2013, 25). The MacDougall Report did argue for a common fiscal policy. In its report, the working group highlighted the necessity of a common fiscal system and argued that a monetary union would demand a large community budget for common fiscal policies (European Commission 1977; see also Sawyer 2017, 10). As a result, it argued for a European federal taxation system, much like the US federal structure (Mody 2018, 56). The authors estimated that the community budget for a monetary union would require about 5–10 per cent of the EU's GDP in an earlier stage and even more in a fully federalized Europe in order to cope with asymmetrical socio-economic developments, such as asymmetrical crises and regional economic shocks (European Commission 1977; Mody 2018, 56; Verdun 2013, 25; Schlosser 2019, 26).

The focus of EMU and common instruments to cope with asymmetric developments changed in the 1980s and 1990s, when monetarism became an influential school of economic thought that underlined fiscal stability as a central goal of economic and fiscal policymaking in Europe (Stützle 2013, 133–67; see also Schlosser 2019, 29). Central changes to the role of economic governance in EMU and the question of fiscal integration came with the Delors Report in 1989 and the subsequent Stability and Growth Pact. Unlike the Werner Report, which focused on demand-oriented economic policy, and the MacDougall Report, which primarily argued for fiscal integration, the debate on economic governance and fiscal policy in the late 1980s turned its focus towards supply-oriented policies (Höing 2016, 20; see also Mody 2018, 65–122). After the end of the Bretton Woods system and with the advent of increasing inflation rates, price stability became a central policy issue (Stützle 2013, 133–40). Supply-oriented policies and price stability therefore became a central aspect of the Stability and Growth Pact and thus the European Economic and Monetary Union (Höing 2016, 20). The reports illustrate this change in predominant economic thought from the 1970s to the 1990s (Heipertz and Verdun 2004, 771).

The highly influential Delors Report of 1989, composed by a group of experts with shared beliefs about the general prospects of economic development (Verdun 1999), proposed a three-stage plan, which laid the groundwork of the European Economic and Monetary Union. In addition to the three-stage plan, it already included the main components of the future Maastricht criteria for EMU and served as a blueprint for the Monetary Union (Verdun 1999, 309). As Heipertz and Verdun (2004, 771–2) argue, the Delors Plan did not put forward an institutional design for EMU that is vastly different to the design envisioned in the Werner Plan. However, the Delors Plan was published in a situation that differed from the 1970s, especially in terms of changes in the status quo of economic and monetary integration as well as in terms of ideational changes in monetary policy (Heipertz and Verdun, 771).

EMU, as envisioned by the Delors Report, was deliberately asymmetric (Verdun 1996): the Delors Report argued for centralized monetary policy, but it did not put forward a proposal for centralized fiscal and macroeconomic policy (Salines, Glöckler, and Truchlewski 2012, 666). The report highlighted the need for community-wide budget coordination but did not incorporate central arguments for fiscal policy centralization.[4] Instead, it saw a disciplinary function for financial markets and argued in favour of national fiscal policy adjustments rather than financial assistance mechanisms (Committee for the Study of Economic and Monetary Union 1989, 20).

In a similar way, the Maastricht Treaty visibly rejects former proposals for community budgets and common financial instruments. The treaty set the convergence criteria asymmetrically on budgetary and fiscal indicators, leaving fiscal policy competences with the member states, but subjecting them to rule-based budgetary coordination. Furthermore, it already included the no-bailout clause and therefore prohibited the establishment of financial assistance instruments for the euro area (e.g., Mody 2018, 86). This central political choice, as Salines, Glöckler, and Truchlewski have argued, was already included in the treaty (Salines, Glöckler, and Truchlewski 2012, 671). It remained a central aspect of the Stability and Growth Pact even throughout the euro crisis, as it framed how financial assistance was debated. The way that the ESM is able to grant financial assistance in today's EMU is clearly shaped by this period of European integration (see below).

The Stability and Growth Pact, which followed the Maastricht Treaty in 1997, has been central to the development of the single currency and the way fiscal policy is coordinated in EMU. In the resolution adopted by the European Council on 17 June 1997 in Amsterdam, the member states

> commit themselves to respect the medium-term budgetary objective of positions close to balance or in surplus set out in their stability or convergence programmes and to take the corrective budgetary action they deem necessary to meet the objectives of their stability or convergence programmes, whenever they have information indicating actual or expected significant divergence from those objectives. (European Council 1997, 1)

The Stability and Growth Pact further defined the rules-based fiscal coordination within EMU with an emphasis on national fiscal policy decisions. Furthermore, it included a corrective arm in order to cope with excessive deficits (Buti and Carnot 2012, 900). While the SGP was amended in 2005 after France and Germany breached the deficit criteria, in order to allow for more counter-cyclical fiscal policy (Heipertz and Verdun 2010, 128–53; Buti and Carnot 2012, 900), the pact's preventive functions are still significant today, as it lays out the budgetary ground rules for the single currency and has been strengthened during the crisis with the Six Pack and Two Pack (Verdun 2015, 228–9). While it has been suspended during the COVID-19 pandemic, the Stability and Growth Pact remains critical for EMU's fiscal framework. At the time of writing, reforming its debt criteria is heavily debated.

The integration of monetary policy has been a central aspect of the different steps towards the monetary union. All of the reports discussed above highlight the fact that monetary integration was an essential step for the establishment of the single currency. However, in term of fiscal policy and financial assistance between member states, especially during asymmetric shocks, the picture is not as clear. In the beginning of the debate on EMU, economic and fiscal integration via central budgetary instruments and financial assistance was thought to be a necessity of the single currency (Verdun 2015, 220–1). However, in its original institutional set-up, EMU coordinated fiscal policy through rules-based coordination without common financial assistance mechanisms. This put the responsibility to react to asymmetric developments solely on the member states (see also 2.2). The ESM is an intergovernmental institution that has its ideational origins in both debates.

4.2 Institutional Development of the ESM

When the global financial crisis materialized in Europe, governments reacted with sizable fiscal measures, including financial support for their banking sectors and counter-cyclical stimulus packages within the context of reduced tax revenues (Buti and Carnot 2012, 903). The German car-scrapping bonus and short-term working allowances are two prominent examples of this strategy of using automatic stabilizers and fiscal means to cope with the recession. However, this common reaction to the crisis led to very different outcomes in terms of sovereign debt: increased sovereign debt in Europe led to asymmetric perceptions of financial markets that put some countries in fiscal stress while other countries paid comparatively lower interest rates for their debt.

While there has been a long-established debate about EMU and the need for financial assistance in times of asymmetric shock (see 4.1), the single currency did not have institutions or devices to deal with such a severe, asymmetric recession and the consequent problems with sovereign debt and access to financial markets. The only instrument that was available before the crisis was Medium-Term Financial Assistance (MFTA), which had been increased at the beginning of the global financial crisis to assist Hungary, Latvia, and Romania in 2008 (Salines, Glöckler, and Truchlewski 2012, 675). However, the MFTA was not a viable option for reacting to the emerging crisis of the euro area.

At the beginning of the crisis, the risk of sovereign defaults as a consequence of lost access to financial markets was seen only as a problem for Greece. The Greek government's liquidity gap of 20 billion euro in January 2010 was perceived at first as containing no risk to other EMU members (Schwarzer 2015, 613). However, this perception proved quickly to be wrong as other countries started to develop balance-of-payments problems as well. Governments tried to reach a common and united response. However, they appeared to be politically paralyzed and could thus not gain the trust of financial markets, which led to further volatility (Gocaj and Meunier 2013, 241; see also Gianviti et al. 2010). The way the EU reacted to the crisis had much to do with institutional deficiencies. As Verdun argues, the EU was unable to engage in an effective coordination role as it was lacking financial means and effective instruments to tackle the crisis. Furthermore, the intergovernmental character of EU decision-making put further emphasis on the Council of the EU and the European Council (Verdun 2015, 224).

In addition, concerns about Article 125 of the Treaty on the Functioning of the EU (TFEU) (no-bailout clause), public opinion concerns about changes to EMU's institutional design, and moral hazard all made it exceedingly difficult for the EU to react to the crisis in a fast and decisive manner (Verdun 2013, 30).

Therefore, in the spring of 2010, different scenarios were discussed at the European level to deal with the risk of sovereign defaults in the single currency (Gocaj and Meunier 2013, 242–4; see also Schwarzer 2015, 607; Verdun 2015, 220):

1 Providing bilateral loans, pooled by the Commission.
2 Creating a Commission-backed stabilization fund.
3 Creating a European equivalent to the International Monetary Fund.
4 Creating an intergovernmental special purpose vehicle.
5 Altering existing national or European instruments.

These scenarios either included the European Commission at the centre or were intergovernmental solutions. The ECB acting as a lender of last resort was not a viable solution, as its statutes prohibit direct state financing (Zagermann 2019, 200). Hence, financial assistance had to come from the members of the euro area, either by new intergovernmental mechanisms or through the European Commission. A second possibility was financing from outside sources like the IMF (Schwarzer 2015, 606).

As Van Rompuy put it in late 2011, the euro area was set with an "empty or de-credbilised tool-box" (European Council 2011, 3). New instruments were needed. Schwarzer highlighted that legal constraints in terms of the no-bailout clause (Article 125 TFEU) sparked further questions about the legality of European financial assistance and shaped the way governments and European institutions discussed possible scenarios to grant financial assistance (Schwarzer 2015, 606).

The crisis and the discussions of possible financial support led to the establishment of new instruments and socio-economic governance mechanisms within the single currency (Verdun 2013). While some of these concerned socio-economic coordination, such as the Euro Plus Pact and the European Semester, others were created to enforce existing fiscal rules, such as the Six Pack, the Two Pack, or the Fiscal Compact. With the EFSF and the ESM, the governments of the euro area have created an institutional architecture to provide financial assistance on an intergovernmental basis outside of EU law (Verdun 2015, 220). After the initial assistance mechanism (Greek Loan Facility, see 4.2.1), it took the heads of states and governments fourteen months to create first a temporary safety mechanism (EFSF and the European Financial Stabilisation Mechanism, or EFSM, see 4.2.2 and 4.2.3), and then the permanent European Stability Mechanism (see 4.2.4; see also Salines, Glöckler, and Truchlewski 2012, 675).

The International Monetary Fund played an important role in the initial provision of financial assistance for Greece, as well as in the establishment of the temporary and permanent financial assistance institutions. According to Schwarzer, the Greek Loan Facility (see 4.2.1) primarily followed IMF standards for granting financial assistance, as the financial assistance institutions "embrace[d] the IMF institutionally" (Schwarzer 2015, 608). Furthermore, their treaties included the IMF as a central partner for financial assistance in the euro area (Schwarzer 2015, 608; see also European Stability Mechanism 2012, 5). The IMF not only took this role because it had international experience in providing financial assistance to sovereign states and working with private creditors; drawing on IMF standards also rendered European financial assistance programs well-suited for IMF operations (Salines, Glöckler, and Truchlewski 2012, 675).

The following chapters provide more insight into the processes related to creating the Greek Loan Facility (see 4.2.1), the temporary European Financial Stability Facility (see 4.2.2), and the European Financial Stabilisation Mechanism (see 4.2.3), as well as the permanent European Stability Mechanism (see 4.2.4). While the general loan-based approach of the Greek Loan Facility did not change as the programs progressed, there are institutional differences between the mechanisms that were used to secure the institutional integrity of the euro (Salines, Glöckler, and Truchlewski 2012, 675).

4.2.1 Greek Loan Facility

The Greek Loan Facility (GLF) was the initial vehicle used by the European Union to organize financial assistance to Greece, after which it was also named. While the GLF was only in use for one program, it constitutes the central starting point of the strategy to secure the single currency's institutional integrity.

The GLF was developed as a reaction to the Greek financial crisis and the fact that the euro area did not have existing instruments to deal with a situation in which member states lose access to financial markets and therefore are unable to refinance their sovereign debt. Greece initially announced financial problems on 20 October 2009. The first informal crisis summit on Greece took place on 11 February 2010. During the first months of the crisis, heads of states and governments were trying to avoid providing financial assistance to a fellow euro area member.

The German government was especially reluctant (Mody 2018, 240–50). However, due to continuous fiscal stress and spill-over risks, the European Council concluded that euro area members would take coordinated action if needed (Mody 2018, 242). According to Mody (2018, 242–3), the heads of states and governments of the euro area hoped that announcing a European action plan for Greece would be able to reduce spreads on Greek bonds and therefore secure Greece's market access.

This was not the case. Greece's yields on long-term bonds increased towards 8 per cent, which was seen as an unsustainable interest rate (Mody 2018, 249–50). In the following months, grounds were prepared to implement a financial assistance package for Greece (Mody 2018, 246–8). The Greek Loan Facility was debated and finally constructed under immense time constraints. As Ioannou, Leblond, and Niemann (2015, 160) have highlighted, the GLF was an ad hoc solution for Greece, established as a reaction to the imminent risk of sovereign default and contagion risks. On 2 May 2010, the Eurogroup formally agreed to give financial assistance to Greece via bilateral loans from other EMU members pooled in the Greek Loan Facility at the European Commission (Eurogroup 2010).

The GLF was based on IMF operations for financial assistance (Verdun 2015, 225–6). Fourteen members of the euro area agreed to provide 80 billion euro for Greece, coordinated by the European Commission (see table 4.1) in cooperation with the ECB and the IMF. Verdun compares this process to Schengen or the Bologna Process as the loan agreement was established outside of EU law but the European Commission was included in coordinating its operations (Verdun 2015, 225–6). The IMF, as it was decided then, would also join the program, both by contributing with financial assistance (30 billion euro) and by being included in drawing up and managing the adjustment program.

The Greek Loan Facility did not have a formal institutional framework supporting its operations, nor did it have any staff. Rather, it was an informal arrangement by which the heads of states and government made sure that financial assistance for Greece would be provided on common grounds, without independent fiscal transfers or problems of delay. Furthermore, by being set up outside EU law, the Greek Loan Facility offered a way out of the dilemma that the European Union faced due to legal restrictions of the TFEU, especially Article 125 (Verdun 2015, 224). By using bilateral loans pooled at the European Commission, the European Union circumvented the restrictions set by the TFEU on financial assistance. Instead of the EU, European member states granted financial assistance on a bilateral basis. However, it can be argued that the bilateral nature of the loan agreements is merely a technicality in order to prevent further debates on Article 125 (Gocaj and Meunier 2013, 242; Illing 2013, 56).

Table 4.1. Greek Loan Facility contributions

Country	%	€ (billions)	Country	%	€ (billions)
Austria	2.86	1.555	Luxembourg	0.26	0.139
Belgium	3.58	1.942	Malta	0.09	0.051
Cyprus	0.20	0.110	Netherlands	5.88	3.194
Finland	1.85	1.004	Portugal	2.58	1.102
France	20.97	11.388	Slovenia	0.48	0.244
Germany	27.92	15.165	Slovakia	1.02	–*
Ireland	1.64	0.347	Spain	12.24	6.650
Italy	18.42	10.008			
			Total	100	52.9

* Slovakia was initially expected to contribute to the GLF. However, Slovakia decided against a contribution of their own. What is more, Ireland and Portugal opted out of the loan disbursements after they applied for financial assistance programs themselves (Colasanti 2016, 10).
Source: Colasanti (2016, 9)

GLF contributions of euro area members were proportional to the capital amounts of each member state of the European Central Bank (Colasanti 2016, 9). While the Greek Loan Facility was supposed to pool bilateral loans from all EMU members, Slovakia decided not to participate in the GLF. Ireland and Portugal initially agreed to join, but then opted out as they applied for financial assistance themselves only a few months later (see 4.4.2). Table 4.1 illustrates the initial financial contributions to the Greek Loan Facility.

The establishment of the GLF therefore marked the first coordinated response of the EU to what would later be known as the euro crisis. Furthermore, the creation of the GLF established the operations of the Troika (European Commission, European Central Bank, International Monetary Fund), which would work on the implementation and supervision of structural reforms that the Greek government needed to put forward in order to gain access to financial assistance (Verdun 2015, 224). While being an ad hoc solution to the crisis, the GLF's mechanism of pooling financial contributions and governing the assistance process on an intergovernmental basis would later come to serve as a model for future financial assistance mechanisms (Verdun 2015, 225).

4.2.2 European Financial Stability Facility

When the GLF was established, it became quickly apparent to heads of states and governments of the EU that the market dynamics that had pushed Greece out of financial markets were threatening to affect other EMU members as well. They could therefore potentially lead to additional countries needing financial assistance due to unsustainable refinancing options on financial markets and severe problems with market access (Ioannou, Leblond, and Niemann 2015, 160).

The necessity of a temporary financial backstop had been debated throughout the establishment of the Greek Loan Facility. After the meeting of the Council of the EU on 9 May 2010, a solution to cope with contagion risks was officially announced (Verdun 2015, 225). The member states of the euro area decided to put forward a temporary firewall with enough financial resources to calm capital markets and effectively reduce yields on long-term bonds. In total, this temporary firewall was supposed to be able to provide 750 billion euro. The resources were drawn from three sources: (1) the European Financial Stability Facility (EFSF) provided 440 billion euro, backed by guarantees of euro area members, (2) the EFSM provided 60 billion euro, backed by EU funds (see 4.2.3), and (3) the IMF agreed to provide up to 250 billion euro[5] (European Council 2010; see also Gocaj and Meunier 2013, 244).

In order to provide the 440 billion euro of this package deal, the European governments established the EFSF as a temporary financial firewall based on a special purpose vehicle (Gocaj and Meunier 2013, 243). The EFSF was created outside of EU law and was fundamentally based on intergovernmental principles (Tooze 2018, 343). On 17 May 2010, its name was officially announced, and the EFSF was formally established on 7 June 2010. After more than 90 per cent of the financial guarantee was ratified by the EFSF member states, it came into force on 4 August 2010. The share of commitments resembled the ECB shares of the euro area member states (Gocaj and Meunier 2013, 246; see also table 4.2).

The EFSF operated without paid-in capital. It worked as a financial institution that borrowed money on financial markets based on guarantee commitments by its member states. These operations were based on contracts between the EFSF and the governments (Illing 2013, 64).

The effective lending capacity of the EFSF was restricted to 440 billion euro. However, its capital guarantee was increased from 440 billion euro to almost 780 billion euro on 21 July 2011. This enlargement of guarantees to 177 per cent was a result of the necessity of having AAA-rated guarantees worth 440 billion euro in the portfolio. Ratification processes of increased guarantees were completed on 13 October 2011. Once Greece, Ireland, and Portugal received financial assistance through the EFSF, they were left out of the guarantees, which effectively reduced the facility's guarantees to 724 billion euro. Shortly after,

Table 4.2. EFSF guarantee commitments

Member State	EFSF max. guarantee commitments, € (millions)	EFSF contribution %	New EFSF max. guarantee commitments € (millions)	New EFSF contribution %
Austria	21,639.19	2.7750	21,639.19	2.9869
Belgium	27,031.99	3.4666	27,031.99	3.7313
Cyprus	1,525.68	0.1957	0.00	0.00
Estonia	1,994.86	0.2558	1,994.86	0.2754
Finland	13,974.03	1.7920	13,974.03	1.9289
France	158,487.53	20.3246	158,487.53	21.8762
Germany	211,045.90	27.0647	211,045.90	29.1309
Greece	21,897.74	2.8082	0.00	0.00
Ireland	12,378.15	1.5874	0.00	0.00
Italy	139,267.81	17.8598	139,267.81	19.2233
Luxembourg	1,946.94	0.2497	1,946.94	0.2687
Malta	704.33	0.0903	704.33	0.0972
Netherlands	44,446.32	5.6998	44,446.32	6.1350
Portugal	19,507.26	2.5016	0.00	0.00
Slovakia	7,727.57	0.9910	7,727.57	1.0666
Slovenia	3,664.30	0.4699	3,664.30	0.5058
Spain	92,543.56	11.8679	92,543.56	12.7739
Total	779,783.14	100	724,474.32	100

Source: European Stabilty Mechanism (2017b, 36)

the funds of the EFSF were officially expanded to 1,000 billion euro (Verdun 2013, 31).

The EFSF was founded as a private company (*société anonyme*) registered and based in Luxembourg. From the beginning, the private company was owned and coordinated by the member states that provided its capital (Donnelly 2018, 88). The temporary EFSF was created as a special purpose vehicle which would be dissolved after its purpose was fulfilled (Donnelly 2018, 88; Verdun 2015, 226). Setting up the EFSF this way meant that putting it into force would only take a short amount of time and would not entail changing EU treaties, which might not have been politically possible (Verdun 2015, 226). It further allowed financial assistance to be intergovernmental and to be available to members of the euro area only (Gocaj and Meunier 2013, 245; Verdun 2015, 226). Due to its intergovernmental nature outside of EU law, the European Parliament was not included in its operations (Illing 2013, 64).

This intergovernmental solution was the result of a "polarised debate on whether the Council of the Commission would lead the new mechanism" (Gocaj and Meunier 2013, 245). During the summit on 9 May 2010, the heads of states and governments discussed whether financial assistance should follow the intergovernmental path set out by the Greek Loan Facility, or whether financial assistance should be provided with more influence from the European Commission via an institutional solution under EU law. An intergovernmental special purpose vehicle without direct control by the European Commission was chosen due to opposition from Germany to more control for the European Commission (Gocaj and Meunier 2013, 245; see also Donnelly 2018, 88–90).

While the EFSF is an intergovernmental financial institution based on Luxembourg law, its operations were first briefly managed by the European Investment Bank (European Investment Bank 2010; see also Verdun 2015, 226) in a limited services agreement. The EIB provided back-office support for the accounting and documentation of loans at a time where the EFSF had only a limited amount of staff (Gocaj and Meunier 2013, 246). Furthermore, the German Debt Management Office was included in debt issuance, cash, and risk management (Gocaj and Meunier 2013, 246). In its first months of operation, the EFSF was not included in day-to-day operations of financial assistance programs. Klaus Regling was selected as the EFSF's chief executive director in 2010. As an interview partner argued, the EFSF at first focused on providing the funds for the financial adjustment programs and strengthening its own institutional architecture:

> This is a natural development, if you keep in mind that at the beginning, we were ten plus people when the first programme started. It is obvious that you cannot play in the same league as the European Commission that went to Ireland with a team of twenty people. Being a small start-up, we had to focus on what was the main task: for us that was the financing of ESM programmes and keeping the financial architecture together. We were so busy with our main task that there was simply no room for other tasks. (Interview 30, 24 July 2018)

However, the EFSF started to recruit more personnel and thus became more active in the daily program processes outside of financing issues. It made for different experiences in terms of cooperation with debtor countries (European Stability Mechanism 2017a, 72).

Financial assistance by the European Financial Stability Facility came with concrete policy conditionality in the form of a Memorandum of

Understanding and thus followed the path the Greek Loan Facility started in 2010 (Verdun 2015, 226). As a prerequisite for being able to apply for support from the EFSF, member states had to lose access to capital markets or be at the verge of losing it due to high interest rates. Once a country applied for financial assistance, the European Commission, in liaison with the ECB and the IMF, negotiated and put together a formal program, including a plan on financial transactions and a Memorandum of Understanding on structural reforms. These terms had to be approved by the Eurogroup before the EFSF was allowed to carry out its operations (Gocaj and Meunier 2013, 246).

The EFSF had an effectively limited tenure of three years. After June 2013, its operations were taken over by the permanent European Stability Mechanism (Gocaj and Meunier 2013, 245). While the EFSF stopped providing new financial assistance programs after the ESM came into force (see 4.2.3), the EFSF continued to administer its financial assistance programs for Ireland, Portugal, and Greece (Verdun 2015, 226).

Initially, the EFSF was created never to be used. Just putting the option on the table was supposed to reduce bond yields and thus decrease risks of losing refinancing access for EMU members (European Stability Mechanism 2019c, 53). At first, the EFSF was met with positive reactions on financial markets (Tooze 2018, 343). However, it did not take long until worries of sovereign default again led to unsustainably high yields (Gocaj and Meunier 2013, 246). Shortly after the EFSF came into power, heads of states and governments came to the conclusion that a temporary firewall for three years would not be enough to secure the single currency. Hence, shortly after its establishment, talks of creating a permanent institution began (Donnelly 2018, 88).

4.2.3 European Financial Stabilisation Mechanism

Shortly after the first Greek program was set up, it became clear that Greece was not the only euro area member with severe balance-of-payments problems. Other members of the shared currency were at risk of losing access to financial markets as well. As it became apparent that other member states might be in the situation to apply for financial assistance, the European Union decided to implement a temporary financial safety net (the EFSF). The European Commission participated in the temporary backstop with a contribution of its own. The EFSM was created by a council regulation adopted on 11 May 2010 (European Commission 2010a). While the EFSM is located at the European Commission, the European Commission shares the responsibility for the

EFSM with the European Council. The decision process to grant financial assistance was twofold: the intergovernmental European Council decides in general whether financial assistance should be granted by the EFSM, and the European Commission is responsible for its daily operations (Schlosser 2019, 77). Thus, the EFSM effectively copies the EU's Balance of Payment assistance to non-EMU countries (Schlosser 2019, 77). Despite efforts by the European Commission, the member states were not convinced that the EFSM should be given the possibility to borrow directly on financial markets using the national budgets of member states as guarantees (Schlosser 2019, 78).

The EFSM supported the operations of the temporary financial backstop with 60 billion euro. This was achieved by raising funds on financial markets with guarantees from the European Commission by using the budget of the European Union as collateral, which effectively included countries that are not part of the euro area. In this way, the EFSM is similar to the Medium-Term Financial Assistance that was used to support Hungary, Latvia, and Romania in 2008 (Salines, Glöckler, and Truchlewski 2012, 675). The EFSM was activated in three cases. It provided 22.5 billion euro to the Irish financial assistance program and 24.3 billion euro (out of 25.6 billion euro) to the Portuguese financial assistance program. While the EFSM was not put in use during the second Greek financial adjustment program, it was reactivated in the political turmoil concerning a possible third Greek financial adjustment program in the summer of 2015.

Due to acute refinancing problems during the negotiation period, the European Commission proposed to reactivate the EFSM in order to grant the Greek government a bridging loan of 7.16 billion euro to cover financial obligations to the IMF and the ECB in July 2015. Greece officially requested the bridging loan on 15 July 2015, which the Council of the European Union agreed to two days later (Council of the European Union 2015; Reuters 2015). The bridging loan had a short-term maturity of three months (Council of the European Union 2015, 6). After the third Greek financial adjustment program was effectively put in place, Greece repaid the bridging loan in August 2015 by using funds from the third program.

The EFSM does not engage in the funding of new financial assistance programs, as this task has been delegated to the permanent European Stability Mechanism. However, it is still an active device for the European Commission to engage in tasks regarding the existing loans for Ireland and Portugal, as well as for future scenarios in which a member of the single currency would need a bridging loan with a very short maturity.

4.2.4 European Stability Mechanism

After the implementation of the temporary financial safety net for the euro area, academic and political debates about the necessity to make changes to the newly implemented EFSF quickly emerged. Its lending ceiling was questioned, as well as its temporary character. The high interest rates euro area members had to pay for financial assistance through the EFSF were criticized as being unsustainable (Gocaj and Meunier 2013, 247). Furthermore, its instruments were put into question: Trichet, at that time president of the ECB, called for further quantitative and qualitative enhancements of the EFSF (Reuters 2011). Even before its official implementation, he also argued for a direct recapitalization of banks via the EFSF (Gocaj and Meunier 2013, 247).

After an initial short period of calming financial markets, sovereign bond holders quickly worried about the prospects of bonds from countries in severe fiscal stress once the temporary EFSF was set to expire, which led to further increases in bond yields (Donnelly 2018, 90). The EFSF was able to contain yield increases for a short period. However, the long-term perspective on the euro crisis, further contagion to other euro area countries, and continued risks of a Greek default put additional pressure on the heads of state and governments in late 2010 (Gocaj and Meunier 2013, 247). In order to provide a setting that would calm financial markets and provide more time to resolve fiscal problems within the euro area, heads of states and governments decided to establish an institution to act as a permanent safety net (Ioannou, Leblond, and Niemann 2015, 160; see also Gocaj and Meunier 2013, 247).

Despite its initial rejection of such a permanent mechanism, the German government agreed to implement an ESM in late 2010, as pressure from financial markets further increased (Donnelly 2018, 88; Gocaj and Meunier 2013). The final decision to implement a permanent stabilizing mechanism was made during the prominent walk taken by Merkel and Sarkozy in Deauville in October 2010 (Young and Semmler 2011, 15). As Tooze shows, the agreement of Germany to the establishment of the ESM was a political concession, especially to France. Several other proposals were discussed, such as Eurobonds, shared liabilities at the European level, or an increase of the EFSF's lending capacities. The German government agreed to none of these proposals but was willing to put the temporary safety net on a permanent basis (Tooze 2018, 418).

After months of debate following the establishment of the EFSF, the European Council generally agreed to establish the ESM during its summit on 16–17 December 2010. A first step towards the establishment of a permanent institution was taken during the council summit on 24–25 March 2011 (Gocaj and Meunier 2013, 248). The ESM Treaty was originally signed by European finance ministers on 11 July 2011 after reluctant support by Germany (Donnelly 2018, 88–9; see also Ioannou, Leblond, and Niemann 2015, 160). After its initial signing the ESM Treaty continued to be discussed, and a reformed treaty was signed on 2 February 2012, including further arrangements between the ESM member states and technical improvements. A central revision revolved around the question of conditions attached to financial aid as well as how much financial assistance could be granted (Donnelly 2018, 89). A second reform would result in an amending agreement in 2021 (see 8.1). The ESM was arranged to take over the financing role of the EFSF after its originally planned expiry date in June 2013. However, due to continuous contagion pressure in EMU and a common perspective of insufficient capitalization of the EFSF, the ESM's inception was brought forward to September 2012 (Gocaj and Meunier 2013, 249): The treaty came into force on 27 September 2012 after 90 per cent of its capital requirements were met after ratification by Germany. On 8 October 2012, the ESM officially started operations with its first meeting of staff. Its first loans were paid out to Spain on 11 December 2012 (Ioannou, Leblond, and Niemann 2015, 160).

The ESM is a separate legal entity, but the EFSF and the ESM share personnel and facilities (European Parliament 2018, 3). Hence, the ESM de facto took over the operations of financial assistance programs financed through the EFSF, while the EFSF continues to operate loan repayments, etc. While the institutional and contractual foundations of the ESM's predecessors (bilateral loans, EFSF/EFSM) have been different, the functionality remains the same: EMU members with severe balance-of-payments problems receive temporary financial assistance while being committed to strict policy conditionality to meet financial and socio-economic targets. As the ESM Treaty came into force in 2012, its predecessors can be interpreted as building steps in an institutional development process.

In its early stages, the ESM could have been described as a permanent special purpose vehicle, as Verdun (2015, 227), for example, argued. Surely there are similarities in the way the institutions operate, the way they are governed by the members of the euro area, and so forth. However, the ESM differs from its predecessor, the EFSF, in several key dimensions. First, it is permanent and thus now a new institution in EMU governance (despite being created outside of EU law), a role that has been further expanded as time progressed (see 4.5). Unlike

Table 4.3. ESM shareholder contributions

Country	ESM contribution key	Capital subscription in billion euro	Paid-in capital in billion euro
Austria	2.7418%	19.42	2.22
Belgium	3.4250%	24.27	2.78
Cyprus	0.1933%	1.37	0.16
Croatia	0.5215%	3.69	0.42*
Estonia	0.2527%	1.79	0.20
Finland	1.7706%	12.54	1.43
France	20.0809%	142.27	16.26
Germany	26.7402%	189.45	21.65
Greece	2.7745%	19.66	2.25
Ireland	1.5684%	11.11	1.27
Italy	17.6457%	125.02	14.28
Latvia	0.2732%	1.93	0.22
Lithuania	0.4042%	2.86	0.33
Luxembourg	0.2467%	1.75	0.20
Malta	0.0892%	0.63	0.07
Netherlands	5.6315%	39.90	4.56
Portugal	2.4716%	17.52	2.00
Slovakia	0.9791%	6.94	0.79
Slovenia	0.4643%	3.29	0.37
Spain	11.7256%	83.08	9.50
Total	100%	708.46	80.97

Source: European Stabilty Mechanism (2023), adjustments by author, *Croatia will provide its 0.42 billion euro paid-in capital over the period of 2023 to 2028 in yearly tranches.

the EFSF, the ESM is not a private company under Luxembourg law (see 4.2.2). Instead, the ESM is a treaty-based, permanent, intergovernmental institution, governed by the members of the euro area (see 4.3). Second, the ESM has a higher capital stock. While EFSF and EFSM combined had an effective capital stock of 500 billion euro, the ESM had a capital stock of 704.8 billion euro (Höing 2016, 17), which was increased to 708.46 billion euro after Croatia joined the euro area (table 4.3). Each member is liable only for its ECB share.

Third, member states paid a deposit into the ESM. The ESM thus currently has a fixed capital stock of 80.97 billion euro and is able to take up additional capital up to 627.49 billion euro. According to the ESM Treaty, the ESM is only able to take up additional capital that is backed with at least 15 per cent of fixed capital (see table 4.3). Fourth, unlike the EFSF and the initial proposal (Verdun 2015, 227), the ESM is able to provide financial assistance to private banks after a decision by European heads of states and governments in June 2013 (Ioannou, Leblond, and Niemann 2015, 163). The ESM's ability to engage in recapitalizing private banks is effectively limited to 60 billion euro and is based on an instrument which is restricted by the Single Supervisory Mechanism and the bail-in rulebook included in the Bank Recovery and Resolution Directive of the EU (Ioannou, Leblond, and Niemann, 163). This institutional role for financial market security has been further expanded as the ESM is also the central backstop for the banking union's Single Resolution Fund,[6] which was first agreed to by European heads of state or governments in December 2018 (European Council 2018; see also 8.1).

Drafting the ESM Treaty was not only a European matter. As the IMF was perceived as having credible experience with crises surrounding sovereign debt, its staff and managing director engaged in drafting and constructing the ESM Treaty "through direct interaction with national and European officials and elected policy-makers" (Schwarzer 2015, 619). They not only interacted on the issue of a permanent solution but also provided best practices for handling financial assistance matters, as well as delivering blueprints to national administrations (Schwarzer 2015, 620).

Furthermore, the ESM Treaty, for the first time, formalized the role of the IMF and the ECB in euro area rescue management. Whereas the GLF and the EFSF/EFSM assistance programs already de facto included the IMF and the ECB in their operations and gave both institutions central roles, the ESM Treaty formalized this arrangement (Lüggert 2017, 120; Obwexer 2012, 237–42; see also European Stability Mechanism 2012, 5). However, the perception of close cooperation with the IMF has changed over the years. As the crisis lost its immediate risk of further contagion and the IMF became weary of its European commitments, the partnership with the IMF lost its importance. Regarding the inclusion of the IMF in future programs, an interview partner argued:

> The wording in the ESM Treaty is "whenever possible," which means that if a country has applied for ESM support, it is expected to apply for IMF support as well. However, this was not possible for Spain, because the IMF does not have a corresponding financial sector programme. In that regard, a different form of cooperation was needed. To that end, changing the "whenever possible" into a clause according to which a country may ask the IMF for support might be a possibility. If you read the Meseberg Declaration, it already says "may ask for support," which I believe is where the future discussions will focus on. (Interview 30, 24 July 2018)

This is especially the case since the IMF started to develop a perspective on the financial assistance programs that is different from that of its European partners (e.g., Blanchard and Leigh 2013; Obstfeld and Thomsen 2013). Re-evaluation of the role of the IMF led to stronger calls for greater European autonomy (Hacker 2018, 5) and thus strengthened the role of the ESM in Europe's crisis management. During the third Greek financial assistance program, the European Stability Mechanism was upgraded, now directly negotiating with the country applying for financial assistance about the program's conditions, along with the European Commission, the European Central Bank, and the International Monetary Fund (Höing 2016, 15).

The ESM does not provide financial transfers. Like the GLF and the EFSF, it grants financial assistance via loans, which, according to the ESM Treaty, must be paid back in full. It therefore respects Article 125 of TFEU, which forbids member states to assume the financial commitments of other member states (Höing 2016, 18). However, depending on future reforms, the ESM could play a viable role in a financial compensation mechanism across the euro area (Höing 2016, 16–17). While financial assistance by the ESM is no form of fiscal transfer, the establishment of the ESM does pose the question of its influence on EMU, as applying for financial assistance does result in severe structural reform programs.

The EFSF started with about 10 to 15 staff members (Interview 30, 24 July 2018), but the ESM operated with about 180 staff members in 2018 and planned to increase its personnel by 20 per cent over the next years (Frankfurter Allgemeine Zeitung 2018). In 2022, the ESM had approximately 220 employees (European Stability Mechanism 2022a, para. 6). The personnel running the operations overlap with the EFSF, which underlines the continuity between both mechanisms. Its managing director is appointed for five years and can be re-elected once. The current managing director is Pierre Gramegna, who was appointed by the ESM board of directors on 25 November 2022 and started his position on 1 December 2022 (European Stability Mechanism 2022c). Klaus Regling, his predecessor, was first appointed in 2012 and re-elected in 2017 for a second term until 2022 (European Parliament 2018, 4). Regling also was the CEO of the predecessor EFSF.

4.3 Decision-Making inside the ESM

This section provides insights into the ESM's decision-making. First, it presents in more detail the ESM's organizational structure and its decision-making bodies (see 4.3.1). Second, it provides insights into the central role of the Eurogroup (4.3.2) and describes the role that parliaments play in ESM decision-making (4.3.3). Last, it describes the relationship between the ESM and the European Commission (4.3.4).

4.3.1 *The Governance Structure of the ESM*

The governance of the ESM is based on two central decision-making bodies that reflect and underline its intergovernmental character. The ESM's highest decision-making body is the board of governors. The board of governors is responsible for essential decisions in ESM governance, such as new financial assistance programs or the general direction of existing programs. Its members are representatives of the twenty member states of the ESM Treaty and mirror the members of the Eurogroup (Salines, Glöckler, and Truchlewski 2012, 676; see also 4.3.2): The board of governors consists of members of national governments who are responsible for finances (European Stability Mechanism 2012, 13) and is chaired by the president of the Eurogroup, although the board of governors could also decide to choose a different member of the board as its chair (European Stability Mechanism 2012, 13). According to the treaty, the board of governors must meet at least once a year, or whenever the operations of the ESM make it necessary. De facto, the board of governors officially meets more often, at least three to four times per year and mostly in combination with Eurogroup meetings. The ESM managing director is often invited to speak at the Eurogroup press conferences, which highlights the strong institutional link between the ESM and the Eurogroup.

The member states' voting share is weighted according to their ESM shares (see table 5.3) The board of governors has to decide unanimously on matters of financial assistance, although in defined cases of emergency, a majority of 85 per cent will allow the board of governors to grant financial assistance as well (Höing 2016, 17). Larger member states such as Germany therefore have a blocking minority when it comes to financial assistance programs. If there is a dispute among the shareholders (and thus the board of governors) about the interpretation of the ESM Treaty and ESM governance, the dispute must be settled at the Court of Justice of the European Union (European Stability Mechanism 2012, 51).

The board of directors is the second central decision-making body. Each governor can appoint to the board of directors one director and one alternate director from national pools of people with high competence in financial affairs. The board of directors effectively mirrors the Eurogroup Working Group (Schlosser 2019, 74). It has to ensure that

Figure 4.1. ESM governance structure

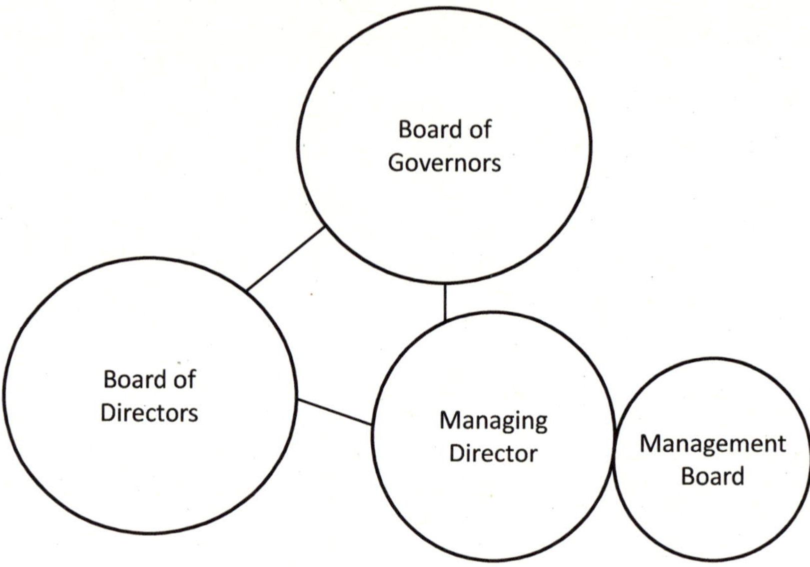

Source: European Stability Mechanism (2022b)

the operations of the ESM are in accordance with the ESM Treaty (European Stability Mechanism 2012, 19), is responsible for decisions in daily operations, and takes on tasks that the board of governors delegates to it (European Stability Mechanism 2012, 19). As the body responsible for daily operations, the board of directors plays an important role in decision-making processes concerning financial assistance programs and is the operational centre (Schlosser 2018, 85). Unlike the board of governors, the board of directors decides via qualified majorities, unless otherwise stated (European Stability Mechanism 2012, 19). The member states' voting share is weighted according to their ESM shares (see table 4.3).

In addition to the two boards, the managing director of the ESM is of key importance. The board of governors appoints the managing director for a duration of five years. The managing director is the ESM's chief of staff and legal representative, acting for the ESM in public. A central task of this position is running the everyday business of the ESM, as directed by the board of governors, as well organizing and appointing ESM staff (European Parliament 2018, 4). The managing director chairs the board of directors meetings, participates in the meetings of the board of governors, and speaks for the ESM during Eurogroup press conferences. The managing director is therefore a central figure, in terms of both administration and representation.

All members of the board of governors, the board of directors, the ESM director, and further staff are immune to legal proceedings in respect to acts performed as a part of their position. Documents of the decision-making bodies, as well as those of staff members, are also inviolable (European Stability Mechanism 2012, 48; see also Karatzia and Markakis 2017, 236).

These two central decision-making bodies and the position of the ESM director reflect the intergovernmental character of the ESM and remove the Commission from the daily proceedings of financial assistance programs to a certain degree (Schlosser 2019, 85), but not from the policy conditionality processes, where the Commission continues to play a key role (see 4.4.3). The ESM Treaty states in Article 5(3) and 6(2) that both the member of the European Commission in charge of Economic and Monetary Affairs and the president of the ECB are able to participate in the meetings of both the board of governors and the board of directors (European Stability Mechanism 2012, 14, 19; see also Karatzia and Markakis 2017, 234). Including the Commission and the ECB is a central aspect of meetings of the Eurogroup, which also invite the ESM managing director to its meetings.

The treaty defines these roles as observatory, and it is somewhat unclear to what extend the European Commission and the ECB are involved in the discussions of the ESM. As Karatzia and Markakis argue, legal provisions concerning the role of the European Commission and ECB in ESM decision-making bodies are mostly concerned with restricting the information both institutions are able to present publicly (Karatzia and Markakis 2017, 237). Furthermore, Article 5(4) and 6(3) underline that the board of governors and the board of directors are able to include non-euro area member states as observers to the discussion, if they are also engaged in stability support operations within the single currency (European Stability Mechanism 2012, 14, 19). Articles 5(5) and 6(4) of the ESM Treaty also allow other institutions, such as the IMF, to be included on an ad hoc basis (European Stability Mechanism 2012, 14, 19).

4.3.2 The Central Role of the Eurogroup

As Salines, Glöckler, and Truchlewski (2012) highlighted, the governance structure of the European Stability Mechanism underlines intergovernmental decision-making processes that were put forward to cope with the crisis (see also 4.3.1). As a consequence of its decision-making structure, the ESM puts additional power in the hands of the Eurogroup and the Eurogroup Working Group (EWG) for the bailout programs. Especially during the first period after its establishment, the ESM relied on EU institutions for administrative support, negotiation of policy conditionality, and combined program surveillance. As Salines, Glöckler, and Truchlewski have argued: "[t]he overlap in terms of composition between the EU Council and ESM structures is [...] significant" (2012, 676). This is especially the case in terms of the Eurogroup and the EWG. While being informal bodies, they have been discussed as de facto governing bodies of the euro area, as the Eurogroup is the central decision-making body for EMU governance (Abels 2018a, 2018b, 2019; Puetter 2006).

Thus, the Eurogroup and its preparatory body, the EWG, play central roles in the way the ESM is governed. They also are in a powerful position in terms of the overall design of financial assistance programs. This is especially the case for the Eurogroup Working Group, as the Eurogroup's preparatory body. Already empowered by the EFSF, the EWG is accorded strong influence over the day-to-day operations of the permanent ESM, including direct engagement with program missions (Interview 25, 9 July 2018). While the European Commission negotiated the Memorandum of Understanding (MoU) during the euro crisis and signed it on behalf of the ESM, the Eurogroup (as the ESM's board of governors) and the Eurogroup Working Group (as the ESM's board of directors) have to approve the MoU. As Schlosser has put it, "[...] it is the Euro Working Group that retains the final word and that decides on the main terms of the financial assistance facility" (Schlosser 2019, 83).

As the governance structure of the ESM (see 4.3.1 and figure 4.1) and the process towards financial assistance (see 4.4.1. and figure 4.2) highlight, the board of governors and board of directors are the central decision-making bodies within the European Stability Mechanism. Not only do they decide on applications for financial support, they are also influential in the negotiations, despite the inclusion of the European Commission and the ECB in MoU negotiations. Although they are formally different decision-making bodies, they de facto hold the same meetings in which the participants change hats during a short break between the official Eurogroup and the official ESM meetings. Thus, as Schlosser argues, "[t]he ESM has, in a feedback loop, converted the Eurogroup from a deliberative informal body into an executive decision-making institution" (Schlosser 2019, 74), which strengthens the influence of the Eurogroup and the EWG, not only in terms of ESM governance, but of EMU governance as a whole.

Since the ESM and its temporary predecessor EFSF are intergovernmental mechanisms outside of the Commission's competences, it is not surprising to see intergovernmental bodies at the heart of the institution. The EFSF framework agreement prominently mentions the EWG as a central decision-making body for its day-to-day operations, as well as central decision processes, such as approvals of Memoranda of Understanding (European Commission 2011a). The ESM Treaty does not include the Eurogroup or the Euro Working Group directly (European Stability Mechanism 2012). However, as the board of governors and the board of directors mirror the Eurogroup and the EWG, "the ESM is informally subordinated to the Eurogroup" (Schlosser 2019, 86), which underlines the centrality of the Eurogroup in ESM decision-making and thus the strong link between the Eurogroup and the governance of financial assistance (Schlosser 2019, 86).

The predominance of intergovernmental bodies was visible throughout the crisis, as the European Council, and the German government in particular, did not want the European Commission to be in the driving seat of the financial assistance process. The member states also decided against the European Commission to be the main financing institution, using guarantees of member states as collateral (see above). The Commission was an influential institution in this process (see 4.4.3) and has developed a strong working relationship with the ESM (see 8.1). However, its officials are "agents for the member states, insofar as we have to take care of whether the EFSF credits will be paid back. And we take care of this on behalf of the member states" (Interview 25, 9 July 2018), as an interview partner argued. The temporary European Financial Stability Facility and the permanent European Stability Mechanism reflect the reluctance of the European Council to let the Commission be in charge of the bailout programs, as an interview partner highlighted (Interview 25, 9 July 2018).

An MoU is primarily negotiated by the Commission, the ECB, and potentially the IMF. However, the ESM's governing bodies have gained a "decisive say in the provision of crisis loans" (Abels 2018b, 520; see also 4.4.1). The intergovernmental dynamics that shaped the crisis management and found resonance in the institutional set-up of the ESM can also be seen in terms of program design, as willingness to pay and political feasibility of the creditor countries play an important role in the design (Interview 5, 7 March 2018).

4.3.3 The ESM and Parliamentary Participation

The ESM, as an intergovernmental institution based on a treaty outside EU law (see 4.2.4), is primarily accountable to its member states and thus their national governments. Furthermore, the national finance ministers play a prominent role, as they are the members of the ESM's central decision-making body (see 4.3.1 and 4.3.2). Furthermore, the ESM Treaty only requires that the board of auditors' annual report be sent to national parliaments (Karatzia and Markakis 2017, 246).

However, national parliaments are included in the decision-making processes, albeit to different degrees.[7] The degree of parliamentary influence depends on the parliaments of the ESM member states. As Kreilinger (2019, 149–52) shows, based on the third Greek program, there are national parliaments with strong participation rights, such as Germany, Finland, Estonia, and Austria. Here, parliaments or special parliamentary committees must vote in favour of a new ESM program before negotiations start and must approve the new financial assistance program after the negotiations are concluded. In the German case, the Bundestag must approve every tranche transferred to a program country. In other countries, such as Latvia, the Netherlands, and Spain, parliaments only have ex post approval rights for new financial assistance programs, either via the parliament or via a special committee. A third category of countries have no voting rights for their national parliaments concerning ESM programs. In Belgium, Cyprus, Ireland, Italy, Lithuania, Luxembourg, Malta, Portugal, Slovakia, and Slovenia, decisions on new and already existing financial assistance programs lie solely with the government (Kreilinger 2019, 150).

This asymmetry of parliamentary influence on ESM decision-making (Höing 2015) does come with some friction. While it is generally agreed that each ESM member state decides on its own how national parliaments are included, there have been cases where this asymmetry did lead to political problems, as the Irish case highlights: a German parliamentary committee received information concerning the Irish program prior to the Irish parliament. This information was picked up by an Irish newspaper (Interview 20, 18 April 2018).

Asymmetric voting rights can thus lead to asymmetric information and hence could lead to political tensions. Furthermore, asymmetric parliamentary influence does challenge accountability relations in EMU, especially in terms of the ESM (Höing 2015, v).

Unlike national parliaments, the European Parliament (EP) has no direct influence on ESM decisions, whether broader strategies or the everyday operations of the ESM. The European Parliament is also not mentioned in the ESM Treaty (Karatzia and Markakis 2017, 246). Since the ESM is based on an intergovernmental treaty outside EU law, it is not accountable to the European Parliament (European Parliament 2018). Although European Council President van Rompuy put forward the idea of parliamentary control by the EP during the TFEU amendment process, as he said in the European Parliament that the ESM "operation will also be subject to the scrutiny of your Parliament" (European Council 2012, 3), no formal control rights have been granted to the EP so far. This has been heavily criticized by MEPs, as the ESM is viewed as having a major influence on European economic governance while lacking parliamentary control at the European level (Interview 26, 10 July 2018; see also Salines, Glöckler, and Truchlewski 2012, 676).

Informally, however, the EP does have some control over the ESM, albeit only to a very small degree and without direct influence on its operations. The ESM's managing director participates in informal Q&A sessions in the EP's Committee on Economic and Monetary Affairs (ECON). Klaus Regling first participated in a meeting of the ECON committee on 24 September 2013. While this practice is not formalized, the ESM does participate in these debates in a semi-regular manner (European Parliament 2018, 11). What is more, the ESM answers written parliamentary inquiries. Klaus Regling, during his time as managing director of the ESM, has spoken in favour of an agreement between the EP and the ESM in order to formalize these hearings (European Parliament 2018, 18). The EP, however, is not entitled to have its questions to the ESM answered. The ESM's managing director has always started the debate with a remark that these meetings are an exchange of views, as the ESM has no accountability towards the EP. This lack of accountability to the EP has been criticized by interview partners. For example,

> The first argument he [Klaus Regling] has used ... is to say: I am 100 per cent accountable to national parliaments. And, well I tell him, is that, well it is not true, because he never speaks to the parliaments, the national parliaments as a whole. (Interview 26, 10 July 2018)

Improving the ESM's accountability has been discussed during early stages of EMU reform deliberations in 2017 and 2018. However, proposals to include the EP in governing the ESM's operations were dismissed early in the process. Hence, the ESM remains an institution that is accountable only to parliaments of its member states.

4.4 Financial Assistance Programs

Since the initial financial assistance program for Greece in 2010, the ESM and its institutional predecessors have provided financial assistance to several states. Except for Spain, all of the recipients have been issued loans within a macroeconomic adjustment program, a key instrument of the ESM (and its predecessors).[8] While the first programs were created in a very short amount of time and without a formalized procedure, financial assistance in the euro area has now become formalized and institutionalized. The following sections first describe how financial assistance in the single currency is organized (see 4.4.1). Second, they provide an overview of the past programs (see 4.4.2). Last, they explain the ESM's position within the financial assistance architecture (4.4.3).

4.4.1 Overview of the Financial Assistance Procedure

While the first financial assistance programs were established in an ad hoc manner, as there were no institutions or instruments to deal with risks of sovereign default in the euro area, an institutional architecture was quickly developed (see 4.2). Requests for financial assistance follow a formalized procedure, which is laid out in the ESM Treaty (European Stabiliy Mechanism 2012, 28–30), to which an amending agreement will make changes (see 8.1). At the time of writing, the ratification process for these changes is still to be finished. The following section thus focuses on the procedure used during the euro crisis. A discussion of amendments will be presented below (see 8.1).

The ESM is able to grant financial assistance if such assistance is "indispensable to safeguard the financial stability of the euro area as a whole and of its Member States" (European Stability Mechanism 2012, 27). However, member states applying for financial assistance will be subject to strict policy conditionality that includes socio-economic adjustment and respects previously established eligibility criteria for the euro area.

One of the most prominent pre-established criteria for access to financial assistance is the ratification of the Fiscal Compact (TSGC), which includes binding balanced-budget rules in national legislation and preferably constitutional self-correcting fiscal mechanisms (Ioannou, Leblond, and Niemann 2015, 161). Furthermore, the country applying for financial assistance must show that a lack of financial support will endanger the financial stability of the euro area or of its member states.

Financial assistance can only be granted if the member state's debt is perceived as sustainable[9] (Höing 2016, 17).

Another important aspect of the procedure is the involvement of the IMF. According to the treaty (European Stability Mechanism 2012), members applying for financial assistance from the ESM should, "whenever possible" (European Stability Mechanism 2012, 5), also apply for financial assistance from the IMF. However, since decision-making processes of the two institutions work separately, it is not only up to ESM members to fulfil this criterion (Höing 2016, 17). As the discussion concerning the third Greek program and the future role of the ESM in EMU governance shows, the IMF will play a less important role in the future. While it will still be a possibility to apply for financial assistance via the IMF, the treaty's "whenever possible" might become a "may ask for support," as also the Meseberg Declaration highlighted (Presse- und Informationsamt der Bundesregierung 2018).

The formalized procedure of ESM financial assistance permanently establishes an intergovernmental process to grant and distribute financial assistance to euro area members in severe fiscal stress (Gocaj and Meunier 2013, 250). While the procedure does hold important and influential tasks for the European Commission, the European Central Bank, and, to an increasingly lesser degree, the International Monetary Fund, the composition of central decision-making bodies of the ESM and their central function within financial assistance underline its intergovernmental character.

The procedure of granting financial assistance includes five steps. The first is application for support: if a member state seeks financial assistance from the ESM, it has to formally apply for support to the head of the ESM's board of governors (European Stability Mechanism 2012, 28–30; European Stability Mechanism 2017b, 39). This underlines the centrality of the Eurogroup in ESM affairs (see 4.3.2).

The second step is an assessment. After the head of the ESM's board of governors receives the application, the European Commission, the European Central Bank and, if requested, the International Monetary Fund evaluate the situation in terms of actual risk for the member's financial stability and the implications for the stability of the euro area, on behalf of the ESM. The institutions assess whether the country's debt is sustainable. Furthermore, they assess the amount of financial assistance needed (European Stability Mechanism 2012, 28–30; European Stability Mechanism 2017b, 39).

Third comes the proposal. After the evaluation and based on the institutions' assessment, the ESM's board of governors will decide in

Figure 4.2. Financial assistance application process

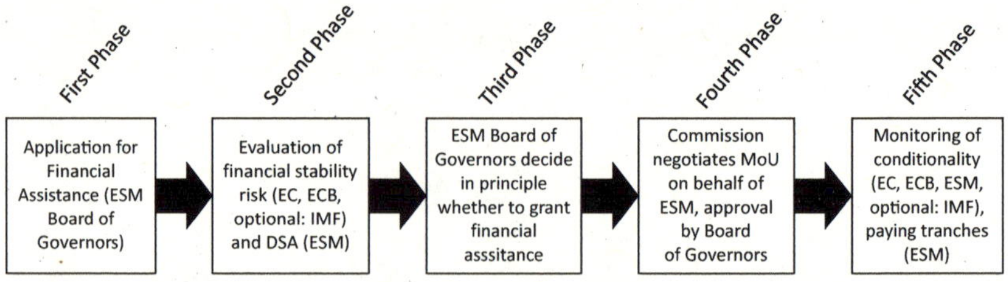

Source: author's compilation, based on European Stability Mechanism (2012, 28—30)

principle whether to grant a financial assistance facility. If the board of governors agrees to grant financial assistance, the ESM managing director will present a proposal to the board of governors for a Financial Assistance Facility Agreement (FFA) including the terms and conditions and choice of instruments (European Stability Mechanism 2012, 28–30; European Stability Mechanism 2017b, 39).

The fourth step is approval of support terms. The European Commission (and the IMF, if asked for) and the applying country establish a common Memorandum of Understanding setting out the policy conditionality for the financial assistance program. The ESM managing director further prepares the Financial Assistance Agreement, which establishes the financial terms in compliance with policy conditionality. The FFA is adopted by the ESM board of directors (European Stability Mechanism 2012, 28–30; European Stability Mechanism 2017b, 39).

The fifth and final step is financial support. After monitoring the applying member state's compliance with the policy conditionality set out in the Memorandum of Understanding, the ESM releases the tranches of financial support after approval by the board of governors (European Stability Mechanism 2012, 28–30; European Stability Mechanism 2017b, 39).

4.4.2 Overview of Existing Programs

The ESM and its institutional predecessors have granted financial assistance seven times in three different forms since 2010. Financial support was given to Greece, Ireland, Portugal, Spain, and Cyprus. Greece was the only euro area member that was granted financial assistance more than once (three times in total). As figure 4.3 shows, six of these programs were granted between 2010 and 2014, at the height of the

Figure 4.3. European financial assistance programs

Source: author's compilation. Grey represents the GLF, light grey represents the EFSF/ EFSM, and black represents the ESM as central European financing instruments.

euro area crisis. Furthermore, only five out of seven programs were cofinanced by the International Monetary Fund. In the case of Spain, financial assistance was granted as an indirect bank recapitalization program, for which the IMF does not have an equivalent instrument and was thus not included in the program. In the case of Greece, differences between the IMF and European counterparts concerning the sustainability of Greek sovereign debt and possibilities of debt relief were a central issue of conflict. The IMF argued in favour of debt relief for Greece (e.g., Obstfeld and Thomsen 2016), whereas the European institutions declared the Greek debt to be sustainable. In the end, the IMF did not participate financially in the third Greek program.

Each financial assistance program came with a Memorandum of Understanding that included similar policy obligations (Greer 2014), monitored by the European Commission, the European Central Bank, the International Monetary Fund, and, in later programs, by the European Stability Mechanism. The programs are generally described as having two objectives: (1) strict consolidation of budgetary deficits, and (2) structural reforms of socio-economic models, including severe reforms to labour markets (e.g., Seikel 2017, 345). Furthermore, the programs focus on reforming national banking sectors.

While the process leading to a financial assistance program (see 4.4.1) stipulates that the European Commission, in liaison with the ECB, assesses the resources necessary to secure financial stability, it is noticeable that most programs are worth 70–80 billion euro. Of that sum, the ESM and its institutional predecessors cover around two-thirds.

4.4.3 The ESM's Role in the Financial Assistance Architecture

The ESM, despite having a central position within the financial assistance procedures (see 4.4.1), does not operate the bailout processes alone. Other institutions, namely the European Commission, the European Central Bank, and the International Monetary Fund, are financially and administratively involved. As explained above (see 4.4.1), the ECB, the European Commission, and, if included, the IMF, hold strong competences concerning policy conditionality attached to financial assistance and the monitoring processes. The competences of the included institutions, however, have changed over time, in line with the institutionalization process of the European Stability Mechanism.

In an early analysis on the dynamics within the Troika – at that time the European Commission, the ECB, and the IMF – Pisani-Ferry, Sapir, and Wolff (2013, 25–6) found no evidence for a systematic division of labour between the institutions. However, as the same analysis argued, the institutions brought different expertise to the table (Pisani-Ferry, Sapir, and Wolff 2013, 25–6). The IMF clearly had the strongest experience with similar crises, albeit outside of the institutional setting of EMU. In addition to the IMF's experience, the European Commission was empowered as a central European agent in these programs by the first financial assistance program for Greece and the institutional setting that was used to provide financial support (Greek Loan Facility, see 4.2.1). While under the supervision of the Eurogroup, the European Commission had a powerful position within the program's governance, as the Commission was responsible for the GLF's coordination and administration. Furthermore, the Commission was responsible for disbursement of tranches to Greece (Schlosser 2019, 76). The ECB was very much involved due to its strong engagement with financial markets.

This division of competences quickly changed after the establishment of the European Financial Stability Facility. Whereas the European Commission was responsible for providing the funds for the program, the administrative part of borrowing money on financial markets was quickly taken over by the EFSF (Interview 30, 24 July 2018). The EFSF started its operations with ten to fifteen employees. Hence, it was unable to engage directly in reviewing the reform process of program countries. At first, the EFSF focused on strengthening the financial aspects of the MoUs, whereas the European Commission was strongly involved in monitoring the program countries in socio-economic issues (Interview 25, 9 July 2018). After the EFSF started to employ more personnel and continued to be more involved in the financial assistance programs, its influence vis-à-vis the European Commission started to increase. A central aspect of gaining competences, however, was the establishment of the ESM and thus the intention to put the financial assistance architecture on a permanent intergovernmental basis.

The division of labour between the ESM and the European Commission emerged and developed over time. It was formalized in a "Memorandum of Understanding on working relations between the Commission and the European Stability Mechanism" in 2018 (European Commission 2018a). In the MoU, both organizations agreed to work together in the policy conditionality and financial design of the programs. While the MoU respects the competences of the European Commission, it includes the ESM as a central partner organization in almost all steps of the financial assistance process (European Commission 2018a). However, as was discussed by interview partners, the MoU between the ESM and the European Commission mostly describes the current state of working relations and not necessarily the working relations the ESM or the European Commission might aim for in the future (see 8.1 for a discussion of possible ESM reforms and treaty amendments).

Hence, the European Stability Mechanism has gained institutional importance as part of the responsibility for financial assistance programs has shifted towards it. The ESM is now in charge of providing the financial framework for such programs, as well as the disbursement of tranches, which also makes the availability of critical information necessary (Interview 30, 24 July 2018). Furthermore, the ESM took over specific tasks during the third Greek program that go beyond the financial aspects.

The ESM already engaged with program countries on a regular basis before the third Greek MoU (European Stability Mechanism 2017a). However, the third Greek program saw a few critical shifts in the tasks the ESM is responsible for. First, the ESM took over the task of providing an Early Warning System to analyse risks in loan repayment, which led to different results than the IMF's debt sustainability analysis. In this regard, it took over central tasks from the IMF, which did not participate in the third Greek program financially. Second, the ESM took over the responsibility for the Greek privatization program (see also 5.2.2.4).

Although the role of the ESM was strengthened and it now participates in ground missions, the European Commission still has an important position in providing policy conditionality, as socio-economic coordination is a responsibility laid out by the EU treaties for the Commission. Hence, the European Commission provides central analyses on different policy areas, such as product markets, labour markets, or fiscal policy. In that way, the ESM does not copy treaty-based competences of the European Commission. Rather, the ESM shares key competences and processes particularly with the European Commission and the ECB, which remain key institutions in drawing up policy conditionalities and compliance procedures.

4.5 Interim Conclusion

This chapter explored the origins of financial assistance instruments within the Economic and Monetary Union, analysed how the implementation process of the ESM and its institutional predecessors took place, and examined the role of the ESM within the financial assistance process at the European level. As analysis of the discussion leading into the creation of EMU highlighted, the necessity of financial assistance instruments within a European currency union was raised already in the early stages of EMU discussions. The ESM's creation stands within the tension field of the Werner Report's broader argument for financial transfers at the European level to counterbalance asymmetric economic developments within a European currency area, and the Delors Report's focus on rule-based monetary integration at the expense of such instruments (see 4.1). In this regard, the ESM is neither an institution of what might be called a transfer union nor an institution that is solely based on the notion of a rule-based stability union (Höing 2016).

The process that led to the current form of the ESM went through different stages of institutionalization, internal organization, and competences in the financial assistance process. It went from an ad hoc mechanism of pooling the financial resources for the Greek program at the Commission to a temporary, intergovernmental special purpose vehicle with a handful of staff in Luxembourg that was supported by a financial instrument of the European Commission, and concluded in a permanent, intergovernmental organization with about 220 staff members in 2022, regular program responsibilities, and participation in country missions (see 4.2).

The process initially strengthened the role of the European Commission, as the GLF and the EFSM were attached to the Commission. However, as European governments were reluctant to give the European Commission more influence and thus focused on intergovernmental solutions, the EFSF and the ESM essentially strengthened the role of the Eurogroup in EMU decision-making process and thus also in financial assistance programs. Until the COVID-19 pandemic, the ESM was the central organization to be approached in terms of an asymmetric socio-economic crisis in the euro area (for a discussion of the ESM's changing role during the COVID-19 pandemic, see 8.2). Its board of governors and board of directors are essential decision-making bodies that decide whether financial assistance should be granted and engage in daily operations. Members of these boards are the same as for the Eurogroup and the Eurogroup Working Group, which essentially links the ESM to the decision-making of these bodies (see 4.3).

While the European Commission has considerably more staff, broader competences, stronger capacities to monitor policy conditionality, and certainly plays a larger role in day-to-day procedures, the ESM and thus the Eurogroup remain the focal points of financial assistance governance in the euro area. The European Commission signs the Memorandum of Understanding for the financial assistance programs, but it does so on behalf of the ESM and only after the MoU is approved by the ESM's Board of Governors (European Stability Mechanism 2012, 29; Interview 25, 9 July 2018). Without a positive decision by the ESM's Board of Governors (and thus the Eurogroup), no program will be granted. Tranches of a financial assistance program will also only be paid out if the ESM agrees to do so (see 4.3 and 4.4).

This central position of the ESM within European financial assistance developed over time, as was analysed above. It became more visible as the institutionalization process of European financial assistance went further and became clearly visible in the Greek crisis of 2015.

The Greek Case: Policy Conditionally and Externally Induced Socio-economic Change

Greece is a central case in the development of the ESM's role in the euro area crisis management. As this chapter highlights, the Greek case offers valuable insights into political economic convergence of EMU members as a consequence of financial assistance. Furthermore, Greece offers important empirical evidence on ideational processes attached to the programs in central policy fields, as well as incentive structures provided by the financial assistance programs, and identifies the euro area crisis as a critical juncture in Greece's political economic development that has enabled central changes.

Chapter 5 proceeds as follows: First, the chapter provides a short historical introduction into central developments of the Greek crisis (see 5.1). Second, it analyses changes in the dependent variable (socio-economic model) from 2009 to 2018, based on institutional changes in Greek labour markets and fiscal policy (see 5.2). Third, the chapter explains the influence of the central independent variable (financial assistance programs, administrated by the ESM and its predecessors) by analysing ideational, interest-based, and historical-institutional processes related to the financial assistance programs (see 5.3 and 5.4). Last, the chapter draws conclusions on how the financial assistance programs changed the Greek socio-economic model and gives an outlook on future developments of Greek capitalism (see 5.5).

5.1 Central Developments of the Greek Crisis

Greece is an interesting case of a mixed-market economy with strong governmental influence in economic affairs that has seen severe institutional change over the last ten years. The economic institutions of Greece – a country on EMU's periphery and with a specific Southern European political economic development (e.g., Manow 2018) – experienced extreme pressure due to a deep and lengthy socio-economic crisis that developed after the initial phase of the global financial crisis of 2007–8.

The Greek crisis had structural differences compared to the problems in other countries with financial assistance programs. After the bankruptcy of Lehman Brothers in September 2008, other countries were much more exposed to the banking crisis and fell into severe economic recession shortly thereafter due to their banking sectors' engagement in subprime markets. Ireland is a prime example of this development (see 6.1). The Greek banking sector, however, was only marginally affected by the global financial crisis of 2008. Its balance-of-payments problems of 2009 resulted from a contraction of its comparatively small export sector and tourism, which play an important part for the Greek economy. The state's automatic stabilizers reacted with higher deficits while tax revenues started to decrease. This accelerated the crisis dynamics (Tooze 2018, 323).

Greece certainly had long-lasting structural economic problems before the crisis (Kentikelenis 2018, 43), despite being a country with high productivity levels in the 1990s (Schweiger 2014, 164), unit labour costs only slightly above the OECD average, and being the second fastest growing economy in the single currency from 2001 to 2007 (Karamessini 2015, 97). A central factor of its structural problems was its weak state capacity and underdeveloped tax-collection system (Featherstone 2011, 196). Furthermore, government spending was highly uncoordinated (Blyth 2013, 63). As was revealed in 2009, the official budget did not include the total Greek government expenditure. Furthermore, sovereign debt was hidden in a multi-level system of social security. Not only did Greece have severe fiscal problems (see table 6.1); it also lacked the economic basis to counter them in a short period of time, as an interview partner highlighted (Interview 4, 5 March 2018).

The southern periphery of the euro area experienced comparatively stronger demand for credit, either by private households, firms, or governments. A key reason for this development was the interest rate harmonization in the first years of EMU in combination with neutralized exchange rate mechanisms and above-average domestic demand. Greece was no exception, as its precrisis growth model was based on two central pillars that accelerated the increase of debt: government expenditure and consumption by private households (Lux and Kompsopoulos 2019, 189; see also I. Kompsopoulos 2016). In the absence of a flexible exchange rate, this combination led to large current account deficit as well as above-average government debt. Hence, the financial crisis intensified structural problems of the Greek socio-economic model within the single currency and thus produced additional vulnerability after the euro crisis materialized (Theodoropoulou 2016, 28).

Greek capitalism was characterized by strong, centralized institutions before the crisis, in terms of both labour markets and fiscal policy. The state played an important coordinative role for the economy. Not only did the government use public employment as a tool to reduce unemployment, which gave the public sector an influential role in the labour market, it also used fiscal means to increase aggregate demand via government consumption and direct economic investments (Theodoropoulou 2016, 28). As Featherstone has highlighted, the Greek government focused on anticompetitive economic regulation (Featherstone 2011, 197). Precrisis Greece can therefore be described as a mixed-market economy with predominantly state-based coordination mechanisms.[1] This was not only the case in terms of economic regulation but also in terms of state presence in certain economic sectors (Spanou 2020, 136). The state's economic presence materialized through state-owned enterprises, semi-states, and direct engagement in business affairs. An above-average amount of the Greek economic turnout was based on public expenditure.

The magnitude of the socio-economic problems in Greece became publicly known only after a change in government following the Greek legislative election on 4 October 2009. The newly elected PASOK (Panhellenic Socialist Movement) government came into office and immediately had to cope with severe financial problems. The European Council put Greece in the excessive deficit procedure as early as April 2009 (Frangakis 2014, 35). Furthermore, the outgoing New Democracy (ND) government had already informed the Eurogroup in July 2009 that the government deficit might amount to 10 per cent. However, the real magnitude of the Greek deficit became known only later in the year (Tooze 2018, 324). The balance-of-payments problems of the Greek government fully materialized after the PASOK government revealed at the Eurogroup meeting in October of 2009 that the Greek deficit would be much higher than expected (Featherstone and Papadimitriou 2017, 238; Mody 2018, 234).

The Greek government announced that the deficit would to be 12 to 13 per cent (Tooze 2018, 324). This figure was updated later to 12.7 per cent of GDP (Tooze 2018, 324). The newly elected government tried to engage in fiscal consolidation, but they faced severe obstacles, both in terms of administrative capacity and in terms of developments on financial markets. Greece's twin deficit in government and current accounts, as well as already high public debt, effectively excluded the Greek government from financial markets as the country's creditworthiness came under severe pressure, leading to unsustainable spreads on government bonds (Spanou 2020, 135–6; Theodoropoulou 2016, 27;

Table 5.1. Selected socio-economic indicators, Greece, 2008–17

Indicator/year	2008	2009	2010	2011	2012	2013	2014	2015	2016	2017
GDP growth (1)	–0.3	–4.3	–5.5	–10.1	–7.1	–2.5	0.5	–0.2	–0.5	1.1
General government debt (% of GDP) (2)	109.4	126.7	147.5	175.2	162.0	178.2	180.3	176.7	180.5	179.5
General government surplus/deficit (% of GDP) (3)	–10.2	–15.1	–11.4	–10.5	–9.1	–13.4	–3.7	–5.9	0.2	0.6
General government spending (% of GDP) (4)	50.8	54.1	52.5	55.1	56.7	62.8	50.7	54.1	49.9	48.5
Employment (20–64) (5)	n/a	65.4	63.5	59.3	54.5	52.5	53.1	54.8	55.9	57.4
Unemployment (6)	n/a	9.8	12.9	18.1	24.8	27.8	26.6	25.0	23.9	21.8

Authors compilation. Sources: (1) Eurostat (2023d); (2) Eurostat (2023e); (3) Eurostat (2023e); (4) Eurostat (2023f); (5) Eurostat (2023a); (6) Eurostat (2023b)

this point was also emphasized by interview partners, e.g., Interview 3, 4 March 2018). In order to prevent a sovereign default and potential loss of its EMU membership, the Greek government turned to its European partners for financial support. What followed was months of negotiations and a continuous worsening of the Greek socio-economic situation overall (Mody 2018, 232–55).

On 23 April 2010, the Greek prime minister announced Greece's official application for financial assistance by the EU and the IMF (Reuters 2010). During the program period of 2010 to 2018, Greece's GDP suffered a cumulative recession of almost 27.4 per cent. The structural adjustments are generally recognized as a central reason for the sharp recession (Kentikelenis 2018, 43; see also Karamessini 2015; Matsaganis 2014). In addition, the adjustment had distributional effects that led to an increase in inequality (Perez and Matsaganis 2018). Greece's unemployment rate surpassed 25 per cent at the height of the crisis. Youth unemployment surpassed 50 per cent. Greece experienced one of the worst economic crises of Western industrialized countries since the Great Depression.

After its initial program in 2010, Greece had to apply for two additional financial assistance programs and became the only country that received more than one program (see also figure 5.3). According to an OECD report on economic policy reforms from 2015, Greece was the most reform-responsive OECD country from 2007 to 2014 (OECD 2015). The third program pursued the structural reforms and fiscal

Table 5.2. Codings related to the socio-economic model, Greece

	First program	Second program	Third program
Socio-economic model			
Change	480	461	318
Persistence	13	5	0
Neither	2	12	0

Source: author's compilation

consolidation strategy from 2010 to 2015 further. The Greek economy, after years of economic depression, started to recover in 2017, but on marginal growth rates (OECD 2018b). The institutional change of the Greek socio-economic model during this period, however, can be described as extensive and transformative (see below). As the economy contracted and implementation processes became harder, the programs changed as well, both in terms of focus as well as in terms of detailed policy conditionality. As an interview partner highlighted: "The [first Greek program] is tailored to balance-of-payment needs, but actually Greece's problems were much more structural and long-term than just a balance-of-payment [problem]" (Interview 32, 1 August 2018).

Fiscal consolidation was accompanied by wide-ranging structural reforms, which were supposed "to modernize the public sector, to render product and labour markets more efficient and flexible, and create a more open and accessible business environment for domestic and foreign investors, including a reduction of the state's direct participation in domestic industries" (European Commission 2010b, 15; see also Spanou 2020, 141). As coded passages in the Greek program documents highlight, changing the socio-economic model of Greece was a central aspect of the financial assistance approach (see table 5.2).

Results from the qualitative document analysis highlight that in the data, the Greek economy is characterized as rigid, static, lacking competitiveness, and overly influenced by the government (e.g., European Commission 2010b, 10; 2012e, 2, 108–10). Modernization of the Greek economy and improving its competitiveness serve as framing objectives within the program documents throughout all three financial assistance programs. Furthermore, modernizing the Greek economy is often synonymous with general ideas of socio-economic liberalization. While passages concerning socio-economic change and labour markets are not bluntly arguing for a more liberalized market economy, the general socio-economic ideas included in the financial assistance programs are clearly identifiable. As a medium-term goal for the adjustment of the Greek economy, the first MoU highlights:

> improv[ing] competitiveness and alter[ing] the economy's structure towards a more investment- and export-led growth model. In parallel with short-term anti-crisis fiscal measures, there is a need to prepare and implement an ambitious structural reform agenda to strengthen external competitiveness, accelerate reallocation of resources from the non-tradable to the tradable sector, and foster growth. Structural reforms that boost the economy's capacity to produce, to save and to export are critical for the success of the programme and recovery of the economy. *Reforms are, in particular, needed to modernize the public sector, to render product and labour markets more efficient and flexible, and create a more open and accessible business environment for domestic and foreign investors, including a reduction of the state's direct participation in domestic industries.* (European Commission 2010b, 15; author's emphasis)

Changing the Greek socio-economic model in the direction illustrated above is a perspective that is regularly brought up in the documents related to the first two programs. The list of policy areas that the MoUs included in the policy conditionality grew over time. They "increased sharply in the second programme, and liberalisation extended to further sectors (privatisation and asset divestment, deregulation in energy and transport sectors, opening up of regulated professions, etc.)" (Spanou 2020, 141). As the following sections highlight, institutional change in Greece was severe and included a multitude of aspects.

5.2 Institutional Change 2010–18

In the following sections the transformation of two central policy fields of the Greek socio-economic model, labour markets (see 5.2.1) and fiscal policy (5.2.2), are illustrated in order to analyse institutional change in the dependent variable.

5.2.1 Institutional Changes in Greek Labour Markets

The financial assistance programs included extensive structural reforms, which focused particularly on labour markets as a central factor for socio-economic adjustments. Although Greece had already brought forward liberalization policies to its labour markets and industrial relations before the crisis (Kentikelenis 2018, 44), the programs aimed at strong structural reforms of multiple labour market aspects. Since the single currency has institutional constraints on possible adjustment strategies, such as currency devaluation (Armingeon and Baccaro 2012; see also 2.2.1), internal devaluation in terms of wage reduction, decreased government expenditure, and less government influence on the economy became the central policy strategy (Kentikelenis 2018, 44; see also 3.2.1), despite the apparent limitation of this approach to the crisis (Armingeon and Baccaro 2012; Walter 2016; see also Blyth 2013). As a review of the Greek program by the institutions highlighted in 2012: "Greece has to restore competitiveness through an ambitious internal devaluation, i.e., a reduction in prices and production costs relative to its competitors, as well as a shift from a consumption-led to an export-led economy" (European Commission 2012e, 2).

Before the crisis, Greek labour markets were characterized by strong, centralized institutions, collective bargaining at the national or sectoral level, and a strong influence of the public sector. However, this scenario also included low job growth, as well as high levels of precariousness and high wage inequalities. Greek industrial relations were confronted with high levels of undeclared work, inefficient labour inspection mechanisms, as well as comparatively high levels of youth and female unemployment (Karamessini 2015, 102–3; Lanara 2012, 5).

The precrisis institutional setting of Greek labour markets was essentially created in 1990 when Law 1876/1990 was passed. It established collective autonomy between social partners and reduced the previously omnipresent government influence (Koukiadaki and Grimshaw 2016, 6). However, despite legislation intended for social partner autonomy, the government still played an interventionist role, which, according to Koukiadaki and Grimshaw, was included in the institutional setting to regulate industrial conflict. Including a strong component of state-based labour market coordination effectively supported the industrial relations system established in the 1990s (Koukiadaki and Grimshaw 2016, 12).

The reforms of the 1990s further established a multi-level bargaining system with institutionalized bargaining processes at the firm, sectoral, and national level (Koukiadaki and Grimshaw 2016, 7). The principle of favourability played an important role in this system, as collective agreements concluded on lower levels were legal only if they included better conditions for workers than sectoral agreements. At the same time, the extension of collective agreements was a regular practice as the Greek economy is predominantly characterized by very small firms (Schulten 2015, 2; Koukiadaki and Grimshaw 2016, 7). Thus, collective agreements were mostly concluded at the national or sectoral level. Furthermore, each side of industrial relations had the right to request arbitration by the Organisation for Mediation and Arbitration (OMED) unilaterally, which effectively strengthened the position of trade unions (Koukiadaki and Grimshaw 2016, 7; see also Interview 1, 12 October 2017). Greek industrial relations are characterized as adversarial, but in the precrisis institutional setting 70 to 80 per cent of workers were covered by wage agreements. Centralized wage-setting was largely supported by the employers' organizations, despite the asymmetry among social partners in terms of arbitration (Interview 11, 12 March 2018). Smaller firms wanted to avoid engaging in wage-bargaining themselves as the centralized bargaining system reduced advantages of their competition via wage differentials; furthermore, centralized bargaining also led to less trade union activities at the firm level and relieved most Greek firms, which have five employees or less, of the need to provide the resources for wage bargaining at the firm level.

This institutional setting of labour markets and industrial relations has been severely reorganized as a consequence of the three financial assistance programs (Kennedy 2016, 2018; see also Lanara 2012, 7). The wide-ranging institutional change was also recognized by the European Commission in 2014 during a review of the second MoU: "Greece was at the top of the countries in adopting measures that decreased the stringency of labour market regulations" (European Commission 2014, 49). Industrial relations and labour market reforms have been a central part of the agenda from the first MoU on, as Greer highlighted: "In the case of Greece, the first EAP meant an 'ambitious' set of labour market reforms. These included the reduction or elimination of sector-wide bargaining, ending the extension of wage-setting agreements across entire sectors" (Greer 2014, 58). Not only does the MoU mention rigid product and labour market regularities, it also proclaims the need to alter Greece's growth model into a direction which allows for more direct foreign investment and export-led growth (European Commission 2010b, 15).

The most transformative reforms were implemented in the first phase of the Greek adjustment programs (see table 5.7 and figure 5.1). However, the year 2012 is generally discussed as the most decisive year in terms of labour market reforms. As interview partners argued: "the major government intervention and interference […] in the Greek labour relations [were] made in 2012" (Interview 8, 9 March 2018). After 2012, labour market reforms were still proposed and implemented. However, in later years labour market reforms were not as severe and numerous as before (see also figure 5.1). Two reasons for this were the political climate in Greece and the severe social effects of the previous reforms (Matsaganis 2018, 59).

Figure 5.1. Labour market reforms in Greece, 2000–18

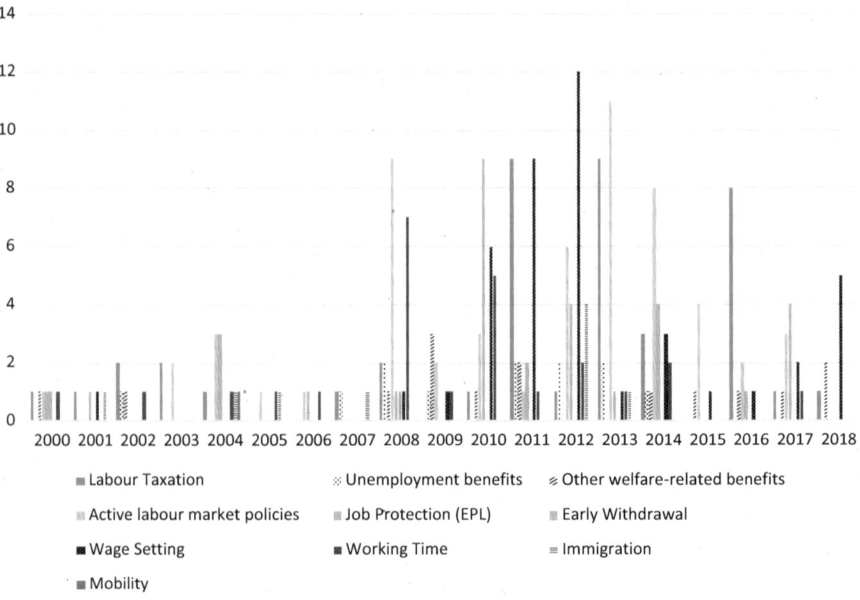

Source: European Commission (2022b)

In terms of the policy mix, the reforms undertaken in the Greek labour markets touch almost all major labour market areas (see also table 5.7). As figure 5.1 shows, two central areas of labour market reforms were wage setting and employment protection legislation. Active labour market policies also played a key role in Greek labour market reforms.

As table 5.3 illustrates, Greek industrial relations have seen severe changes throughout the crisis. Typical for mixed-market economies, Greece's trade union density was lower than in countries with corporatist institutions, such as Finland or Sweden. However, at 24.9 per cent in 2001, trade union density was comparatively high, especially so in strongholds of trade unions, such as the public sector, and significantly lower in the tertiary sector (Chasoglou 2015, 248–9). At first, trade union density was remarkably resilient. By 2017, however, Greece's trade union density was reduced by 5.9 percentage points (see table 5.3). Trade unions, less so than employers' organizations, lost their social

Table 5.3. Changes in Greek industrial relations, 2001–16

	2001	2007	2013	2016	Change		
					01–07	07–13	13–16
Trade union density (1)	24.9%	22.6%	23.1%	19.0%	–2.3	+0.5	–4.1
Bargaining coverage (2)	72.0%	70.1%	42.3%	17.8%	–1.9	–27.8	–24.5
Centralization of wage bargaining (3)	5.75	5.75	1.25	n/a	0	–4.5	–
Predominant level of wage bargaining (4)	5*	5**	2	2	0	3	0
Employment protection legislation (5)	2.8	2.8	2.12	n/a	0	–0.68	–
Minimum wage setting (6)	3	3	9	9	0	6	0
Mandatory extension of wage agreements (7)	3	3	0	0	0	–3	0

Adapted from Iversen, Soskice, and Hope (2016, 177)
Sources: (1) OECD/AIAS (2021); (3) Visser (2016); (4), (6), and (7) Visser (2019b); (2) ILO (2022); (5) OECD (2013)
Notes: (3) higher scores represent higher levels of collective bargaining centralization (4) 1–5 scale, higher scores represent higher levels at which bargaining takes place (5) 1–5 scale, higher scores represent stricter employment protection legislation (6) 0–9 score, 0 indicates no minimum wage, higher scores represent higher centralization of minimum wage setting (7) 0–3 score, higher levels represent higher levels of trade agreement extension
*: Data from 2002; **: Data from 2008

role because they were increasingly less able to engage in collective bargaining, as an interview partner highlighted (Interview 2, 20 February 2018). Collective agreement coverage declined severely throughout the crisis. In 2001, 72 per cent of workers were covered by collective agreements. In 2016, only 17.8 per cent of workers were covered by collective agreements (see table 5.3).

Greek industrial relations were characterized by a high ratio of sectoral agreements and comparatively high levels of centralization of collective bargaining. However, the Greek wage-bargaining system was radically decentralized (see table 5.3). During the crisis, the predominant level of collective bargaining shifted to the firm level, with some sectoral exceptions (see table 5.3). Mandatory extensions of collective agreements were an important factor in Greece's industrial relations before the crisis. Legislation on the extension of collective agreements has been fully abolished (see table 5.3).

5.2.1.1 DECENTRALIZATION OF COLLECTIVE BARGAINING

Decentralizing collective bargaining systems and a decline in private and public sector wages were central policy goals of the Greek programs (Kennedy 2016). The first MoU included provisions for tripartite discussions on wage-bargaining reforms between the state, business, and labour with the aim of enhancing the price competitiveness of the Greek economy (European Commission 2010b, 27). These provisions failed, according to the second MoU, as no agreement was possible (European Commission 2012e, 147). In contrast to the first MoU, the second MoU put forward unilateral state-based measures to enhance a rapid adjustment of labour costs, economic competitiveness, and further decentralizations (European Commission 2012e, 147). As table 5.7 highlights, the first program focused on market-based adjustments of labour markets with some top-down reforms of the bargaining system and employment protection legislation. However, the second program intensified unilateral state-based policies to enforce market-based coordination and lower levels of collective bargaining (see table 5.2, table 5.3, and table 5.7). This change in strategy was put forward due to failed tripartite dialogues in 2011 and 2012, which did not deliver the kind of strategy for wage adjustment the institutions deemed to be necessary (European Commission 2012e, 47).

The Greek industrial relations system was characterized by multilevel collective bargaining processes whose results could not deviate from nationally established standards (Kennedy 2016, 260). Collective bargaining was mandatory if one of the social partners demanded a collective agreement. If social partners were unable to reach an agreement, they were able to address an arbitration body, from which trade unions could demand a binding conciliation (Schulten 2015, 1). This institutional setting came under severe stress during the years of crisis. The suspension of the favourability clause was first subject to legislation in 2010, when PASOK passed Law 3899/2010, suspending the favourability clause for firm-based collective agreements. While the amendment for firm-based collective agreements was later revoked, Law 4024/2011 abolished the principle of favourability as well as legislation to extend the scope of collective agreements (Lanara 2012, 7; Schulten 2015, 2). Furthermore, the right of trade unions to represent workers was subject to retrenchment under Law 4024/2011, as it is now easier to conclude non-union-based agreements at the firm level (Kennedy 2016, 261). In addition, special arbitration rights of unions have been abolished (Schulten 2015, 2).

Institutional changes in bargaining processes caused severe changes to the conclusion of trade agreements. In the precrisis institutional setting, collective agreements were concluded at the sectoral and the firm level. Before 2008, 150 to 250 new collective agreements were concluded at the firm and sectoral level per year. The dual collective agreement system ended in the wake of the Greek crisis. Since 2011, there has been a fundamental shift from the sectoral to the firm level. Sectoral agreements began to decline in 2009 (2009: 120 agreements; 2011: 63 agreements; 2015: 19 agreements; see Schulten 2015, 3). Firm-level agreements peaked in 2012 and remain at comparatively high levels (2012: 937 agreements; 2013: 409 agreements; 2014: 286 agreements; 2015: 193 agreements; see Schulten 2015, 3).

The minimum wage was the object of legislation in 2012 when the government passed Law 4093/2012. The minimum wage had been set by the social partners in line with the General National Collective Agreement (EGSEE) since the 1950s. However, after a central legislative amendment in 2012, the minimum wage is now unilaterally set by the government (see table 5.3). The EGSEE, while still in place, has lost in significance for the Greek industrial relations system (Kennedy 2016, 260–1; Lanara 2012, 7). Employer organizations and trade unions still conclude yearly declarations, but in terms of wage setting no longer have direct influence (Interview 8, 9 March 2018; Interview 2, 20 February 2018). The EGSEE does, however, continue to set working conditions that are not wage related.

In effect, trade unions and employers are less able to conclude trade agreements at the national or sectoral level, and collective bargaining has seen a strong decentralization shift. Greek labour markets are now predominantly shaped by market-based wage setting, as trade agreements are possible at the firm level but are rarely concluded. The government is still able to influence the bargaining process. However, during the program this influence was mostly used to engage in enabling market-based wage developments, reducing wages, and decentralizing wage determination processes. In that sense, the government has become a market enabler.

5.2.1.2 EMPLOYMENT PROTECTION AND EMPLOYMENT DEVELOPMENTS
The Greek crisis led to a strong increase in unemployment: Greece's unemployment rate increased from 9.8 per cent in 2009 to 24.8 per cent in 2012 at the first climax of the Greek crisis, thus making Greece the EMU member with the highest unemployment rate by far. Because the Greek economy, unlike that of Ireland, did not start to grow again after 2012 (see chapter 6), unemployment increased until 2015 to 25.0

per cent (see table 5.4), with the peak of 27.8 per cent in 2013 (Eurostat 2023a). Greek youth unemployment was comparatively high. In 2013 the youth unemployment rate (from 15–24 years) peaked at 59.2 per cent and it remained high throughout the crisis (Eurostat 2023a). Long-term unemployment (LTU, workers unemployed for more than twelve months) is another serious development in the Greek employment sector. In 2009, Greece's LTU rate stood at 3.6 per cent. As unemployment became a bigger problem as a consequence of the economic depression, so did long-term unemployment. In 2012, the Greek LTU rate in the workforce increased to 13.1 per cent. As the Greek depression continued, LTU rates increased further. In 2015, 16.4 per cent of Greek workers had been unemployed for more than twelve months (see table 5.4). While the wage share has declined by 2 per cent since 2010, real wages have decreased by almost 23 per cent (Lübker and Schulten 2017, 429–30). Poverty, including severe material deprivation, has become a more pressing issue in Greece throughout the programs (Darvas and Tschekassin 2015; see also table 5.1). Therefore, Greece continues to face severe social cohesion problems.

Institutional changes to Greek employment protection legislation enabled these developments. Many employees have been affected by wage freezes or wage cuts, first in the public sector and later in the private sector as well. Given that Greece is a country with already high levels of low-wage workers and precarious work environments, wage declines are a common instrument in companies: 74.9 per cent of new firm-level collective agreements from 2011 to 2013 included cuts to wages. Only 1.5 per cent of new collective agreements included higher wages (Schulten 2015, 4). Hence, wages predominantly declined during the recession of the Greek economy. Wage structures have become more fragmented as the collective bargaining system has been decentralized (see 5.2.1.1). Collective dismissals have been a common instrument for small and medium-sized companies (Mitsopoulos 2016, 162). Making collective dismissals easier for firms was included in the policy conditionality attached to the program (see table 5.7).

Reforms of employment protection legislation further reduced the rights of workers and thus the power recourse of trade unions. The probation period was extended from two months up to twelve months with Law 3899/2010 (Karamessini 2015, 116). The possible duration of temporary contracts was extended from eighteen to thirty-six months (Kennedy 2016, 263). Thresholds for collective dismissals have been reduced with Law 3863/2010, including reductions of the duration of dismissal notifications and severance pay reductions (Kennedy 2016, 263).

Table 5.4. Changes in labour and unemployment, 2009, 2012, and 2015

	2009	2012	2015	% Change	
				2007–12	2012–15
Employment (000) (1)	4,459	3,608	3,534	−19.08	−2.05
Employment rate (%) (2)	60.7	50.4	50.7	−16.97	0.60
Unemployment (000) (3)	491	1,208	1,198	146.02	−0.83
Unemployment rate (%) (4)	9.8	24.8	25.0	153.06	0.81
LTU rate (%) (5)	3.6	13.1	16.4	263.89	25.19

Sources: (1) Eurostat (2023a); (2) Eurostat (2023a); (3) Eurostat (2023b); (4) Eurostat (2023b); (5) Eurostat 2023c. Table adapted from O'Connell (2017, 233).

Further liberalizations of collective dismissal regulation followed (see table 5.7). Employment protection thus has been reduced to a larger degree, which further strengthened market-based coordination mechanisms in Greek labour markets.

5.2.1.3 UNEMPLOYMENT SUPPORT AND ACTIVE LABOUR MARKET POLICIES The fiscal consolidation strategy of the financial assistance programs (see 5.2.2) did have a strong effect on unemployment support and the possibility of active labour market policies in Greece. As government expenditure in social affairs decreased, the social welfare systems were less able to cope with rising unemployment numbers (see table 5.1). Greek social welfare did not include a guaranteed minimum income scheme (GMI) before the crisis. Hence, unemployment support only lasted for the first year of unemployment if the newly unemployed met the eligibility criteria. With rising LTU rates (see table 5.4), households regularly had no income of their own (Kentikelenis 2018, 40). A common development of this period was financial transfers from retired parents to their unemployed children. Furthermore, social welfare such as unemployment support was subject to severe retrenchment in the first two programs as a part of the fiscal consolidation strategy. Proposals for social investment only started to develop in a perceptible way during the third program (table 5.7).

Unemployment numbers were not the only problem confronting the Greek social welfare system, as fiscal consolidation strategies also included reductions in social spending despite increased unemployment. Furthermore, the Greek unemployment support system was considered to be a very passive system with only limited activation instruments.

Including active labour market policies into the Greek welfare system was thus a central aspect of the programs' policy conditionality in later years of the adjustment (see table 5.7). However, despite an implementation of active labour market policies throughout the financial assistance programs, participation levels remain very low. The OECD underlined in its Economic Survey of 2018 that the reason for low participation levels lay predominantly in limited capacities and problems with financial resources. Furthermore, Active Labour Market Policies (ALMP) have a limited scope of eligible workers (OECD 2018b, 40).

A guaranteed minimum income was implemented only in the last stages of the third financial assistance program – in form of the Social Security Income program (SSI) – although it had been on the policy agenda since 2012. In February of 2017, after initial smaller pilot projects starting in 2015 and further gradual implementations of the program, the Social Security Income program was launched. It is the first "universal means-tested income support programme targeted to households at risk of poverty and exclusion" (European Commission 2017d, 6; see also Marini et al. 2019). The SSI is planned to be closely connected to activation, granting "priority access to a number of active labour market schemes" (European Commission 2017d, 6) and provision of social services.

Taking its eligibility criteria into consideration, up to 750,000 households were expected to have access to a GMI (European Commission 2017d, 6). However, according to a quantitative study provided by the World Bank in January 2019, the program achieved only low coverage among the eligible households (Marini et al. 2019, 2). Only about 40 per cent of eligible beneficiaries applied. Furthermore, the implementation of active labour market policies and the provision of social services in the SSI is limited (Marini et al. 2019, 19).

5.2.2 Institutional Changes in Greek Fiscal Policy

Fiscal policy was a major cornerstone of all three MoUs, as the deficit announced by the Greek government in 2009 started the financial assistance process. Greece's fiscal development also was a key narrative for most of the crisis period (Matthijs and McNamara 2015). Over the three programs, Greek fiscal policy experienced severe changes, not only in terms of expenditure and revenue developments but also in terms of its institutional setting.

Fiscally, the state played an important role for the economic development of Greece before 2008. However, despite having a government with strong constitutionally based powers, the Greek administration has historically lacked strong policy implementation capacities (Featherstone 2011, 195). Greece's comparatively weak expenditure control mechanisms became apparent during the crisis, as did its lack of capacity for effectively raising taxes (Featherstone 2011, 196). Tax collection also was a key issue throughout the program, as in 2012 only 57 per cent of due taxes were actually collected (Troost and Ötsch 2019, 7).

Fiscal consolidation in the Greek program focused on three central aspects. The first was expenditure reduction in line with the goal to reduce the deficit from over 15 per cent in 2009 to under 3 per cent of GDP in 2014 (see 5.2.2.1). The second was increasing government revenue as well as administrative capacity regarding tax collection (see 5.2.2.2). Reforming the budgetary process and thus strengthening deficit controls (see 5.2.2.3) was the third. In effect, the program led to institutional change in Greece's fiscal framework. Furthermore, the consolidation strategy had a strong influence on socio-economic coordination in Greece, as fiscal policy developments effectively reduced and limited the government's role in economic affairs (see 5.2.2.5).

It is noteworthy that, according to Commission services, the Greek government had already implemented fiscal measures worth 5.5 per cent of GDP before the first MoU was signed (European Commission 2010b, 18). The newly elected PASOK government legislated fiscal consolidation measures in 2009 for the 2010 budget, as well as in January, February, and March 2010 (European Commission 2010b, 19) in an effort to reduce the deficit as well as to convince financial markets and European partners that the Greek government was willing to make hard decisions (Interview 5, 7 March 2018).

From a fiscal policy perspective, the three financial assistance programs Greece received are consistent in their broader fiscal consolidation strategy, as the policy conditionality focus underlines (see table 6.5). However, throughout the three programs, there has been a shift in emphasis for the fiscal policy conditionality (Interview 3, 4 March 2018; Interview 5, 7 March 2018). The first program mostly focused on government expenditure reductions. In the second program, fiscal consolidation was supposed to be achieved through a mix of expenditure reductions and revenue increases. The third program put a stronger emphasis on increasing government revenue and kept government expenditure comparatively stable. In sum, the programs achieved fiscal consolidation: Greece is running primary surpluses and is slowly reducing its debt. Furthermore, as the program reviews highlight, Greece has outperformed its fiscal targets of 2016 and 2017 by achieving higher primary surpluses than originally agreed with the institutions (European Commission 2017c, 7; 2018b, 4).

The following sections analyse the changes in fiscal policy by focusing on government expenditure (see 5.2.2.1) and revenue developments (see 5.2.2.2). Furthermore, the reforms of the budgetary process and fiscal rules are analysed (see 5.2.2.3). The privatization process, a central aspect of the Greek financial assistance programs, is illustrated (see 5.2.2.4). Last, an analysis of the effects of fiscal policy forms on the government's role is presented (see 5.2.2.5).

5.2.2.1 FISCAL CONSOLIDATION BY REDUCING GOVERNMENT EXPENDITURE

Reducing government expenditure is an essential part of the financial assistance program's approach to fiscal consolidation. In line with the general interpretation of unsustainable debt and irresponsible government spending as the central cause for the euro crisis (Illing, Jauch, and Zabel 2012, 156), as well as a special focus on debt and government expenditure in the Greek case (Illing 2013, 31–5; Priewe and Stachelsky 2015), reducing government expenditure played a key role in the MoUs (see below).

The policy focus on expenditure reduction is clearly visible in the development of government spending. In terms of government expenditure in Greece, several trends are identifiable. The government's total spending has been reduced by 30 per cent in nominal terms from 2008 to 2018. In comparison, government spending in relation to GDP remains stable. When Greece exited the financial assistance programs in 2018, its expenditure-to-GDP ratio was reduced by 8 per cent in comparison to 2008 (see figure 5.3). This comparatively smaller reduction in expenditure to GDP primarily results from the depression of Greek GDP, culminating at 25.7 per cent during the period of 2009 to 2015 (Eurostat 2023g). Developments in government expenditure and GDP are connected as the government played a key role in GDP growth (Theodoropoulou 2016, 54).

The sharpest reductions in government spending were undertaken during the first and second bailout programs (2010–12 and 2012–15; see figure 4.3 and 5.3). The strongest reduction in government expenditure within one year was implemented in 2014, when expenditure was reduced by 20.3 per cent (see figure 5.3). In comparison, government spending remained stable during the third program (2015–18; see figure 5.3).

As figure 5.2 illustrates, the fiscal consolidation strategy affected all ten sectors of government expenditure, as provided by Eurostat COFOG data (see figure 5.2, for a short description of COFOG data see chapter 3). Three sectors of government activity stand out.

First, as figure 5.2 illustrates, Greece's expenditure in social protection has decreased by 15 per cent, despite increased unemployment numbers (see table 5.4). This development underlines a common trend

Figure 5.2. Greece's government expenditure by function (COFOG)

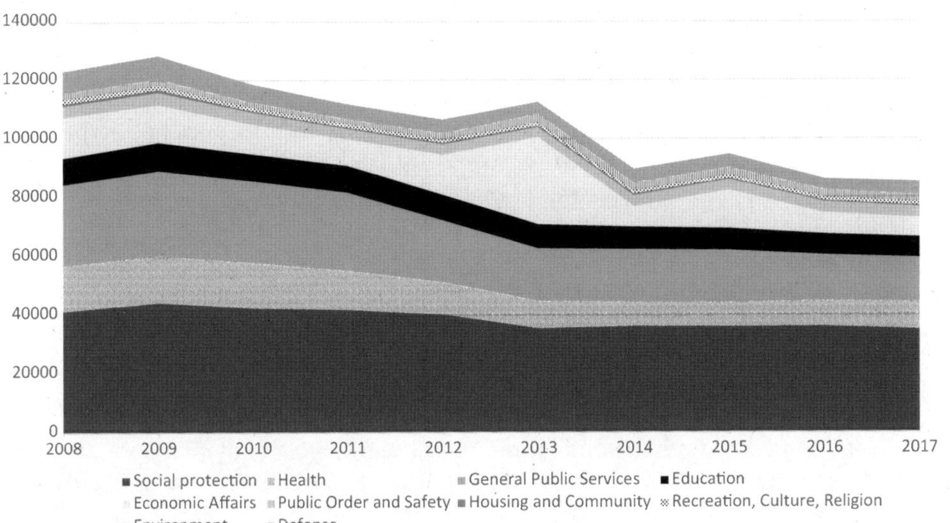

Source: Eurostat (2019)

of welfare retrenchment in line with the fiscal consolidation strategy in order reduce the fiscal deficit, despite higher unemployment numbers (see also 5.2.1.3). Most expenditure reductions were implemented during the first two programs. After 2015, social protection spending remained comparatively stable (see figure 5.2).

Second, government expenditure in economic affairs is particularly interesting, as the government played an important part in precrisis economic coordination. The general direction of expenditure in economic affairs, despite a higher expenditure in 2013, underlines a reduction of the government's engagement with the economy. From 2008 to 2017, expenditure on economic affairs was reduced by 49.4 per cent (see figure 5.2). Beyond a general reduction, however, a clear trend is not visible. While most reductions took place during the first two programs (2010 to 2015), with the sharpest reduction taking place in 2014, economic affairs expenditure increased and then decreased further after the third program was agreed upon in 2015 (see figure 5.2).

Third, a similar trend can be analysed for general public services. As the government had a key role in precrisis economic coordination, its expenditure in economic affairs was not the only relevant factor in the classification of Greece's socio-economic model. Furthermore, expenditure on general public services played a role in producing aggregate demand in the Greek economy. The data highlights a strong reduction in general public services. From 2008 to 2017, a reduction of 45.63 per cent can be measured (see figure 5.2). In terms of general public services, the same pattern can be identified as for the total government expenditure reduction: most reductions took place during the timespan of 2010 to 2015, and the sharpest reduction within one year occurred in 2012. After the third program was agreed to in 2015, general public service spending was relatively stable, albeit at a level approximately 45 per cent lower than before the crisis.

5.2.2.2 INCREASING GOVERNMENT REVENUE

The strategy of fiscal consolidation focused on two central strategies: reducing government spending and increasing its revenue, albeit at different weighting of importance in the policy mix. Thus, increasing government revenue is an additional strategy to achieve fiscal consolidation and reduce the deficit in Greece. As the government's revenue development highlights, it developed in a similar way as government expenditure. In nominal terms, government revenue was reduced by 13.3 per cent from 2008 to 2017. Government revenue started to decrease in 2009. The nominal reduction in revenue continued until 2015. After 2015, government revenue remained stable (see figure 5.3). In terms of revenue-to-GDP ratio, government revenue increased from 2008 to 2018 by 7.1 per cent. The highest revenue-to-GDP was measured in 2016, when revenue accounted for 49.4 per cent of GDP.

The asynchronous development of total government revenue in nominal terms and in terms of the revenue-to-GDP ratio was caused by the Greek economic depression from 2008 to 2015 and the decline of the Greek GDP by approximately 27 per cent. As GDP decreases, total government revenue decreases as well if the tax code remains unchanged. In this regard, the asynchronous development of both indicators illustrates that general taxation has changed across the years. As a central aspect of the fiscal consolidation strategy, the financial assistance programs put forward tax reforms that aimed at broadening the tax base and thus creating more revenue (see table 5.4). In addition, the policy conditionality attached to the financial assistance aimed at strengthening tax collection and thus creating more revenue as well (see table 5.4). This is especially visible from 2010 to 2013 onwards. As was highlighted above, these were the years with the strongest recession (see table 5.1). However, revenue decreased by relatively lower rates. The strongest reduction in revenue occurred from 2014 to 2015.

The programs, as table 6.5 underlines, emphasized revenue increases to different degrees. The first program only put forward broader

Figure 5.3. Total government expenditure and revenue developments, Greece, 2008–18

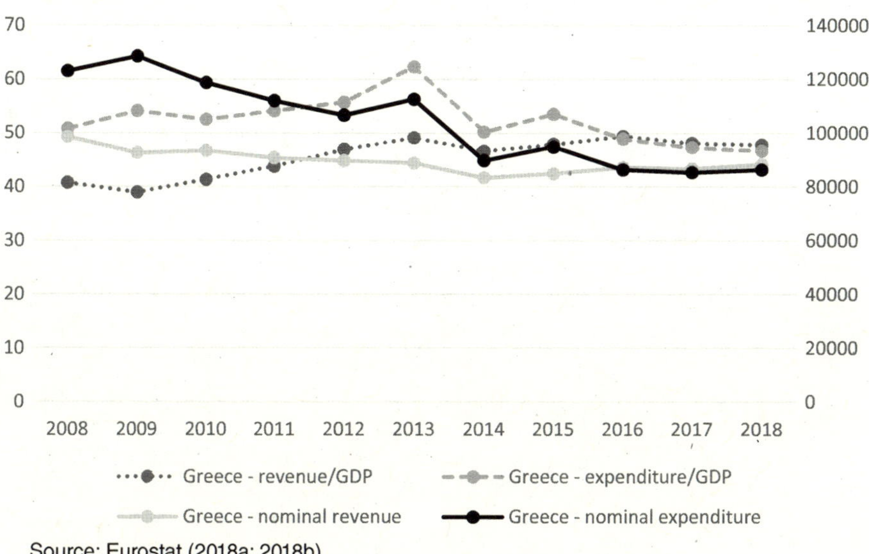

Source: Eurostat (2018a; 2018b)

revenue-related goals and aimed at an increase of 4 per cent of GDP in taxation increases, without specifying which taxes were supposed to be increased, and an improvement in the government's capacity to generate revenue (European Commission 2010b, 15, 19). The second program had a similar focus in terms of revenue increases. Furthermore, it put additional focus on taxation system reform and broadening of the tax base, while reducing higher marginal taxation rates (European Commission 2012e, 34). These reforms were supposed to improve the competitiveness of the Greek economy (European Commission 2012e, 99). As table 6.5 highlights, the third program put additional focus on increasing revenue via increasing taxation in several fields.

5.2.2.3 FISCAL RULES, BUDGETARY REFORMS, AND THE REDUCTION OF GOVERNMENT DISCRETION

The Greek financial assistance programs put additional emphasis on strengthening fiscal policy institutions and implementing fiscal rules. Furthermore, reducing government discretion in fiscal policy was a key objective. Greece, as argued above, had comparatively weak institutional capacity to react to severe financial difficulties. Implementing stronger revenue collection mechanisms as well as reducing government expenditure were difficult program objectives (see 5.2). As it was reported by several interview partners, implementing already-legislated expenditure cuts and getting information on government spending was hard to achieve (e.g., Interview 5, 7 March 2018). The fiscal framework of the Greek government was changed in three central regards: (1) independent oversight, (2) a reform of the budgetary process, and (3) the implementation of new fiscal rules.

The fiscal framework of Greece did not include independent supervisory bodies before the crisis. As a consequence of the large deficit and weak institutional capacity in fiscal policy, the MoUs included the establishment of independent supervisory bodies as key reforms. As the European fiscal framework changed as a reaction to the euro area crisis, the MoU included the implementation of changes at the European level into the Greek fiscal framework as well. The implementation of independent bodies in the budgetary process started in 2010. In line with the first MoU (European Commission 2010b, 24), Greece created a Parliamentary Budget Office (PBO) by implementing Law 3871/2010. The PBO produces quarterly and interim budget reports, supports the Hellenic Parliament with information on fiscal policy developments, and thus provides a parliamentary fiscal policy control to the government. Before the PBO was established, the parliament was unable to access financial data outside of budgetary publications by the government, which made parliamentary control of budgetary processes more difficult (e.g., Interview 9, 9 March 2018).

As a key policy deliverable, the second MoU included the establishment of the Hellenic Fiscal Council, an independent fiscal council whose role goes beyond independent oversight of budgetary processes. As an independent administrative authority, the council monitors fiscal and macroeconomic projections of the Greek government. The Hellenic Fiscal Council furthermore oversees the compliance of Greece with the EU's fiscal rules framework, especially in terms of the Fiscal Compact[2] (European Commission 2012d, 32) and medium-term fiscal targets. In addition, the Hellenic Fiscal Council analyses the macroeconomic projections the government uses to develop the annual budget, as well as the medium-term fiscal strategy (Hellenic Republic, Ministry of Finance 2019, 26). It was established in 2014 and publishes two central reports per year in line with the schedule of the European Semester. The implementation of the Hellenic Fiscal Council also included automatic corrections of undesirable fiscal developments (Kazákos 2015, 47).

The programs furthermore aimed at depoliticizing revenue collection in order to strengthen institutional capacity. To achieve this goal, the independent General Secretariat of Public Revenues was created in 2013 (Kazákos 2015, 47). As a key policy goal determined by the institutions, central tax-relevant services were split from the Ministry of Finance and transferred to the General Secretariat of Public Revenues (European Commission 2013e, 2). The reform and depoliticization of revenue collection was advanced in the third MoU for Greece, where the establishment of an independent revenue agency, was a key policy goal in 2015 (European Commission 2015e, 11). After a year and a half of preparations for its implementation, the General Secretariat of Public Revenue was reformed into the Independent Authority for Public Revenue (IAPR) on 1 January 2017.

A second central aspect of reforming the Greek fiscal framework, under the financial assistance program, aimed at reforming the budgetary process. In 2011, as a central policy conditionality of the financial assistance program, the Greek government engaged in a reform of its Organic Budget Law, the central law for its budgetary process. The reform introduced Medium-Term Fiscal Strategies (MTFS) to the budgetary process, which provide detailed budgetary plans for the current budget year and the next three years ahead. This, as interview partners highlighted, is a strong contrast to the budgetary process precrisis, where the Greek government provided a budget for the current budget year, without additional plans for the years ahead (Interview 10, 12 March 2018). Medium-term financial plans are now discussed in economic committees of the Hellenic Parliament three months before the parliament votes on the budget, which was described as a fundamental structural change by interview partners (Interview 10, 12 March 2018).

Not only did the introduction of MTFS implement financial plans for three consecutive years, the MTFS furthermore include binding expenditure ceilings for ministries, as well as balanced-budget rules for local governments. State-owned enterprises were issued performance targets (if these were missed, the enterprise would be privatized). The health sector, a large expenditure sector (see figure 5.2), received multiannual expenditure ceilings as well, which effectively lowered health expenditure (European Commission 2014, 37)[3]. Hence, the reforms of the Greek Organic Budget Law put forward stronger fiscal planning and the institutional possibilities to prevent larger fiscal deficits. However, the reforms did lower the government's discretion to use fiscal policy as a coordinative mechanism in economic affairs.

As the implementation of independent agencies and reforms to the budgetary process highlight, the Greek fiscal policy framework has experienced wide-ranging institutional change over the financial assistance period, which is also highlighted by the European Commission's fiscal governance database[4] (see table 5.5).

Table 5.5. Fiscal rule index, 2008–17

Country	'08	'09	'10	'11	'12	'13	'14	'15	'16	'17
Coordinated market economies										
Germany	−0.22	0.18	−0.05	0.22	0.22	1.35	1.35	1.35	1.35	1.35
Austria	−0.03	0.30	0.30	0.38	0.57	0.57	0.57	0.54	0.54	1.31
Belgium	−0.21	−0.21	−0.21	−0.21	−0.19	−0.19	1.00	1.00	1.08	1.23
Finland	0.10	−0.20	−0.20	−0.08	−0.12	1.09	1.07	1.07	1.13	1.13
Netherlands	0.36	0.36	0.36	0.36	0.42	0.42	2.68	2.62	2.76	2.37
Slovenia	−1.02	−1.02	−1.02	−1.02	−1.02	−1.02	−1.02	0.44	0.44	0.44
Luxembourg	0.34	0.34	0.03	0.03	0.03	0.26	0.75	0.78	0.78	0.78
Malta	−1.02	−1.02	−1.02	−1.02	−1.02	−1.02	1.33	1.33	1.33	1.33
Liberal market economies										
Ireland	−0.90	−0.90	−0.90	−0.90	−0.91	0.68	0.68	0.61	0.61	1.07
Estonia	0.79	0.79	0.92	0.92	0.44	0.77	1.34	1.34	1.34	1.34
Latvia	−0.69	−0.69	−0.69	−0.69	−0.69	0.65	1.16	1.20	1.20	1.20
Lithuania	0.11	0.11	0.11	0.11	0.12	0.12	0.12	2.07	2.20	2.20
Mixed-market economies										
France	−0.40	−0.25	−0.33	−0.02	0.85	0.79	0.85	0.85	0.85	0.85
Spain	0.47	0.47	0.47	1.05	1.48	1.48	1.72	1.84	1.84	1.84
Italy	−0.24	−0.18	−0.15	−0.13	−0.13	−0.10	2.33	2.35	2.33	2.33
Greece	−1.02	−1.02	−1.02	−1.02	0.11	0.11	0.18	0.26	0.66	0.66
Portugal	−0.36	−0.36	−0.36	−0.36	−0.24	1.03	1.13	1.96	1.96	1.96
Slovakia	−0.35	−0.36	−0.36	−0.36	0.92	0.92	1.42	1.42	1.42	1.42
Cyprus	−0.94	−0.94	−0.94	−0.94	−0.94	0.79	1.12	1.12	1.12	1.12

Source: European Commission (2022a)

While the Greek fiscal rules indicator is still one of the lowest, it improved by over 1.5 points. Furthermore, the fiscal rules Greece implemented place a strong focus on binding targets for the country's primary balance in relation to GDP in combination with medium-term fiscal goals and nominal debt targets in relation to GDP (European Commission 2022a).

5.2.2.4 PRIVATIZATION

Privatization was a central fiscal policy goal in the Greek financial assistance programs to reduce Greece's general government debt. The MoUs included targets of divesting assets and state-owned enterprises (SOEs), as well as decreasing government involvement in economic affairs through public businesses and semi-states in order to create additional financial resources. While privatization at first was only a small part of the financial adjustment strategy, the scope of this strategy increased over time. During the first program, the Greek government was supposed to prepare a plan to privatize assets and enterprises amounting to at least 1 billion euro per year for the years 2011 to 2013 (European Commission 2010b, 71). However, the target was increased quickly. In autumn of 2010, during the second review of the first program, the Greek government was expected to raise 7 billion euro via privatization over the period of 2011 to 2013 (European Commission 2010c, 2). During the third review of the first program, the privatization goal was increased to 50 billion euro until the end of 2015 (European Commission 2011d, 2). Furthermore, the legislation of Law 3986/2011 established the Hellenic Republic Asset Development Fund (HRADF) in 2011, a central institutional authority for privatizing state assets and enterprises and reducing government involvement in economic sectors (European Commission 2011b, 42)[5]. After the establishment of the HRADF, the privatization strategy was further pursued but remained unchanged until 2015.

During the negotiations for the third MoU, the institutions and the Greek government renegotiated the terms of the privatization strategy. The HRADF published an asset development plan with detailed information concerning state assets which were planned to be privatized (Hellenic Republic Asset Development Fund 2015). This asset development plan was continuously updated throughout the third program, and further updates were published after Greece exited from the third program in 2018.

Two aspects of the renegotiated privatization strategy stand out. First, the HRADF was joined in its privatization efforts by the Hellenic Corporation of Assets and Participations (HCAP), an independent fund (European Commission 2015e, 28–9), which was established in 2016 by Law 4389/2016 (European Commission 2017c, 46) and oversees the privatization processes of the HRADF. State assets that are planned to be privatized are transferred to the HCAP for ninety-nine years and cannot be transferred back to the Greek government. Its five-person supervisory board includes three board members appointed by the Greek government and two by European institutions (European Commission and ESM) (European Commission 2016a, 11). The second important aspect of the renegotiation of the privatization strategy is the use of financial resources. Before 2015, all funds from privatization were supposed to be used for repayment of financial assistance loans. After the strategy was negotiated again, parts of the financial resources can now be used for investments in the Greek economy[6] (European Commission 2015e, 29).

While privatization has been a central point of the fiscal consolidation strategy, privatizing Greek state assets proved to be a complicated issue. From 2011 to 2017, Greece privatized state assets worth 4.7 billion euro, which is less than 10 per cent of the 50 billion euro targeted in the financial assistance program. In addition, the Greek government projected additional sales worth 2.7 billion euro for 2018 (Tugwell 2018). Hence, the additional financial resources were only used to reduce Greece's sovereign debt, as the privatization revenues did not reach the targets negotiated.

Thus, the privatization strategy did not have a strong influence on budgetary developments as such. It did reduce the government's debt but only to a very small degree. However, as the Greek socio-economic model was predominantly based on state-based coordination before the crisis, the privatization strategy influenced the socio-economic model of Greece and supported more market-based coordination of Greek capitalism (see 5.2.2.5).

5.2.2.5 EFFECTS ON THE GOVERNMENT'S ROLE IN THE ECONOMY

The fiscal policy developments, especially the broad reductions in government expenditure (see 5.2.2.1), the development of government revenue (see 5.2.2.2), and the privatization of state-owned enterprises and state assets (see 5.2.2.4) had visible effects on the government's role in the Greek economy. The OECD's product market regulation database illustrates that the Greek state, albeit coming from a significant coordinative role, lost a large part of its influence on the economy. The reduction of coordinative influence is visible both in terms of fiscal engagement of the government with economic affairs (see 5.2.2.1 and 5.2.2.4) as well as in terms of regulation (see 5.2.2.5). State-based coordination of the economy is still an important factor in the Greek socio-economic model. However, the government has lost influence in economic affairs to a significant degree, as table 5.6 highlights.

The broad indicator for state control of the economy has been reduced by over 25 per cent from 2003 to 2013. State control of the economy in Greece has been approximated to the state control of other non-MME states in the single currency (OECD 2018a). Public ownership, a central issue for the Greek socio-economic model before the crisis, has seen a reduction of over 10 per cent from 2003 to 2013 (see table 5.6). Data from 2018 suggests a reduction of over 50 per cent, but due to a changed methodology, the data is not comparable (OECD 2018a). While the scope of the still existing SOEs is higher than the EU average, the government's general involvement in network services has also been reduced. Privatization of SOEs and state assets, a central fiscal policy objective of the Greek bailout programs (see 5.2.2.4), is an important factor in this development. In addition to the government's reduction of direct engagement in the economy, its involvement in business operations and its command and control regulation were reduced by over a third. The strongest reduction appeared during the time Greece received financial assistance (see table 5.6).

Table 5.6. Greece, OECD indicators on Product Market Regulation

	2003	2008	2013
State control (1)	3.81	3.33	2.82
Public ownership (2)	3.14	3.22	2.84
Scope of state-owned enterprises (3)	3.60	3.60	3.40
Government involvement in network sectors (4)	4.55	4.27	2.86
Involvement in business operation (5)	4.48	3.43	2.79
Command & control regulation (6)	4.19	3.94	2.58

Source: OECD (2018a)

Considering these developments, the Greek government experienced a strong change in its own role within socio-economic coordination. This development correlates with the implementation of the financial assistance programs. In comparison to precrisis levels, it has lost significant influence on business activities and is less capable to effectively regulate market developments. Furthermore, the government's reduced scope of public enterprises gives the government less influence on market developments in central parts of the economy. These institutional changes lead to more market-based socio-economic coordination and a weaker coordinative role of the government for the Greek economy.

5.3 Labour Market Reforms

Labour markets have been identified as a central adjustment variable for the Greek socio-economic model within the Memoranda of Understanding (see table 5.7). Hence, wide-ranging institutional changes in Greek labour markets are a central development associated with the financial assistance programs (see 5.2.1). Structural labour market reforms were an explicit requirement by the ECB, the European Commission, the IMF, and the ESM (Koukiadaki and Grimshaw 2016, 1). These reforms, as was also shown above (see 5.2.1), went beyond the public sector and heavily influenced the institutional setting of wage-setting mechanisms and employment protection legislation in the private sector as well (Koukiadaki and Grimshaw 2016, 1; see also Kennedy 2016; Schulten 2015).

One the one hand, policy paradigms and ideational processes concerning labour market developments present an interesting point of analysis: Where do ideas within the financial assistance programs about liberalizing and decentralizing labour markets, as well as recommodifying labour, come from? What kind of policy goals are associated with

Table 5.7. Labour market reforms proposed in the MoUs

	Ireland	Greece
Collective bargaining	First program (2010–13) • Termination of national collective agreement system (happened before the official program) • Extension of sectoral wage agreements will be reviewed, focusing on inter-sectional adjustments • Review of sectoral wage agreements in line with sectoral adjustments, which set higher minima than the minimum wage • Review of extensions of collective agreements in line with sectoral adjustments • General modernization of sectoral wage agreements to improve responsiveness to sectoral and economy-wide shocks • Removal of non-wage settings from EROs • Amending the Industrial Relations Act • Formal review of all employment regulation orders (EROs) and registered employment agreements (REAs) to provide required reallocation of labour force within and across sectors	First program (2010–12) • Reform wage-bargaining system in the private sector, including local territorial pacts to set wage growth below sectoral agreements • Introduce variable pay to link wages to productivity performance at the firm level • Amend regulation of the arbitration system • Suspension of the favourability clause Second program (2012–15) • Previously agreed wage increases are suspended • Reduction of maximum duration (three years) • Reduction of time expired agreements stay in force (three months instead of six months) • Further amendment of arbitration (guaranteeing that arbitration reflects the need for wage adjustment), arbitration only possible if both social partners agree to it Third program (2015–18) • Increasing the quorum for first-degree unions to vote on a strike • Review of the list of protections for the termination of contracts for trade union members • Further amendments to arbitration systems Supplemental MoU (2017) • Legislation to ensure that the collective bargaining reforms of 2011 stay in force at least until the end of the third program.

(Continued)

Table 5.7. Labour market reforms proposed in the MoUs (*Continued*)

	Ireland	Greece
		• Development of a reliable administrative system for sectoral agreements in order to increase the representativeness • Legislation for fast-track judicial procedure on industrial action • Digital registry for trade unions • Review of justified reason to terminate contracts of workers under protection as trade unionists • Rationalization of leave benefits for trade unionists • Review of mediation and arbitration procedures by February 2018 Supplemental MoU (January 2018) • Development of a reliable administrative system for sectoral agreements in order to increase the representativeness • Digital registry for trade unions • Increase of the quorum for first-degree trade unions on strikes from 20 to 50% • Development of a reliable administrative system to assess representativeness of sectoral collective agreements • Creation of a digital registry for trade unions • Review of current mediation and arbitration systems
Minimum wages	First program (2010–13) • Reduction of 12% (€1) per hour • Enlarging the scope of the "inability to pay" clause	First program (2010–12) • Introduction of sub-minimum wages Second program (2012–15) • Unilateral state-based reduction of the minimum wage by 22% (32% for workers aged under twenty-five years)

(Continued)

Table 5.7. Labour market reforms proposed in the MoUs (*Continued*)

	Ireland	Greece
Private sector wages	First program (2010–13) • Review of regulated wages in order to exert downward pressure on private sector wages (directly and indirectly through spill-over effect)	First program (2010–12) • Flexibilization of private sector wages for cost moderation • Flexibilization of overtime work • Creation of minimum entry-level wages • Reduction of pay rates for overtime work Second program (2012–15) • Reduction of non-wage costs (e.g., reduction of social contributions by 5%)
Employment protection legislations	First program (2010–13) • Extension of the "inability to pay" clause for employers	First program (2010–12) • Extend the probationary period for new jobs to one year • Reduce the overall level of severance payments which should apply equally to blue- and white-collar workers • Raise the minimum threshold for activating rules on collective dismissals especially for larger companies • Put measures in place to guarantee that current minimum wages remain fixed in nominal terms for three years • Facilitate use of temporary contracts and part-time work • Adjust legislation to introduce annual time accounts and reduce overtime pay • Recalibrating rules concerning collective dismissals Second program (2012–15) • Reduction of privileged working conditions in previously state-owned enterprises Third program (2015–18) • Collective dismissals with a maximum notification procedure of three months and no ex ante approval

(Continued)

Table 5.7. Labour market reforms proposed in the MoUs (*Continued*)

	Ireland	Greece
		Supplemental MoU (2017) • Collective dismissals with a maximum notification procedure of three months and no ex ante approval • Streamlining and rationalization of existing labour laws into a Labour Law Code and a Code of Labour Regulatory Provisions
		Supplemental MoU (January 2018) • Streamlining and rationalization of existing labour laws into a Labour Law Code and a Code of Labour Regulatory Provisions
Employment	First program (2010–13) • Priority to activation policy • Reform of unemployment and social assistance, designed to reach budgetary savings of 750 million euro • Enhancing the conditionality for work and training • Strengthening activation measures via increased profiling, more effective monitoring, and sanction mechanisms for unemployed workers • Reduction of inactivity traps	Supplemental MoU (2017) • Achieving EU best practice labour market institutions and fostering constructive dialogue among social partners • Review of labour market institutions (the government implemented an international expert group to review labour market reforms) • Development of mechanism to find out labour market needs • Implementation of quality frameworks for vocational education and training (VETs) and apprenticeships • Development of institutional capacity in labour and employment administration in order to implement and monitor activation policy • Further improvement of the impact of Active Labour Market Policies (ALMP) and their impact on employment

(*Continued*)

Table 5.7. Labour market reforms proposed in the MoUs (*Continued*)

	Ireland	Greece
		Supplemental MoU (January 2018) • Personalized active labour measures for at least 10 per cent of SSI beneficiaries by February 2018 • Implementation of a new ALMP strategy, which includes reformed mutual obligations, reviewed quality specifications for ALMP training providers, a blueprint for evaluation and monitoring, and the introduction of a new delivery model
Public sector wages	First program (2010–13) • New entrants to public sector receive a 10% pay reduction • Effective public sector pay reductions of 14% • Nominal pay freeze until 2014 • Reducing 23,500 full-time positions in public employment • Pensions will be indexed to consumer prices • Pensions will be based on career average earnings • Cuts to public sector pensions (4% on average)	First program (2010–12) • Cuts to thirteen and fourteenth monthly income (seasonal bonuses), additional seasonal pay • Flat bonus of 1,000 euro for wages under 3,000 euro, paid for by cutting salary allowances for higher salaries • Cuts to public pensions over 1,400 euro by an average of 8% Third program (2015–17) • Establishment of ceilings for the wage bill relative to GDP and fiscal targets
Public sector employment	First program (2010–13) • Reduction of public employment by 25,000 people • Pay cut for new entrants by 10% • Public sector pensions adjustment (progressive reduction of an average of 4%) • Linking public sector retirement age to state pension retirement age • Effective pay cut 2009/2010 of 14% • Pay freeze until 2014	First program (2010–12) • Reduction of public employment • Replacement of only 1:5 Second program (2012–15) • Further reduction of public employment • Dismissal of 150,000 public employees • Third program (2015–17) • Lowering the replacement rule from 1:5 (2016) to 1:4 (2017) to 1:3 (2018)

Sources: author's compilation based on European Commission (2010b; 2011e; 2012e; 2015e; 2017c; 2018b)

paradigmatic shifts? Do the ideational processes attached to the MoU adjustment process lead to a new understanding of labour markets in Greece? On the other hand, it is fruitful to analyse the role of actor constellations and political incentive structures in central decisions within the adjustment process. Furthermore, the influence of the previously existing institutional setting of Greek labour markets on possible reform implementation is a third and particularly interesting aspect. All three aspects are analysed in the following sections.

5.3.1 Labour Market Paradigms and Ideational Processes

Ideas and ideational processes, as this section highlights, have explanatory value for the policy change visible in Greek labour markets and collective bargaining structures. This is particularly the case for the specific nature of the liberalization policies that were proposed and implemented as a condition of the financial assistance programs. It is worthwhile to note that the Greek MoUs were created under immense time pressure[7] during critical moments in the history of the euro area crisis. In this regard, they were not necessarily the result of thorough deliberation between the institutions and the Greek government.

As a document analysis unveiled, the MoUs include specific ideas on labour market development in Greece, which are visible in quantitative and qualitative terms. In terms of quantity, passages that focus on the liberalization of collective bargaining, firm-based wage setting, and the recommodification of labour clearly outweigh state-led and sectoral coordination passages (see table 5.8). A similar trend is visible for employment protection, as a clear majority of the passages focus on liberalizing existing employment protection legislation. There are only a few passages identified in the documents that address preserving or strengthening Greek employment protection legislation (EPL) (see table 5.8). Social welfare, such as unemployment support and active labour market policies, shows a slightly different tendency. The first program largely focused on the retrenchment of unemployment support and social security. Passages that focus on social investment, rather than retrenchment, became a more common topic within the documents in the third program (see table 5.8). Hence, there is a development towards social investment from 2010 to 2018, albeit at different frequencies (see table 5.8).

Public employment is characterized by similar trends in the data. Most passages in the first and second financial assistance programs focus on the reduction of public employment, either in numbers or in

Table 5.8. Document analysis, labour markets, Greece

	First Program	Second Program	Third Program
Wage-setting mechanisms			
State-led coordination	9	9	0
Sectoral coordination	2	0	3
Liberalization	114	99	10
Employment protection segislation			
Liberalization	72	58	8
Stricter protection	0	3	0
Unemployment and activation			
Retrenchment	37	39	5
Social investment	2	79	82
Public employment			
Reduction	109	115	19
Preservation	3	16	47
Increase	0	28	3

Source: author's compilation

public sector pay. There are only a few passages that focus on preserving or increasing public employment. The third program, as table 5.8 highlights, includes more passages concerning the preservation of public employment, albeit at lower frequencies than the first two programs. As the quantity of passages highlights, these differences exist mainly between the program periods of 2010–15 (first and second program) and 2015–18 (third program).

The qualitative document analysis supports the quantitative results. The passages concerning labour market adjustments include specific ideas of labour market adjustment. To give an example, the Memorandum of Economic and Financial Policies attached to the first MoU specifies the program's vision for Greek labour markets:

> In line with the lowering of public sector wages, *private sector wages need to become more flexible to allow cost moderation* for an extended period of time. Following consultation with social partners and within the frame of EU law, *the government will reform the legal framework for wage bargaining in the private sector, including by eliminating asymmetry in arbitration. [...] Employment protection legislation will be revised, including provisions to extend probationary periods, recalibrate rules governing collective dismissals, and facilitate*

greater use of part-time work. (European Commission 2010b, 53; emphasis by the author)

The labour market reforms within the first and the second MoU largely follow the initial goal of making labour markets more efficient and flexible (see 5.2). Central passages concerning labour markets focus on reducing wages, both in the public and the private sector, reducing employment protection legislation, and decentralizing wage-setting mechanisms or reducing employment protection legislation:

Excessively expensive statutory severance pay slows down the labour market adjustment and hampers job creation. This also hinders labour mobility to dynamic sectors and firms as acquired severance payment entitlements would be lost in case of taking up a job elsewhere. Statutory requirements on severance payments, which were visibly higher in Greece compared with other European countries will from now on be capped at 12 months of pay. [...] *Looking forward, this reform is an important complement to the product market reforms of the programme: as the latter are expected to give rise to more dynamic market entries and exits of firms and thereby of potential employers, proper framework conditions enhancing labour mobility need to be in place.* (European Commission 2012d, 55; emphasis by the author)

Reducing social welfare rates and transforming unemployment support from a traditionally passive transfer system into active labour market policy is another central part of the labour market paradigm included in the documents; it comes up regularly and is a dominating topic. Most aspects of the labour market reforms are found separately in the data. However, in combination, they form a coherent policy paradigm that supports market-based coordination mechanisms for labour markets that does not allow deviations. This has also been described by interview partners: "At the period between 2010, 2011, 2014, many of the people, I think, felt that they, there is no way out. They are trapped for years in a specific path of neoliberalism, of austerity without any kind of benefit" (Interview 11, 12 March 2018).

Hence, the labour market policy paradigm is clearly identifiable. As an interview partner argued, "the three memoranda, they come under the [...] neoliberal ideas [...] on how labour markets work. [...] [I]t's not only wages that have to go down, but also it has to do with employment protection programs, it has to do with a number of issues concerning flexible labour markets" (Interview 4, 5 March 2018). Similar descriptions of the labour market reforms are given by other interview partners as well. An interview partner summarized the policy goals of labour market developments in Greece as a liberalized labour market with less employment protection legislation and reduced wages (Interview 8, 9 March 2018). The apparent goal was to reduce unit labour costs: "The main argument of the government was that in this way, they will reduce, they will lower the so-called unit labour cost and to boost competitiveness" (Interview 8, 9 March 2018).

As the 2011 International Labour Organisation (ILO) Report of the High Mission to Greece highlighted, employment was an issue that was usually not deliberated during the meetings between the Greek government and the institutions. Rather, the labour market reforms were put forward by the institutions as the policy conditionality attached to the financial assistance (International Labour Office 2011; see also Koukiadaki and Grimshaw 2016, 24–5). Hence, labour market ideas included in the MoUs have their origin in the institutions rather than the Greek government. Interview partners argued in a similar way: the government engaged in talks and social partners were consulted, but without any perceived effect on the direction of the program (e.g., Interview 8, 9 March 2018; Interview 11, 12 March 2018).[8]

The qualitative document analysis furthermore highlights that there are adjustments within the policy paradigm throughout the years. Not only has the frequency of labour market reforms decreased (see also figure 5.2); the strategies of adjustments in the private sector have also become a central issue. Whereas the first program me argued for private flexibilization through tripartite dialogues, the second MoU put forward unilateral private sector liberalizations through the state (see tables 5.7 and 5.8). The most obvious change in the policy paradigm included in the programs occurred after the Coalition of the Radical Left – Progressive Alliance (SYRIZA) was elected in 2015. As the labour market reforms of 2010 to 2012 had already developed their impact on Greek labour markets, the focus shifted (see tables 5.7 and 5.8).

A central qualitative shift in this process is the notion of achieving "EU best practice across labour market institutions and [fostering] constructive dialogue amongst social partners" (European Commission 2015e, 21), albeit without specifying said EU best practices. Before 2015, the central notion in terms of labour markets had been to render labour markets more flexible. The new framing indicates a change in the emphasis of reforms. Furthermore, the third MoU contains a clause on including an independent expert group to review the reforms of 2010 to 2015 and to make proposals for future labour market reforms, albeit without reversing past reforms (European Commission 2015e, 21–2).[9]

The MoUs therefore transport ideas about labour market reforms that materialized in Greek labour markets through policy conditionality. The institutions – at first the European Commission, the European Central Bank, and the International Monetary Fund, and later also the European Stability Mechanism (see chapter 4) – thus acted as policy entrepreneurs (see 2.3.3; see also Schmidt and Radaelli 2004, 195–7). They constructed a discursive element about the need for reform of Greek labour markets based on ideas concerning liberalization, decentralization, and recommodification – as is visible in the document analysis. This discursive element enabled them to implement policies that did not fit in the previous legacy of state-based economic coordination. However, while the institutional changes in Greek labour markets are empirically visible and resemble the labour market paradigms included in the programs (see 5.2.1), ideational change of labour market paradigms is neither apparent within the Greek political system, nor among Greek social partners.

As several interview partners highlighted, the ideas in the programs concerning labour market reforms were challenged by other actors, both the government and social partners. Interview partners associated with business organizations argued that enterprises in Greece would prefer to engage in national and sectoral wage bargaining and would like to restore the system in place before the crisis, albeit with more possibilities to adjust agreements according to the needs of their respective business sectors (Interview 1, 12 October 2017; Interview 11, 12 March 2018). The trade unions' main priority is the re-establishment of collective bargaining, at both the national and the sectoral level: "Our main priority, among other things of course, the main priority [...] [is] the re-establishment of the normality as far as the conclusion of collective agreements is concerned" (Interview 8, 9 March 2018).

As interview partners highlighted, restoring the collective agreement structure was also a central issue for the SYRIZA-led government (Interview 12, 12 March 2018). Furthermore, a Member of the Hellenic Parliament highlighted that the programs' reforms of the labour markets were very substantive. However, not all of them were necessary as the labour market itself was not the central problem of the Greek economy (Interview 9, 9 March 2018).

The institutions, including the ESM and its institutional predecessors, were thus able to materialize specific ideas about wage-bargaining decentralization and the liberalization of employment protection legislation, as well as a stronger recommodification of labour that went beyond the precrisis policy legacy. However, the program did not produce a new policy legacy that would support the socio-economic ideas included in the MoUs. To the contrary, the precrisis policy legacy of labour markets appeared to be still intact, as the general objective of reinstating precrisis labour market institutions highlights. The MoUs do account for the lack of ideational change within the Greek society concerning its labour markets. They include socio-economic thresholds that Greece must meet before the government is able to engage in taking back some of the reforms (Interview 2, 20 February 2018).

5.3.2 Actor Preferences and Incentive Structures

Actor preferences, strategic interaction, and incentive structures within the specific institutional setting of Greece, in combination with financial assistance programs and policy conditionality, potentially have significant effects on institutional changes of Greek labour markets, as rational choice institutionalism identified these as strong explanatory factors (Hall and Taylor 1996, 942–6; for an overview, see 2.3.1). The specific economic context of Greece effectively losing its market access to refinance its debt indicates strong actor preferences towards preventing a sovereign default. Furthermore, this incentive is linked with the specific policy conditionality structure attached to financial assistance in the single currency. Thus, the programs can be identified as powerful incentive structures for institutional change, despite different policy preferences by the Greek governments.

Structural adjustments of the labour markets are, as argued above, disputed within the different Greek governments, especially those of the political left. PASOK and SYRIZA both campaigned for higher wages and stronger employment protection before they were elected. In government, however, they implemented labour market reforms that went in a different direction. Their parliamentary factions regularly argued for less severe adjustments or different labour market reforms in general. As Mody showed, the run-up to the parliamentary vote for the first MoU saw PASOK MPs argue for lower wage cuts and less labour market decentralization. However, they were unable to change the path of adjustment as they were told that no changes to the program were possible (Mody 2018, 257). An interview partner argued that the labour market reforms were mostly unnecessary as, from the interview partner's perspective, the Greek problems were situated elsewhere. However, they had to be implemented because the institutions insisted on the reforms, and otherwise they would have gone into sovereign default (Interview 9, 9 March 2018).

Hence, given the strong ideational differences between the institutions and the Greek governments, the benefit-risk assessment of sovereign defaults vs. unwanted labour market reforms gave a clear incentive towards institutional change of labour markets, even when there was no consensus on the direction of the reforms. The incentive structures thus gave the Troika a lot of political influence. Not only did the governments implement reforms that were against their political positions, social partners were not substantially included in the discussions concerning employment, as Koukiadaki and Grimshaw argued (Koukiadaki and Grimshaw 2016, 24).

The lack of social partner involvement in the programs' reforms of Greek labour markets was also underlined by interviewees from social partner organizations (e.g., Interview 1, 12 October 2017; Interview 4, 5 March 2018; Interview 7, 8 March 2018; Interview 8, 9 March 2018; Interview 11, 12 March 2018). While the business organizations did engage in talks with the institutions (Interview 1, 12 October 12017; Interview 11, 12 March 2018), they did not feel that their input was considered for the reforms. As an interview partner highlighted: "Well, they, the way they operate is: they are come, they listen to everybody, but in the end […] it's their decision. […] I have seen situations where you try to explain [to] them things that are [...] absolutely reasonable and they simply, flatly reject it" (Interview 1, 12 October 2017). Trade unions, according to the interview partners, did not engage in direct talks. This was in part due to an adversarial attitude towards the institutions. An interview partner described the institutions as an enemy without political legitimacy (Interview 7, 8 March 2018).

A clear dispute between actor preferences and new incentive structures established through the European Stability Mechanism and its institutional predecessors is visible after the coalition between SYRIZA and the Independent Greeks (ANEL) came into power in 2015. Whereas previous governments were critical of certain aspects of the financial assistance programs, they generally accepted the necessity of thorough structural reforms. SYRIZA and ANEL reacted differently to the prospect of a third financial assistance program. As an interview partner highlighted: "We have tried and implemented our best within the given framework and the given framework was, naturally, given the European power relationships, catastrophic for Greece" (Interview 12, 12 March 2018). Given their political programs and their "anti-Memorandum, pro-welfare rhetoric" (Prodromidou 2018, 196), SYRIZA and ANEL would have been candidates to reject the MoU's labour market policies, which fundamentally did not fit with their party manifestos. However, despite campaigning for reversing previous labour market reforms, they were strong program implementers throughout the program – even while continuing to argue that they did not support the program but had to implement it to prevent a sovereign default. Instead, as the qualitative document analysis highlighted, by agreeing to the program in the summer of 2015, the SYRIZA-led government engaged in a form of constant renegotiation and achieved smaller qualitative changes to the general focus of the program and the included labour market reforms over time (see table 5.7).

The euro area crisis can thus be interpreted as an exogenous shock to Greek labour market policy that changed previous strategic interaction and, to a smaller degree, actor preferences. With the financial assistance architecture and the ESM as its institutional focal point, new incentive structures for the Greek government developed. While exiting from the single currency might have been a political, strategic threat voiced by parts of the government, it was commonly accepted in Greece that an exit from the euro was not a viable option for the country (European Commission 2015b, 8).[10] Therefore, the government accepted labour market reforms that it had earlier campaigned against.

In short, the SYRIZA-led government agreed to further labour market reforms because it would have been irrational for it to agree to an exit of Greece from the euro, despite severe differences on the labour market terms of the bailout program. In return, they agreed to implement reforms and opted for a strategy of being inside the financial assistance program but engaging in constant renegotiations in order to gain more policy space (e.g., Interview 12, 12 March 2018). The ESM and its institutional predecessors played an important role in this regard, as they were the central institutions to provide financial assistance and thus opened up the possibility of preventing sovereign default scenarios, albeit at the cost of structural adjustments.

5.3.3 The Crisis as a Critical Juncture in Greek Labour Market Policy

Feedback loops, historical legacies, and path dependence are generally perceived as key factors in explaining why institutional settings tend to be stable even if they are exposed to external pressures (Steinmo 2008; Steinmo, Thelen, and Longstreth 1992; Thelen 1999; see also 2.3.2). However, critical junctures can start historical developments which lead to institutional changes of political economies (Hall and Taylor 1996, 942).

The euro crisis has been described by some scholars as a critical juncture of institutional development at the European level (e.g., Verdun 2015; Gocaj and Meunier 2013). Focusing on Greek labour market developments, the severe crisis of the Greek economy starting in 2008 can also be analysed as a situation in which the countries' "formal or informal procedures, routines, norms and conventions embedded in the organizational structure of the polity or political economy" (Hall and Taylor 1996, 938) became unstable. As the danger of a sovereign default grew in 2009–10 and the Greek economy started to fall into a deep recession, the institutional equilibrium was punctured (see also 2.3.2), thus opening the possibility for institutional change of the Greek economy.

Historical and political economic developments of financial assistance programs are concentrated at the points in history when the Greek government and the institutions negotiated and agreed to the three Memoranda of Understanding (see figure 4.3). They can be interpreted as critical junctures where different developments come together: perceived and real risk of a sovereign default, the risk of losing EMU membership, and severe economic crises, which reduced the influence of institutional feedback loops and historical policy legacies. In this regard, policy paradigms included in the MoUs were able to forge a new path of labour market development (see also 5.3.1). While new policies and reforms were introduced throughout the entire program period, the path of adjustments was set during the negotiations and conclusion of the MoUs. In addition, the ESM's strict conditionality approach to financial assistance programs supported the changing of socio-economic paths in terms of labour markets as well (see also 4.4). Once the policy path was changed, feedback loops and path dependence started to keep the institutional reforms intact. As several interview partners highlighted, they did not expect Greek labour markets to return to their precrisis settings (e.g., Interview 4, 5 March 2018; Interview 8, 9 March 2018; Interview 11, 12 March 2018).

Between the conclusion of the MoUs, the direction of labour market developments was only changed to smaller degrees. In addition, the new historical legacies and feedback loops turned out to be strong, as after the programs ended, the labour market reforms remained stable. There were some initiatives by the Greek government after the country officially exited the third bailout program. In February 2019, the government increased the minimum wage by 11 per cent (Seralidou 2019). However, unlike what trade unions and employer organizations had previously demanded, the Greek government did not restore the autonomy of social partners to set the minimum wage under the National

General Collective Agreement. Rather, they set the new minimum wage unilaterally, stabilizing the institutional change of 2012, which was implemented to reduce the minimum wage (Seralidou 2019; see also table 5.3). Post-program adjustments to the minimum wage system thus followed the policy legacy of the financial assistance program.

A critical juncture in form of the euro crisis and subsequent institutional change in Greek labour markets is clearly identifiable (see 5.2.1). However, as the development of the Greek crisis shows, past institutional settings and policy legacies did not cease to exist. Rather, they influenced the institutional change of labour markets in Greece to a certain degree. The way Greek labour markets were composed before the crisis made some reforms more feasible than others. Hence, the analytical assessment of institutional change in Greek labour markets shows severe changes in a more market-based direction, but no full convergence with the ideal-type liberal market economy.

The missing expertise in some areas of labour market policy, as well as the severe threat of a sovereign default, made it hard to implement coordination mechanisms that went beyond market-based coordination. While the first MoU put forward the idea of tripartite coordination (European Commission 2010b, 27), such non-market coordination mechanisms were quickly abandoned as they did not produce the adjustment results asked for by the institutions (European Commission 2012e, 38; see also table 5.8). Due to the specific path dependence of the Greek state and the strong focus on expenditure reduction, changing the developmental path of labour markets proved not to be easy. In this regard, the program predominantly focused on market-based coordinative instruments and enabling market mechanisms in labour markets. Furthermore, due to feedback loops of previously existing labour market institutions, the precrisis institutions in Greek labour markets were not fully abandoned,[11] but changed in a way that supported the general objectives of the program.

As the evaluation of Greek labour market reforms by international experts highlighted, the reforms appear stable (Expert Group for the Review of Greek Labour Market Institutions 2016). In addition, several interview partners argued that they would not expect the institutional setting of labour markets to change again in the near future (e.g., Interview 2, 20 February 2018; Interview 4, 5 March 2018; Interview 6, 7 March 2018), despite the growth of precarious employment and high poverty rates as a result (Kennedy 2018). Furthermore, the third MoU provided thresholds for further reforms, which made it unlikely to reverse some of the reforms implemented during the program. Other scholars also do not see strong policy reversals after the exit of the program (e.g., Moury et al. 2021, 157–60). While the institutions including the ESM agreed to have to a review process for labour market reforms, including collective bargaining and employment protection legislation, the third MoU makes clear that after the reform process ended, Greek labour market policies should be brought "in line with best practice in the EU" (European Commission 2015e, 22), and "a return to past policy settings" (European Commission 2015e, 22) was specifically ruled out (European Commission 2015e, 22).

The expert group published its recommendations for the Greek labour market in 2016. While its twelve recommendations[12] went beyond the scope of policy proposals envisioned in the third MoU, it argued in some instances to return to precrisis settings, albeit with some modifications (e.g., in terms of minimum wage determination processes, see Expert Group for the Review of Greek Labour Market Institutions 2016); however, most of its proposals have not yet been implemented.

In sum, critical junctures played an important role in the reform of Greek labour markets. The negotiations and conclusions of the three MoUs are central points in the history of the crisis in Greece. They were negotiated in situations of severe socio-economic crisis and extensive political disputes, which can be identified as critical junctures due to the high amount of uncertainty around future prospects. In this situation, the financial assistance programs associated with the ESM and its institutional predecessors were able to change the developmental path of Greek labour markets and establish new feedback loops.

5.4 Fiscal Policy

Fiscal policy is a central pillar of the Greek financial assistance programs, as bringing down the Greek deficit to below 3 per cent and reducing government debt were key objectives of all three programs (European Commission 2010b, 45; 2012e, 24–6; 2015e, 6–7). To regain financial stability and thus regain access to financial markets, fiscal consolidation and reforming fiscal governance in Greece were central policy goals in the adjustment process (see table 5.9). The precrisis government expenditure and weak tax-collection capacities were identified in the political debate as central problems of Greek fiscal policy (European Commission 2010b, 7–10; see also Matthijs and McNamara 2015). Furthermore, budgetary processes were identified as institutionally weak and as leaving too much space for the government to run up fiscal deficits despite existing fiscal rules. Finally, the government's engagement with the economy was identified as harmful for fiscal stability, as well as for Greece's economic development (European Commission 2010b, 7–8).

As for labour market reforms, policy paradigms and ideational processes related to the fiscal consolidation strategy in the programs are fruitful points of analysis: What is the origin of central fiscal consolidation ideas? Which policy goals are connected to it, aside from reducing the deficit? Do the ideational processes within the realm of fiscal policy include a changing vision of the Greek state's role in the economy? In addition to ideational aspects of the institutional change, what role did political and institutional actors and interests play in the fiscal consolidation strategy? Furthermore, how did previously existing paths of fiscal policy development enable or inhibit fiscal policy strategies?

In order to provide an analysis of the institutional change in Greek fiscal policy, the following sections proceed as follows. First, fiscal policy paradigms and ideational processes within the financial assistance programs are analysed (see 5.4.1). Second, the role of actor preferences and institutional incentive structures for fiscal policy are examined (see 5.4.2). Last, the impact of existing fiscal policy trajectories, feedback loops, and the role of the euro crisis as a critical juncture in fiscal policy are highlighted (see 5.4.3).

5.4.1 Fiscal Policy Paradigms and Ideational Processes

Interview partners argued that there was no coherent fiscal policy strategy within the programs, as the policy focus shifted throughout the programs (Interview 3, 4 March 2018; Interview 5, 7 March 2018; Interview 10, 12 March 2018), which is visible in the way fiscal policy put emphasis on expenditure reductions and revenue increases (see 5.2.2).

However, the document analysis points out several aspects that ideationally structure the Greek fiscal adjustment process. First, fiscal policy proposals predominantly focus on restricting fiscal policy as a means of engaging in economic affairs. There are only very few passages which highlight the need to expand government expenditure, although these become more frequent in the third program. Most passages concerning the direction of fiscal policy in Greece argue for reducing government expenditure, either in general or in relation to specific aspects of the budget. Within the third program, however, there are considerably fewer passages that argue for restricting fiscal policy, which indicates a small change of strategy after 2015 (see table 5.9).

Table 5.9. Document analysis, fiscal policy, Greece

	First program	Second program	Third program
Budgetary process			
Restrained	192	263	97
Flexible	1	10	0
Fiscal policy direction			
Restrictive fiscal policy	543	350	151
Expansionary fiscal policy	8	5	21
Government discretion			
Less government discretion	223	224	117
More government discretion	0	2	3

Source: author's compilation

Second, the budgetary process as a key reform project is regularly brought up in program-related documents. A clear majority of passages focuses on reforming the budgetary process in a way that restricts the budgetary leeway of the current government. Examples of stricter formalization and stronger fiscal rules can be found in proposals for fixed expenditure ceilings, medium-term fiscal strategies, or institutional oversight by non-majoritarian, expert-based institutions. Passages including more budgetary flexibility can rarely be identified in the material. This is predominantly less the case in the third program (see table 5.9)

Third, the government's influence in economic affairs is a key issue in the data. The MoUs and further related documents include a variety of passages within the broader field of fiscal policy that discuss a reduction of the government's influence on the economy via fiscal means. Topics discussed in the coded passages include SOEs and government participation in economic activities, as well as financial aid for economic sectors. The documents rarely include passages that argue for a stronger usage of fiscal means for economic coordination. However, there are considerably fewer passages arguing for less discretion in the third MoU (see table 5.9).

Based on the qualitative analysis, a specific fiscal policy paradigm can be identified. The ideal-type fiscal policy outlined in the documents underlines the necessity for fiscal stability, rule-based fiscal and long-term budgetary processes, stability commitments in fiscal terms, and balanced budgets (European Commission 2010b, 2012e), a perspective on fiscal policy that is associated with German economic thought (Brunnermeier, James, and Landau 2016). In this regard, the MoUs resemble the Brussels-Frankfurt Consensus, as described by Erik Jones (Jones 2013).[13] The first MoU's main program objective for fiscal policy, visible throughout the documents, is as follows: "Sustainability-enhancing fiscal consolidation is urgently needed. The immediate priority is to contain the government's financing needs and reassure markets on the determination of the authorities to do whatever it takes to secure medium- and long-term fiscal sustainability" (European Commission 2010b, 15). Fiscal policy adjustments are thus supposed to achieve the overarching goal of restoring trust of financial markets in order to regain access to market-based refinancing options (European Commission 2010b, 15–16).

These aspects are central in the second MoU as well. However, fiscal consolidation strategy and financial stability are combined with policy goals of broader socio-economic change, highlighting the role of the state within the Greek economy (European Commission 2012e, 5). As a central program objective, the second MoU therefore puts forward the following:

> To rebalance the economy, support growth and employment, restore fiscal sustainability, and secure financial stability we will [...] [f]undamentally reduce the footprint of government in the economy through bold structural fiscal reforms and by privatizing public assets. Greece's recovery must come from a vigorous private sector response and this cannot happen with the government controlling access to key assets. (European Commission 2012e, 95)

The fiscal policy paradigm does have strong policy entrepreneurs in the institutions involved in the programs. Furthermore, as the program progressed, the ESM joined the institutions to promote the fiscal policy goals included in the programs in Greece. In this regard, the ESM is acting on behalf of its shareholders and puts forward the perspective of the Eurogroup (see chapter 4).

Over the years, the fiscal policy paradigm became a point of contention between the institutions, more so than labour market policy (see 5.3.1).[14] While the institutions initially developed central fiscal policy strategies together within the first MoU, differences about the necessity of further deep expenditure cuts and the possibility of debt relief became visible as the program progressed further. Within the IMF, concerns about the fiscal strategy and its effects on the economy were publicly discussed (e.g., Blanchard and Leigh 2013). The IMF, as was pointed out by interview partners, also voiced concerns about Greek debt sustainability and argued for debt relief, an issue that led to the

IMF's not participating within the third program as a creditor (e.g., Interview 6, 7 March 2018). However, as the ESM was fully operational in 2015, it effectively took over the IMF's position and engaged as a policy entrepreneur against debt relief by providing its own perspective on debt sustainability. In this regard, it supported the fiscal policy paradigm put forward by the Eurogroup. The ESM is engaged especially in the fields of fiscal policy, debt sustainability analysis, and privatization (Interview 30, 24 July 2018; Interview 32, 1 August 2018).

5.4.2 Actor Preferences and Incentive Structures

Greek governments and European institutions developed different fiscal policy preferences for the programs, as well as different strategies to achieve them. For Greece, refinancing in financial markets was not possible during the program period as the country lost market confidence. As a result, bond yields increased to unsustainable heights that could have led to a sovereign default (Illing 2013, 31–3). The possibility of financial assistance thus allowed the country and EMU to prevent that.

Between October 2009, when the Greek government announced its increased deficit, and April 2010, when the Greek government and the institutions signed the first MoU, the Greek government took strong initiatives to reduce the deficit. In October 2009, the government put forward expenditure reductions to reduce the deficit by 3.5 per cent. In January 2010, the deficit was again reduced by 3.5 per cent (Interview 10, 12 March 2018). During that time, the Greek government aimed at reducing its deficit in line with EU fiscal rules by 2012 (European Commission 2010b, 13). As argued by Pelagidis and Mitsopolous, the PASOK government predominantly implemented tax increases and only started to focus on expenditure reductions in March 2010 (Pelagidis and Mitsopoulos 2016, 101). The central aim of the strong fiscal consolidation measures by the newly elected government was coping with increasing fiscal pressure. However, the Greek government at the same time tried to convince European governments that Greece was engaging in difficult reforms in order to gain the support of its European partners and thus receive bilateral loans: "the large part of the fiscal measures that were required were voted [in] before, and this was also part of our effort to convince our European partners to offer us the bilateral loans" (Interview 10, 12 March 2018). After the first MoU was signed, expenditure reductions still took place, but on a smaller scale for the rest of 2010 (Interview 10, 12 March 2018).

A central aspect of the fiscal policy reforms implemented throughout the years of crisis thus came from functional pressures. The central goal of the Greek government was staying within the euro area, while the members of EMU wanted to prevent further financial sector instability (Colasanti 2016, 40–2). Furthermore, an exit scenario could have led to increased social and economic hardship, as well as further economic dependency (Altvater 2013); avoiding such an outcome was a central aspect of the Greek position to implement fiscal policy reforms.

Interview partners highlighted that the institutions initially focused on broader fiscal targets and were open to proposals from the Greek government, which gave the government some policy space. As the program progressed, however, policy conditionality became more detailed. Furthermore, in some areas that are traditionally harder for governments to reform, such as pensions, the institutions made policy proposals in order to drive the reform process forward (Interview 5, 7 March 2018; Interview 10, 12 March 2018). To a certain degree, the Greek government used blame-shifting as a political strategy, especially as fiscal policy decisions tended to affect all parts of the society. Despite common decisions between the institutions and the government, it sometimes was politically easier to argue that the reforms were part of the conditionality and thus not negotiable. Taking this into consideration, the ESM and the institutions on the one hand, and the Greek governments on the other hand, were able to use the policy conditionality approach as an instrument for their different strategies to implement institutional change in difficult policy fields.

Despite its election campaign against a third MoU and its adversarial position to the policy conditionality (Prodromidou 2018, 196), the SYRIZA-led government became a strong implementer of the fiscal policy reforms in the third program. The government argued on a regular basis that the program they were implementing was not theirs, even while, according to several interview partners, they became very active in achieving higher results than the fiscal targets with the institutions set out. As one interview partner argued, SYRIZA campaigned for lower fiscal targets in 2015 because, from their perspective, Greece needed the fiscal space to get the economy growing (Interview 10, 12 March 2018). Primary budgetary surpluses were a central point of contestation between the newly elected government and the Eurogroup. However, according to an interview partner: "Every year since then, the Greek government overshoots the targets" (Interview 10, 12 March 2018).

The financial assistance provided by the ESM in cooperation with the Commission, as well as the IMF and the ECB, hence had a disciplining effect on the Greek government. It put forward a predominant incentive structure. The Greek government faced a sovereign default in the summer of 2015 due to a prominent dispute about the conditionality of a potential third program between the newly elected SYRIZA-led government and the institutions (which included a referendum on such a program on 5 July 2015, a vote against it, and further negotiations after the referendum). The institutions effectively withheld financial support during this period, but their agreement in the end to a third financial assistance program gave the new Greek government an opportunity to prevent a sovereign default. Once the government agreed to the financial assistance program, the ESM offered it additional incentives to engage in strong program implementation in order to gain more space in other policy spheres.

5.4.3 The Crisis as a Critical Juncture in Greek Fiscal Policy

The Greek fiscal crisis of 2008 and 2009, as well as the financial assistance process that followed in 2010, can be clearly identified as a critical juncture in Greek fiscal policy. It had a lasting effect on the institutional setting of Greek fiscal policy and the role the government plays in the Greek economy, based on the wide-ranging and transformative institutional change that took place after the crisis emerged (see 5.2.2).

Greek fiscal policy had already experienced strong adjustments before the euro area crisis. The country had already engaged in fiscal adjustment from 1993 to 1999 in order to comply with the Maastricht criteria and thus become a member of the single currency (Kaplanoglou and Rapanos 2011, 6). This was not only the case in Greece, as adjustments in order to join EMU took place in all countries, albeit at varying degrees (Sadeh 2006, 39–45). In addition, the fiscal adjustments of 1993 to 1999 did not have a transforming effect in socio-economic coordination mechanisms in Greece. This was particularly highlighted by the fact that Greece again started to build up higher deficits after the introduction of the euro and was put under the excessive deficit procedure from 2004 to 2007 (Kaplanoglou and Rapanos 2011, 6–7).

The fiscal engagement of the Greek government in economic affairs was a central aspect of the Greek socio-economic model and continued to be central for socio-economic coordination until the euro crisis (see 5.1 and 5.2.2). The country's fiscal framework remained largely unchanged despite economic recessions, previous consolidation phases, and fiscal malfunctions. Some factors, such as the underdeveloped state capacities and weak tax collection, as well as the strong involvement of the Greek state in economic affairs, were central factors of international concern. However, no institutional change was visible until 2008, despite external criticism and socio-economic pressure.

As the euro crisis started to materialize, Greece's fiscal policy became a central field of institutional change (see 5.2.2). Fiscal consolidation in the form of expenditure reductions and revenue increases was a central aspect of the financial assistance procedure (see 5.2.2.1 and 5.2.2.2) and was also central to previous fiscal consolidation periods. The financial assistance programs were different in the way they transformed norms, institutions, and formal fiscal policy procedures, which are central indicators of critical junctures (Hall and Taylor 1996, 938).

The institutional change of fiscal policy as a consequence of the critical juncture is visible in two dimensions. First, Greek budgetary governance has transformed into an anticipatory, rules-based framework that gives the government less options to engage in fiscal policy on an ad hoc basis (see also 5.2.2.3). The introduction of the Medium-Term Fiscal Strategy in 2010 provided Greece with multi-year fiscal planning mechanisms that are now a central aspect of fiscal policy (Interview 10, 12 March 2018). As the OECD illustrated, the new Organic Budget Law of 2014 included enhanced EU fiscal rules in Greece's fiscal frameworks and thus introduced "a balanced budget rule, a debt rule, a convergence rule and correction mechanisms" (OECD 2019, 186). In addition, new independent agencies were included in the fiscal framework. While the OECD argues that budgetary transparency needs to be improved (OECD 2019, 186), there have been central steps towards more budgetary transparency. Most of the reforms to the fiscal framework and fiscal governance were implemented as part of the policy conditionality attached to the financial assistance programs (see table 5.9). Second, as a consequence of fiscal consolidation and the new fiscal governance, the role of the state in the economy has been transformed and reduced. The government was a central institution of economic coordination, and using fiscal means was a central aspect of its coordinative efforts. Three financial assistance programs later, the Greek government cannot engage in economic affairs to the same extent, due to fiscal constraints (see also 5.2.2.5, especially table 5.6).

Considering these aspects, the fiscal policy reforms do appear to build a new, stable developmental path with increasing feedback loops and a strong policy legacy. While discussions about specific fiscal issues were always a part of the financial assistance negotiations between the Greek government and the institutions, the general route of adjustment remained stable. This was even the case after 2015 when SYRIZA came into power. Despite public criticism of the adjustment programs, the left-wing government proved to be a strong implementer of the fiscal paradigms included in the adjustment process (e.g., Interview 10, 12 March 2018). In addition, as EMU's fiscal rules were adjusted during the euro crisis, there are now more instruments on the European level to engage in fiscal developments at the national level (Verdun 2018).

Furthermore, as the ESM is a key creditor of the Greek state, it will further engage with the Greek government on fiscal issues in order to secure the repayment of loans. Hence, there are strong feedback loops in place that support the newly established path of fiscal policy in Greece.

5.5 Interim Conclusion

Greece was not only the first country of the euro crisis that asked its European partners for financial support; it was also the only country with more than one financial assistance program. Furthermore, Greece was granted financial assistance during all three phases of the ESM's institutional development: the ad hoc Greek Loan Facility, the temporary EFSF in combination with the Commission's EFSM, and the permanent ESM (see 4.2). Hence, the Greek program allows us to analyse different stages of the financial assistance process and thus offers empirical evidence of its influence on institutional change over a longer period.

In the Greek case, institutional change of its fundamental socio-economic coordination mechanisms is clearly identifiable (see 5.2.1 and 5.2.2). Before the crisis, Greece was a key example of a mixed-market economy with predominant state-based coordination mechanisms. This, as was argued above, was the case for labour markets and fiscal policy. While there were some elements of non-market coordination of labour markets between social partners at the national level, such as the setting of the minimum wage, the state played a key role in most socio-economic matters. Before the euro area crisis, the Greek state was a key focal point for social partners to coordinate labour market developments. Furthermore, the government provided substantive parts of economic demand by engaging in expansive fiscal policy, either via direct economic engagement by SOEs, or by using government expenditure.

The Greek financial assistance programs addressed the role of the government in the economy, the centralized coordination of labour markets and fiscal policy developments as central problem areas and focused on reforming them. As the analysis of the labour market and fiscal policy has shown, Greece's socio-economic coordination mechanisms have seen institutional change towards marked-based coordination, to a wide-ranging degree. While the Greek variety of capitalism has not fully converged with ideal-type liberal market economies, markets are included as central aspects of economic coordination in terms of labour markets, as well as the role of the government in economic coordination (see 5.2.1 and 5.2.2).

In the Greek program, three critical aspects came together that facilitated institutional change. First, as was analysed above, the financial assistance programs included ideas and policy paradigms for both fiscal and labour market policy that in effect enabled market-based coordination in central economic spheres (see 5.3.1 and 5.4.1). In both areas, the programs included a clear policy paradigm that focused on the reduction of governmental influence and centralized coordination mechanisms at the national level, as well as the strengthening of markets as the predominant mechanisms of socio-economic coordination.

Second, while there was no ideational consensus among European and Greek policymakers and Greek social partners, policy conditionality and incentive structures of financial assistance enabled wide-ranging reforms. In both policy fields, Greek policymakers and social partners had alternative ideas in mind and would have preferred different strategies to support their interests. However, in the Greek case sovereign default was a key risk during central periods of the financial assistance programs. Hence, there were strong rational incentives to implement policies put forward by the institutions. The ESM's policy conditionality approach thus enabled institutional change, despite severe ideational differences (see 5.3.2 and 5.4.2).

Lastly, the crisis can be identified as a critical juncture, which made wide-ranging institutional change possible. The magnitude of the Greek crisis in 2008 and 2009, as well as the negotiations for the second and third programs in 2012 and 2015, led to a situation in which the institutional settings of precrisis Greece became fluid. Hence, changing paths and implementing central reforms that stood against historical legacies became easier. After the initial institutional reforms, new feedback loops started to develop, which made taking reforms back to precrisis settings much more difficult (see 5.3.3 and 5.4.3).

The ESM (and its institutional predecessors) is a central creditor of Greece. The policy conditionality attached to the program made possible through the ESM (as well as the EFSF and the GLF) certainly supported the stabilization of market-based coordination mechanisms in Greece's socio-economic model.

Chapter Six

The Irish Case: Policy Conditionality and Internal Ideational Change

Ireland is a key case in the euro area crisis as it was the first country to experience severe economic problems during the global financial crisis. Ireland started to adjust to the crisis as early as 2007 but ultimately had to apply for financial assistance because of severe problems in its banking sector. It is the only liberal market economy of EMU that applied for financial assistance and the first country to successfully exit a financial assistance program, in 2013. The Irish case thus provides interesting empirical evidence about the direction of the program's policy conditionality and the possibility for countries to use financial assistance to implement difficult reforms.

This chapter on the Irish case proceeds as follows: First, the case study provides an introduction into how the Irish crisis developed (see 6.1). Second, the chapter provides an analysis of institutional change from 2009 to 2018. The analysis focuses on institutional change in Irish labour markets as well as fiscal policy developments (chapter 6.2). Third, the case study explains how the central independent variable (financial assistance programs provided through the ESM and its institutional predecessors) influences the dependent variable by analysing ideational, interest-based, and historical-institutional processes related to the financial assistance programs (see 6.3 and 6.4). Last, the case study concludes by assessing the degree to which the financial assistance program led to institutional change in the Irish socio-economic model and how this change occurred. Furthermore, the analysis provides an outlook on future developments for Irish capitalism (see 6.5).

6.1 How the Irish Crisis Developed

Ireland, as a peripheral member of EMU, has played a particularly interesting role in the euro crisis. For over a century, up until the country's socio-economic basis started to show signs of severe recession, Ireland was portrayed as a liberal market economy success story. Coming from a peripheral position in the 1980s, Ireland has witnessed strong economic expansion, its economy doubling in size since the 1990s (Grubb, Singh, and Tergeist 2009, 5). Ireland experienced comparatively high economic growth rates, declining government debt, and increasing wages throughout the 1990s and early 2000s. In the late nineties, the Irish economy grew by almost 10 per cent per year (Johnston 2016, 137; see also Wickham 2015, 127; Donovan and Murphy 2013, 16). Net outward migration turned around as more people saw economic futures for themselves in Ireland. Ireland gained the "Celtic Tiger" nickname during this period (Donovan and Murphy 2013, 15–30).

Throughout the late 1990s and early 2000s, Ireland was widely acknowledged as an example of the comparative strength of liberal market economies. Low corporate taxes and flexible labour markets, as well as a strong emphasis on globalized trade, market liberalization, and a government strategy to attract foreign direct investments by American IT companies were key foundations of Ireland's precrisis socio-economic model. The former president of the European Commission, Manuel Barroso, called Ireland "a model for Europe" (Wickham 2015, 127). While there were tripartite elements in Irish industrial relations (see below), the predominant form of economic coordination was market based. The government did not have a strong, influential position (see table 6.6). Rather, it acted as an economic ambassador that opened opportunities for businesses.

Ireland kept its public image as the poster child throughout the euro crisis.[1] Not only was Ireland seen as the proof "that the programs work" (Manuel Barroso, cited in Mackintosh 2013; see Dukelow 2015, 94), Christine Lagarde argued that "Ireland has set standards for the correct measures to follow towards a recovery" (cited in Carswell 2015). Ireland's reform process was argued by Jean-Claude Trichet to be a form of best practice that could also be put to good use by Greece: "Greece has a role model and that role model is Ireland" (Trichet, cited in Brazys and Regan 2017, 411).

Taking the strong fiscal and economic position of Ireland into consideration, Ireland should not have been a candidate for a severe economic recession during the wake of the euro crisis. However, because of unsustainable developments in its banking and construction sectors,[2] Ireland became the second EMU member to apply for fiscal assistance. As Tooze argued, "Ireland was an overgrown offshore banking hub" (Tooze 2018, 323). The Irish crisis was composed of five key elements: (1) a bubble in Ireland's property markets that burst in 2007, (2) a collapse of its banking sector as a consequence of the global financial crisis and the Irish property bubble, (3) an economic recession which had its origin in the Irish construction sector, (4) fiscal problems of the state, and (5) increased unemployment after 2007 (O'Connell 2019, 177).

The magnitude of the Irish banking sector problems posed a severe risk to the Irish and European economy. When Ireland first legislated a 440 billion euro safety net for its banking sector, the Irish administration was convinced that the problems of the Irish banking market would be confined to the Anglo Irish Bank (AIB), worth 4 to 5 billion euro (Interview 18, 17 April 2018). However, it was quickly acknowledged by people in the departments that that they were "looking at anything from a 30 to 50 billion problem in the banking system" (Interview 18, 17 April 2018). When the Irish financial assistance program was signed in 2010, Irish financial sector bailouts cumulated to 46 billion euro (29 per cent of the Irish GDP) (European Commission 2011e, 15).

Ireland could very easily have been the first country to apply for financial assistance, as was pointed out by several interview partners (e.g., Interview 10, 12 March 2018), but Ireland faced problems similar to those of Greece: Germany effectively vetoed collective European action to combat an EMU-wide crisis (Tooze 2018, 323). Nonetheless, rumours of an intervention by the IMF were looming in early 2009, after Ireland bailed out AIB. At this time, Ireland's effective default risk was higher than that of Greece (Toode 2018, 323). However, the Irish government declined a precautionary program offer by the IMF in 2009, despite a budgetary deficit of almost 10 per cent (Mody 2018, 268–9).

The Irish government legislated its first national fiscal adjustment program in 2008 and was one of very few western countries that did not put up expansionary, counter-cyclical programs to react to the global financial crisis of 2008–9. Rather, the country already focused on fiscal consolidation during that period (Hardiman 2014, 150). From July 2008 to the end of 2010, the Irish government legislated six pro-cyclical consolidation packages (Hardiman 2014, 149–51). During this period, the Irish government implemented fiscal adjustments worth 9 per cent of GDP (Dukelow and Considine 2014, 58).

In late 2010, Ireland's GDP had already decreased by 17 per cent. At the same time, its deficit had increased to 11 per cent (European Commission 2011e, 7). Consequently, Ireland lost the confidence of financial markets in autumn 2010 (O'Connell 2019, 178). Ireland's fiscal situation was in severe trouble, but its economy was slowly starting to recover in late 2009 and 2010 (see table 6.1). Nonetheless, contagion processes related to the Greek application for financial support and

Table 6.1. Selected socio-economic indicators, Ireland, 2008–17

Indicator/year	2008	2009	2010	2011	2012	2013	2014	2015	2016	2017
GDP growth (1)	–4.5	–5.1	1.8	0.8	0.0	1.1	8.6	24.4	2.0	9.0
General government debt (% of GDP) (2)	42.5	61.8	86.2	110.5	119.6	119.9	104.3	76.7	74.3	67.8
General government surplus/deficit[3] (% of GDP (3)	–7.0	–13.9	–32.1	–13.6	–8.5	–6.4	–3.6	–20	–0.8	–0.3
General government spending (% of GDP) (4)	41.8	47.0	65.1	47.2	42.5	40.6	37.6	29.1	28.1	26.2
Employment (20–64) (5)	n/a	68.0	65.5	64.5	64.5	66.5	68.1	69.8	71.3	72.9
Unemployment (6)	n/a	12.6	14.6	15.4	15.5	13.8	11.9	9.9	8.4	6.7

Authors compilation. Sources: (1) Eurostat (2023d); (2) Eurostat (2023e); (3) Eurostat (2023e); (4) Eurostat (2023f); (5) Eurostat (2023a); (6) Eurostat (2023b)

Ireland's loss of access to financial markets ultimately led to the Irish application for financial assistance. The application was officially sent out on 21 November 2010 (European Commission 2011e, 7). The MoU was signed on 16 December 2010 by the Irish government on the one side and the European Commission (acting on behalf of the Eurogroup and the EFSF), the International Monetary Fund, and the European Central Bank on the other side. Ireland officially exited its economic adjustment program on 15 December 2013. At the time of writing, Ireland is still in post-program surveillance. The Irish program was the first financial assistance program in the euro area carried out by the temporary EFSF.

A central cornerstone of the Irish program was a four-year adjustment plan proposed by the Irish government in November 2010 and published before the final negotiations of financial assistance for Ireland (Laffan 2017, 185). The plan took into consideration previous adjustment policies implemented by the government since 2008 and provided a detailed fiscal and structural adjustment proposal to cope with the crisis. It included a combination of fiscal targets and front-loaded expenditure reductions. The plan aimed at Irish compliance with the Maastricht criteria by 2014 (Republic of Ireland 2010; see also Laffan 2017, 185). Furthermore, the National Plan for Recovery set out

Table 6.2. Codings related to the socio-economic model, Ireland

	Program (2010–13)	Post-Program (2014–18)	Total
Socio-Economic Model			
Change	199	88	287
Persistence	79	28	107
Neither	90	108	198

Source: author's compilation

a detailed economic adjustment process to improve the competitiveness of the Irish economy (Republic of Ireland 2010, 29–50). Acknowledged by the institutions in the Irish MoU, the plan was used as the foundation for the MoU's policy conditionality (European Commission 2011e, 19).

The Irish socio-economic model came under immense pressure during the economic crisis and structural adjustments. As will be analysed below, its economic institutional setting has been the subject of institutional change throughout the years, albeit to a different degree than the economic institutional setting of Greece. The question of how Ireland's economy should be further developed to regain competitiveness and to thus to strengthen its export-led growth model also played a role in the MoU and quarterly reviews, as table 6.2 shows.

First, changing the socio-economic model as a general topic can be identified in several passages throughout the analysed documents. These are more frequent during the program and are less common during post-program surveillance (see table 6.2). The quantity of passages on socio-economic change does not in itself indicate the preferred direction of change of the economic institutional setting. Second, the image is not as clear cut as the emphasis on socio-economic change might indicate. The data also illustrates a regular argumentation for the persistence of economic structures, albeit to a less frequent degree (see table 6.2). Third, socio-economic structures in the Irish economy are also debated without a preference on changing or preserving precrisis economic institutions (see table 6.2).

6.2 Institutional Change 2009–18

In the following sections, the transformation of labour markets (see 6.2.1) and fiscal policy (6.2.2) and thus of the Irish economic institutional setting are illustrated to analyse institutional change in Ireland's socio-economic model (dependent variable, see 3.1).

6.2.1 Institutional Changes in Irish Labour Markets

The Irish Memorandum of Understanding as well as the National Plan for Recovery focused on structural adjustments of labour markets in order to restore Ireland's competitiveness and to boost employment growth (European Commission 2011e, 36–9; Republic of Ireland 2010, 35–9). Central reforms included in the MoU to achieve this goal focused on labour market liberalization, a reduction of the national minimum wage, reviews of sectoral wage agreements, and reforms of social welfare in order to include active labour market policies and increased incentives to accept work offers (Greer 2014, 58–9; Roche 2017, 194–5). The reforms matched the ideal of Europe 2020 and European Economic Governance and had the potential to further increase the flexibility of Irish labour markets (J. Kompsopoulos 2015, 230–1). As the single currency did not allow for adjustment strategies such as internal devaluation (see 2.2.1) to regain competitiveness, labour market reforms were thus a central possibility of internal adjustment in Ireland. The labour market reforms in Ireland were strongly influenced by the financial assistance program as its policy conditionality included specific labour market policies. In addition, the program's fiscal policy approach also influenced policy choices of the Irish government (Walsh 2015, 6).

Until 2009, the institutional setting of Irish labour markets was characterized by three central aspects. First, the National Social Partnership was an essential instrument of tripartite policymaking by the Irish government in cooperation with leading trade unions and employer organizations[4] that started in 1987 and ended in 2009 when the employers withdrew from the social partnership and the government unilaterally legislated wage cuts for the public sector without including trade unions in this decision (Maccarrone, Erne, and Regan 2019, 316; O'Connell 2019, 180). Not only was the National Social Partnership important for the growth strategy in the 1990s and early 2000s; it also produced floors for wage increases and included a corporatist form of socio-economic governance[5] into a political economy that is generally described as governed by market mechanisms. Seven tripartite social pacts were concluded during the National Social Partnership before it ceased to exist (Doherty 2011, 374).

Second, Irish labour markets were characterized by primarily market-based coordination. Employees enjoyed only weak employment protection (O'Connell 2019, 176). Social welfare focused on modest, means-tested support rates typical for liberal welfare states (O'Connell 2019, 176) and thus included a strong commodification of labour. Despite the central role of national social pacts, Ireland has a voluntarist collective bargaining system. It was the state's responsibility to set a framework in which collective bargaining could take place. Maccarrone, Erne, and Regan highlight that Irish industrial relations were increasingly structured by individual workers' rights as trade union density declined (Maccarrone, Erne, and Regan 2019, 315). Employment negotiations became individualized further (e.g., Doherty 2016).

Third, the Irish labour market was characterized by a strong dualization between employees working for foreign and domestic firms.[6] In comparison to Irish companies, employees in foreign direct investment (FDI) sectors earn higher wages, have higher productivity rates, and were less affected by the economic recession. According to Regan, in 2007, shortly before the crisis, the multinational sector provided 15 per cent of total Irish employment (Regan 2012b, 14). The Industrial Authority Agency, founded in 1949, was particular important in attracting foreign firms by using state aid grants and lower business taxation (Fink 2008, 8–9; Regan 2012b, 14). Due to comparatively higher wages and low unionization rates, foreign firms essentially included market-based modes of labour coordination, whereas certain of the domestic firms were more likely to engage in sectoral or firm-based bargaining.

As figure 6.1 shows, labour market reforms were legislated on an infrequent basis before the crisis. In the years leading up to the crisis, the institutional setting of Irish labour markets remained unchanged for the most part. If reforms were implemented, they focused on active labour market policy initiatives, as their increase in 2005 and 2006 highlights. Labour market reforms became more frequent as the Irish banking and construction sectors fell into deep crises. In an already comparatively liberal labour market, the Irish government started to adjust to the crisis by implementing further reforms concerned with activation policies, beginning in 2008 and 2009. As figure 6.1 underlines, reforms of labour taxation, unemployment benefits, and other welfare-related benefits were legislated throughout the program. This process continued until 2015, two years after Ireland officially exited its financial assistance program.

As table 5.4 and figure 6.1 highlight, labour market reforms were less frequent in Ireland. Policy conditionality for labour markets was also less prescriptive, which might reflect that Ireland, as a liberal market economy, was already better suited for the rescue strategy pursued by the institutions included in the process. Furthermore, with the National Plan for Recovery, the Irish government put forward a detailed

Figure 6.1. Labour market reforms in Ireland, 2000–18

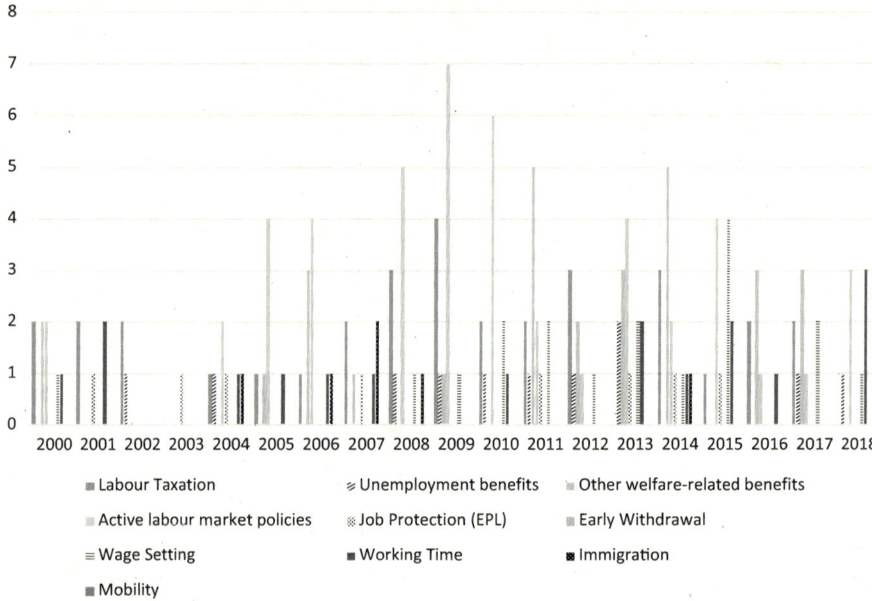

Source: European Commission (2022b)

program of planned reforms. Nonetheless, the structural adjustment conditionality included in the MoU did affect Irish labour markets and deepened its liberal market economy path in terms of wage-setting procedures (6.2.1.1), employment protection and employment developments (6.2.1.2), as well as unemployment support and activation policies (6.2.1.3).

6.2.1.1 DECENTRALIZATION OF COLLECTIVE BARGAINING

Ireland's bargaining system saw several adjustments throughout the crisis. A central development of the reaction to the crisis was a severe decentralization of collective bargaining. As table 6.3 highlights, despite being a liberal market economy, the Irish bargaining system was characterized by a strong centralization of collective bargaining. At the same time, collective bargaining primarily took place at the national level (see table 6.3). Because of the Irish crisis, collective bargaining was decentralized to a strong degree. The predominant level of wage bargaining now is the firm level (see table 6.3). A central, transformative development in this regard was the end of the National Social Partnership. The partnership was a central approach of tripartite socio-economic governance with the aim of maintaining cost competitiveness and industrial peace (Murphy and Mercille 2019, 27).

Ireland's industrial relations were highly characterized by the tripartite social partnership between the state, employers, and trade unions, which was first implemented in 1987 (Regan 2012b, 14; see above). The social partnership, an important instrument during the Irish economic developmental process from the late 1980s onwards, officially ended in the wake of the global economic crisis and thus before the MoU (J. Kompsopoulos 2015, 229–37; see also Regan 2012b; Roche 2017, 194): First the employers opted out, then the government imposed unilateral wage cuts for public sector workers of 5 to 8 per cent and advocated for legislation on minimum wage cuts as well as collective bargaining deregulation as a first reaction to the emerging crisis (Culpepper and Regan 2014, 734). Decentralized collective bargaining in combination with the voluntarist bargaining system has resulted in a decline in bargaining coverage. Over 40 per cent of workers were covered by collective agreements until 2007. In 2013, only a third of workers in Ireland were covered by a collective agreement (see table 6.3).

Currently, only public sector wage bargaining takes place at the national level. Despite the unilateral cuts in public sector wages in 2009, public sector trade unions engaged in negotiations with the government and agreed to several national collective agreements for the public sector starting in 2010.[7] According to O'Connell, these public sector agreements "represent some degree of continuity in social dialogue" (O'Connell 2019, 181). Industrial relations are now putting a stronger focus on minimal individual rights, market-based wage setting, and the relative position of management (Dukelow 2018, 208). This trend was visible earlier and is typical for LMEs, but it accelerated during the crisis.

Wage bargaining is almost exclusively present in parts of the economy with high rates of unionization, which is a consequence of the voluntary industrial relations system (Regan 2012b, 177). This system does not include the option of extending collective agreements, which is a result of the Irish strategy to attract foreign direct investments (Johnston 2016, 142–3; Regan 2012a; 2012b, 177–8; 2014). However, Irish labour markets were partly structured by registered employment agreements (REAs) and employment regulation orders (EROs), which

Table 6.3. Changes in Irish industrial relations, 2001–16

	2001	2007	2013	2016	Change		
					01–07	07–13	13–16
Trade union density (1)	35.0%	30.5%	28.5%	23.4%	–4.5	–2.0	–4.1
Bargaining coverage (2)	44.2%	40.5%	33.5%	n/a	–3.7	–7.0	–
Centralization of wage bargaining (3)	4.65	4.65	1	n/a	0	–3.65	–
Predominant level of wage bargaining (4)	5	5	1	1	0	–4	0
Employment protection legislation (5)	1.44	1.27	1.40	n/a	–0.17	+0.13	–
Minimum wage setting (6)	4	4	6	6	0	3	0
Mandatory extension of wage agreements (7)	1	1	0	1	0	–1	+1

Adapted from Iversen, Soskice, and Hope (2016, 177)
Sources: (1) OECD/AIAS (2021); (5) OECD (2013); (3) Visser (2016); (4), (6), and (7) Visser (2019b); (2) ILO (2022)
Notes: (3) higher scores represent higher levels of collective bargaining centralization (4) 1–5 scale, higher scores represent higher levels at which bargaining takes place (5) 1–5 scale, higher scores represent stricter employment protection legislation (6) 0–9 score, 0 indicates no minimum wage, higher scores represent higher centralization of minimum wage setting (7) 0–3 score, higher levels represent higher levels of trade agreement extensions

set minimum standards for economic sectors above the minimum wage (Maccarrone, Erne, and Regan 2019, 318–19). They were decided by tripartite, sectoral Joint Labour Committees (JLCs). Only 15 per cent of employees worked in sectors that were covered by JLCs, and only 8 per cent worked in sectors with REAs (Duffy and Walsh 2011, 24). In total, 13 JLCs and 73 REAs existed in 2011 (Duffy and Walsh 2011, 98–103).

Sectoral standards came under severe pressure. The institutions questioned their binding character and argued for opt-out clauses (Maccarrone, Erne, and Regan 2019, 319–20). Furthermore, businesses issued legal challenges to EROs and REAs. After a 2011 ruling of the Irish High Court, JLC decisions lost their statutory effect and EROs became unconstitutional (European Commission 2012c, 26). Starting in 2012, the JLCs' ability to set EROs was reformed and finally reinstated via the Industrial Relations (Amendment) Act of 2012. In 2013, REAs were ruled unconstitutional as well. The Industrial Relations (Amendment) Act of 2015 introduced Sectoral Employment Orders (SEOs) as a substitute for the now unconstitutional REAs (Maccarrone, Erne, and Regan 2019, 319).

There are differences in the scope of the new orders. Joint Labour Committees and the Labour Court now have to account for the competitiveness of the respective industries (Maccarrone, Erne, and Regan 2019, 319). In 2019, seven Joint Labour Committees[8] and two EROs (contract cleaning and security) were in place. According to Whitson (2014, 420), the process shows "how the transition from the Duffy–Walsh Report to the 2012 Act has accelerated an already marked shift towards greater reliance on minimal individual rights, market forces and a reinforcement of managerial prerogative" (Whitston 2014, 420).

In sum, the Irish collective bargaining system was severely decentralized during the crisis. Whereas wage setting was dominated by tripartite national social pacts from 1987 to 2009, the tripartite negotiations stopped after 2011. The only national wage-setting mechanism still in place is the negotiation of public sector wages between the government and public sector trade unions. In the private sector, wage setting is now primarily based on the firm level (see table 6.3). Previous sector-wide standards have come under pressure. The voluntary character of Irish collective bargaining puts additional emphasis on union density as a key factor for collective agreements. The decline of Irish union density has made collective agreements harder to achieve (see table 6.3). These developments had a significant influence on the Irish socio-economic model and deepened the focus on marked-based coordination of the labour market. The Irish financial assistance program supported these developments, especially in terms of reviewing sectoral extensions. However, critical developments in the Irish wage-setting systems took place in the lead-up to the Irish financial assistance program's conditionality.

6.2.1.2 EMPLOYMENT PROTECTION AND EMPLOYMENT DEVELOPMENTS

The Irish labour market was characterized by high levels of flexibility. Typical for liberal market economies, the flexibility of the Irish labour market was institutionally supported by comparatively weak employment protection legislation (EPL, see table 6.3). Structural adjustments of labour markets in line with the financial assistance program had different effects on EPL as well as employment and wage developments. According to Walsh, Irish labour markets are more flexible than most other European countries (Walsh 2015, 7) as Irish employees have had only minimum protection for their employment. In this regard, the financial assistance program included no major changes, as table 6.3 indicates. Due to the high flexibility of the Irish labour market, the program focused on different areas (see table 5.7). Employment protection legislation was, for a short period, expanded to a smaller degree. However, it returned to its precrisis status shortly after the program ended.

As figure 6.1 highlights, during the time of the program, two legislative initiatives concerned with employment protection were initiated. In 2011, the state rebate for statutory redundancy lump sums was reduced from 60 per cent to 15 per cent. In 2013, a provision considering pensions was legislated, which secured reduced pensions in cases of insolvent employers and underfunded pension schemes (European Commission 2022b). While EPL remained stable throughout the crisis, the Irish crisis led to a sharp increase in unemployment. During the years of the Celtic Tiger, Ireland experienced a severe reduction of unemployment. However, the labour market was highly fragmented between employees of international enterprises, which set up branches in Ireland in line with the Irish program to attract more FDIs and regional enterprises. The economic growth Ireland experienced before the crisis reduced unemployment for all workers, albeit with high income differentials between the different economic sectors (Fink 2008). During the financial and euro area crises, unemployment became a severe issue again.

Ireland's unemployment rate increased from 4.6 per cent in 2007 to 13.7 per cent in 2012 at the climax of the Irish crisis. Once the Irish economy was growing again, unemployment was reduced to 8.7 per cent in 2015 and is currently at the threshold of full employment in specific sectors. As Walsh argued, workers were affected differently by the crisis, and this was especially the case for employees with technological skills (Walsh 2015, 6). Irish long-term unemployment (LTU) and involuntary part-time workers proved to be problematic during the crisis. Precrisis, Ireland's LTU rate was comparatively low: only 1.4 per cent of all workers were unemployed for more than twelve months. As unemployment intensified during the crisis, so did long-term unemployment. In 2012, the LTU rate was 8.2 per cent. Even as the Irish economy experienced growth again, LTU rates remained problematic. In 2015, 4.7 per cent of workers were still unemployed for more than twelve months (see table 6.4).

Wages declined during the recession (Roche 2017, 204). On average, wages did not decrease more than 4 per cent (Kinsella 2017, 55).

Table 6.4. Changes in labour and unemployment, 2007, 2012, and 2015

	2007	2012	2015	% Change 2007–12	2012–15
Employment (000)	2,156.0	1,848.9	1,983.0	−14.2	7.3
Employment Rate (%)	68.8	59.3	63.9	−13.8	7.8
Participation Rate (%)	63.8	59.6	60.0	−6.6	0.7
Unemployment (000)	104.6	294.6	187.5	181.6	−36.4
Unemployment Rate (%)	4.6	13.7	8.7	197.8	−36.5
Long-term Unemployment (LTU) (000)	31.7	176.4	102.1	456.5	−42.1
LTU Rate (%)	1.4	8.2	4.7	485.7	−42.7

Source: CSO (2015), cited from O'Connell (2017, 233)

However, wage differentials are high across the different economic sectors in Ireland. Whereas the construction, public administration, health, and accommodation/food services sectors experienced median cumulative pay reductions, other sectors such as manufacturing experienced median cumulative pay increases (Walsh 2015, 33). The Irish labour market has witnessed temporary opening clauses of existing collective agreements in recent years in order to cope with its economic recession (Visser 2016). Private sector employers predominantly made cuts to their employment numbers, as well as working hours and wages. Involuntary part-time work became a prominent issue in Irish labour markets (Roche 2017, 196).

In addition, the public sector has seen several cuts in wages and reductions in total employment: From 2008 to 2013, public employment was reduced by 10 per cent. In total, the public wage bill was reduced by 17.7 per cent from 2009 to 2013 (Roche 2017, 199). These wage reductions partly preceded the financial assistance program as they were the initial reaction to the Irish crisis in 2008 and 2009. However, their continuation was central to the fiscal consolidation measures agreed on in the program (Roche 2017, 198). In total, the Irish wage share has declined by 17.1 per cent from 2010 to 2017. Real wages have increased by 6.9 per cent during the same time span (Lübker and Schulten 2017, 429–30). The combination of increased real wages but a declining wage share reflects the strong Irish GDP growth after the crisis, which did not lead to wage increases of the same level. This, in part, is a consequence of the decentralisation of industrial relations during the crisis.

6.2.1.3 UNEMPLOYMENT SUPPORT AND ACTIVATION POLICIES

Retrenchment of unemployment support systems and the implementation of activation policies were central developments in Irish labour market policies. The Irish welfare system went through three central changes: (1) reductions of replacement rates, (2) the implementation of activation policies, and (3) institutional redesigns.

The Irish unemployed support system is built upon two benefit schemes: Jobseeker's Benefits (JB), a support scheme that supports newly unemployed workers for a certain amount of time if they meet the qualifying conditions, and Jobseeker's Allowance (JA), a means-tested, guaranteed minimum income scheme (Dukelow 2018, 202–6). Both support schemes provide minimal financial transfers as "[t]he Irish social protection system has traditionally primarily been oriented towards the goal of poverty alleviation as opposed to income replacement" (Dukelow and Considine 2014, 62). During the crisis, JB and JA have seen severe retrenchments in terms of support rates, stricter qualification conditions, and shorter durations (see table 5.7). Based on the idea that out-of-work income was comparatively high in Ireland and would set negative incentives to take up work (O'Connell 2017, 248), reducing replacement rates was a key policy goal of the MoU (see table 5.7). JB paid a maximum of 204.30 euro per week in 2009. Payment rates were cut in 2010 and 2011 to 188.00 euro per week (Dukelow 2018, 203). The payment rates were increased to 203.00 euro again in 2017. The duration of JB was reduced in 2008 and in 2013 from twelve to fifteen months (depending on contributions) down to six to nine months (depending on contributions) (Dukelow 2018, 203).

Similar trends are visible for JA. Already means-tested, payment rates were reduced by the same margin as JB. JA used to pay up to 204.30 euro per week for adults over twenty-five, which was reduced in 2010 and 2011 to 188.00 euro per week (Dukelow 2018, 207). It was also increased to 203.00 euro in 2017. At the same time, income support for part-time workers eroded while part-time work became a more central characteristic of Irish labour markets (Dukelow 2018, 204).

Furthermore, the implementation of wide-ranging activation measures marks a central structural change in the Irish welfare system. Ireland has been described as a late activation adopter although it implemented several ALMPs in the 1990s (Regan 2012b, 120; Dukelow 2018, 201). Activation measures became a central reform initiative in the initial MoU (Murphy and Mercille 2019, 28; see also table 5.7). According to Dukelow, previous labour market programs focused primarily on direct job creation (Dukelow 2018, 198). However, they "have been somewhat curtailed and new, more market-oriented, programs have been introduced" (Dukelow 2018, 198). The Irish government developed *Pathways to Work*,[9] a central activation and employment strategy, in order to accelerate profiling and activating unemployed workers through one-on-one case management and including sanctions as a central incentive to pick up work (European Commission 2012a, 75). First published in 2012, the strategy has seen regular updates, each emphasizing similar issues and strategies (Dukelow 2018, 209). Activation measures are predominantly based on reinforcing incentives and include a focus on self-employed work (Dukelow 2018, 209). In addition, sanctions for non-compliance were introduced (O'Connell 2017, 242–3; see table 5.7). The general trend in Irish unemployment policies has thus been the retrenchment of social rights (Dukelow 2018, 205). The activation strategy also includes "marketization and privatisation as policy instruments" (Dukelow 2018, 198) to a stronger degree (Dukelow 2018, 198).

In line with the reform of its unemployment support system and the inclusion of a new activation strategy, Ireland has implemented a wide-ranging institutional reorganization of its labour market administration and training agencies. This led to a stronger integration of unemployment support systems with training programs and activation measures (Dukelow 2018, 198). Unemployed workers were assisted by FÁS, the central Training and Employment Authority. Due to changes in the policy direction of unemployment and dissatisfaction with FÁS, its discontinuation was announced in 2011 and became effective in July 2013. FÁS's responsibility for employment services, as well as its staff, were taken over by the Department of Social Protection (Dukelow 2018, 215). The Department of Social Protection created the Integrated National Employment and Entitlement Service (Intreo), a one-stop location for unemployment services. Intreo effectively merged the income support mechanisms of the Department of Social Protection with employment services previously run by FÁS, in branches across the country (Murphy and Mercille 2019, 29; O'Connell 2017, 243).

The reform process, however, has been particularly slow. Intreo was at first only in use for newly unemployed workers (O'Connell 2017, 244). After the initial slow implementation period, activation polices became frequently applied in combination with unemployment support. Whereas in January 2008 52,136 unemployed workers were in activation programs, including community employment, 89,704 unemployed workers participated in activation measures in March 2015 (Murphy and Mercille 2019, 30). In August 2017, with considerably lowered unemployment numbers (see table 7.1), 51,065 workers still participated in activation programs (Murphy and Mercille 2019, 30). These numbers underline the shift to an activation-based welfare system. However, the effectiveness of a range of programs is questionable: their effect is either not visible, or they are working on an insufficient scale (O'Connell 2017, 249).

In sum, the Irish unemployment support system has been the subject of substantial institutional and programmatic reform (Dukelow and Considine 2014, 63). The reforms include a stronger emphasis on marketization to employment allocation, activation services, and unemployment support, which predominantly focus on negative incentives rather than direct job creation. In effect, the reforms of unemployment support influence Irish labour markets in a way that puts additional focus on market-based coordination mechanisms.

6.2.2 Institutional Changes in Irish Fiscal Policy

Fiscal policy has been a key component of the Irish strategy to combat the severe crisis, which started in 2007. Furthermore, fiscal policy has been a central issue of the Irish Memorandum of Understanding, which the Irish government concluded with the European Commission, the IMF, and the ECB in late 2010. Prior to the beginning of the Irish crisis, the Irish government was in a comparatively strong fiscal position. As argued above, the Celtic Tiger period was characterized by strong economic growth and low unemployment. The Irish government accomplished a reduction of Irish sovereign debt to 23.9 per cent in relation to GDP (Department of Finance 2018, 15). However, as the Irish economic and financial crisis started to materialize, Ireland's fiscal position began to deteriorate quickly (see table 6.1). Coming from a period of a government balance surplus of 0.3 per cent in 2007 (Department of Finance 2018, 15), Ireland's "primary fiscal balance shifted to baseline deficits of 11%-12% of GDP in 2009 and 2010" (Kinsella 2012, 224).

The Irish deficit had two key sources: As the Irish construction sector contracted, government revenue started to decrease (see 6.2.2.2). The construction sector accounted for almost a quarter of GDP, which is why its contraction had a severely negative influence on public revenue. In addition, Irish unemployment increased, which led to higher government expenditure for unemployment support (Department of Finance 2018, 15–17). As private sector credit increased by almost 250 per cent from 2003 to 2008, mainly in relation to property (Department of Finance 2018, 10), the Irish banking sector experienced existential problems. Private investments were reduced by 31 per cent in 2009. Irish fiscal policy developed in a similar way, and Irish government expenditure was reduced by 4.4 per cent in 2009 (Kinsella 2012, 224).

As a reaction to the crisis, the Irish MoU predominantly focused on "expansionary fiscal contraction" (Hardiman 2014, 139), a rebalancing of the government's fiscal situation through a combination of cutting government expenditure and revenue increases (Hardiman 2014, 139). It consisted of two-thirds expenditure reductions and one-third revenue increases (Department of Finance 2018, 20). The Irish adjustment followed a pro-cyclical, front-loaded route of adjustments (Department of Finance 2018, 20). The MoU alone planned a total fiscal consolidation of 15 billion euro and planned to reduce current expenditure spending by a total 7 billion euro, mostly by reducing the public sector wage bill and public sector pensions (European Commission 2011d, 28; see also table 6.5). Capital expenditure was planned to be reduced by 3 billion euro over the timespan of 2011–14 (European Commission 2011e, 28). In addition, the consolidation strategy included 5 billion euro in revenue increases (European Commission 2011e, 29).

The adjustment strategy did not comply with the excessive deficit procedure in place for Ireland. Fiscal consolidation, as planned in the National Plan for Recovery and the MoU, would have taken Ireland until 2015 to reduce its deficit to under 3 per cent of GDP. However, as the institutions and Commission services expected the Irish economy to grow again, they extended the deadline of the excessive deficit procedure to 2015, expecting that Ireland would need an additional consolidation of 3 billion euro in 2015 (European Commission 2011e, 31).

The program was successful in addressing the Irish fiscal imbalances as it reduced the current deficit. At the same time, the Irish adjustment program did lead to institutional change in the way Irish fiscal policy is conducted. Therefore, the following sections analyse the changes in Irish fiscal policy by first focusing on government expenditure (see 6.2.2.1) and developments in Irish revenue (see 6.2.2.2). Furthermore, the reforms of Irish budgetary processes and implementation of fiscal rules are analysed (see 6.2.2.3) and the role of privatization is illustrated (see 6.2.2.4). Last, an analysis of changes to the government's role due to fiscal policy reforms is presented (see 6.2.2.5).

6.2.2.1 FISCAL CONSOLIDATION BY REDUCING GOVERNMENT EXPENDITURE

Ireland's fiscal position was comparatively strong prior to the crisis. However, when the Irish construction and banking sectors contracted, the government's revenue started to decrease rapidly. In addition, increased social expenditure in line with increased unemployment and a bank guarantee put the Irish fiscal balance under additional stress (Walsh 2015, 4–5; see above). The Irish fiscal consolidation strategy had already started in 2008, as the authorities, especially in the Finance

Table 6.5. Fiscal policy reforms proposed in the MoUs

	Ireland	Greece
Cumula-tive fiscal consolidation	First program (2010–13) • Cumulative fiscal consolidation of 15 billion euro in 2011–14 • Front-loaded consolidation: 6 billion euro in 2011	First program (2010–12) • Fiscal measures up to 13 per cent of GDP between 2010 to 2014, in addition to previous fiscal measures by the Greek government (5.5 per cent of GDP) • Front-loaded consolidation: 8 per cent of GDP in 2010 (incl. previous measures); 4 per cent in 2011; 2–2.5 per cent in 2012, 2013, and 2014
Government expenditure	First program (2010–13) • 7 billion euro current expenditure reductions (esp. public sector paybill, public sector pensions, and departmental expenditure) • 3 billion euro capital expenditure reductions • Front-loading in 2011: current expenditure reductions worth 2.1 billion euro, reductions in capital spending worth 1.9 billion euro • Reforming public service pensions in order to reduce expenditure (higher retirement age, reform of pension entitlements) • Reducing the public sector wage bill by reducing public employment by 23,500 employees (full-time equivalents)	First program (2010–12) • Expenditure reductions worth 7 per cent of GDP Second program (2012–15) • In order to achieve 2012 fiscal targets: expenditure reductions worth 1.5 per cent of GDP (75 per cent of which are permanent measures) Third program (2015–18) • Re-establishing full INN prescription • Reducing the price on off-patent drugs • Launching a comprehensive social welfare expenditure review • Permanently reducing expenditure ceilings for military spending (2015: 100 million euro; 2016: 400 million euro) • Second-phase reforms of pensions • Extension of Gross Gaming Revenues • Increase of income taxes for rents (below 12,000/year: 15 per cent; above 12,000/year: 35 per cent) • Producing a plan to complete the clearance of arrears and pension claims Supplemental MoU (2017) • Pension reform (expenditure reductions of 1 per cent of GDP in 2019–22)

(Continued)

Table 6.5. Fiscal policy reforms proposed in the MoUs (*Continued*)

	Ireland	Greece
		Supplemental MoU (January 2018) • Additional social policy spending due to fiscal space
Government revenue	First program (2010–13) • 5 billion euro in revenue increases in 2011–14 • Front-loading in 2011: revenue increases worth 1.4 billion euro • Broadening of the taxbase via income tax increases in 2011, as well as increases in VAT, carbon tax, and property tax • No increase of corporate taxes • If revenues are higher than planned, they must be used for debt reduction	First program (2010–12) • 4 per cent of GDP in tax measures (mostly indirect taxes) Second program (2012–15) • Reform of the tax system, broadening the tax base while reducing high marginal rates Third program (2015–18) • Abolishing the refund on excise tax on diesel for farmers • Reform of income tax code (incl. phasing out preferential tax treatment for farmers) • Increasing tonnage tax • Correcting problems with past revenue measures • Eliminating VAT island discounts • Reducing garnishment thresholds to 1,500 euro • Producing a comprehensive plan to fight tax evasion • Strengthening VAT collection and enforcement Supplemental MoU (2017) • Putting forward a national tax-collection strategy in 2017 to improve the collection of tax debt • Centralization of social security contributions in a single fund (EFKA) • Establishment of a continuously declining wage bill ceiling
Primary surplus		First program (2010–12) • Reducing the primary deficit from -8.5 per cent in 2009 to a surplus of 6 per cent by 2014 Second program (2012–15) • Adjusted primary surplus targets: −1 per cent deficit in 2012; 1.8 per cent surplus in 2013; 4.5 per cent surplus in 2014

(*Continued*)

Table 6.5. Fiscal policy reforms proposed in the MoUs (*Continued*)

	Ireland	Greece
		Third program (2015–18) • Gradual achievement of a primary surplus of 3.5 per cent of GDP in 2018 (2015: –0.25 per cent; 2016: 0.5 per cent; 2017: 1.75 per cent) **Supplemental MoU (2017)** • Medium-term primary surplus of 3.5 per cent of GDP, maintained until 2022
Deficit reduction		**First program (2010–12)** • Planned reduction from 14 per cent deficit in 2009 to below 3 per cent in 2014
Budgetary process	**First program (2010–13)** • Reforming the medium-term budgetary framework • Introducing a Fiscal Responsibility Bill that allows for medium-term expenditure provisions, incl. binding sectoral multi-annual expenditure ceilings • Implementing an independent budgetary advisory council	**First program (2010–12)** • Introduction of a medium-term fiscal framework build on rolling three-year expenditure ceilings for different levels of government and social security • Implementing binding expenditure ceilings for each ministry in line with deficit targets • Strengthening the administrative role of the finance minister • Reform of the General Accounting Office, making it more active in budget planning and control • Creating a non-partisan, independent fiscal agency **Second program (2012–15)** • Strengthening public expenditure management, incl. timely provision of social security funds and public investment budget data • Strenghtening revenue administration and fighting against tax evasion • Improvements to tax collection **Third program (2015–18)** • Strengthening the independence of revenue administration by establishing an autonomous revenue agency

(Continued)

Table 6.5. Fiscal policy reforms proposed in the MoUs (*Continued*)

	Ireland	Greece
		• Establishing a fully operational Fiscal Council
		Supplemental MoU (2017) • Medium-term financial strategy for 2018–21 in line with fiscal targets of MoU • Final establishment of the Independent Authority of Public Revenue • Fully functional General Directorate for Financial Services • Making the Fiscal Council responsible for reviewing draft budget laws (compliance with TSCG) • Creation of a new government budget classification structure
		Supplemental MoU (June 2018) • Medium-term financial strategy for 2019–22 in line with fiscal targets of MoU
Privatization	**First program (2010–13)** • 2011: Asset sales worth 700 million euro (unspecified)	**First program (2010–12)** • 2011–13: Privatization worth at least 1 billion euro per year
		Second program (2012–15) • Privatization of assets worth 50 billion euro
		Third program (2015–17) • Relaunch of privatization program (50 billion euro) • Creation of a new independent fund to which ownership of state assets will be transferred (Hellenic Corporation of Assets and Participations – HCAP) • First 25 billion euro of privatization revenue will be used for debt reduction; 50 per cent of second 50 billion euro can be used for investment
		Supplemental MoU (January 2018) • Semi-annually updated asset development plan (ADP)

Sources: European Commission (2010b; 2011e; 2012e; 2015e; 2017c; 2018b; 2018c)

Figure 6.2. Total government revenue and expenditure, Ireland, 2008–18

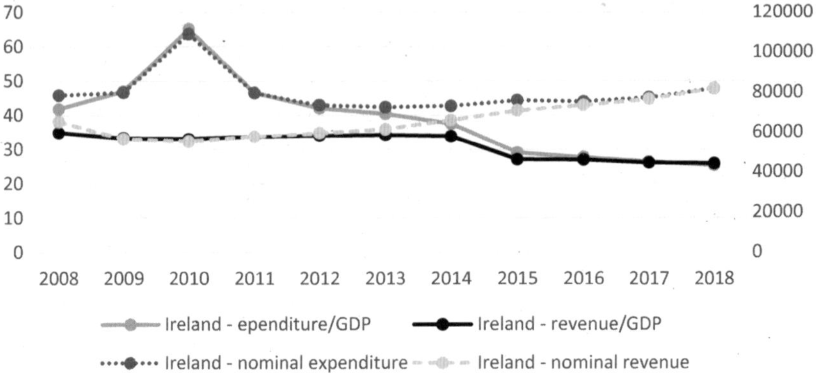

Source: Eurostat (2018a; 2018b)

Department, saw government revenue declining as the global financial crisis started to materialize (Interview 18, 17 April 2018; see also 6.2.2.2). The strategy to reduce expenditure aimed at minimizing the deficit, which sharply increased as the crisis dynamic became more severe (see table 6.1). As public finances further deteriorated and Ireland continuously lost access to financial markets, reducing government expenditure also became an instrument to show financial market participants that the Irish government was able and willing to engage in difficult decisions to prevent a sovereign default and thus regain their trust.

Figure 6.2 underlines that the aim of reducing government expenditure was at first only partly met. Despite austerity budgets and 15 billion in fiscal adjustments between 2008 and 2009, total government expenditure increased between 2008 and 2010 (Laffan 2017, 185). The increase in government expenditure resulted primarily from its bank guarantee (Mody 2018, 268).

Expenditure below the initial nominal value of 78.5 billion euro in 2007 was only achieved in 2012. However, during these years, Ireland implemented broad expenditure reductions over almost all sectors of government spending (see figure 6.3). Except for general public services, economic affairs, and education, all sectors of expenditure were reduced, especially during the period of 2008 to 2013. Two sectors are particularly interesting. First, it is notable that a majority of economic affairs spending consisted of capital injections to struggling financial institutions during 2009 and 2010[10] (European Commission 2011e, 15).

Figure 6.3. Ireland's government expenditure by function (COFOG)

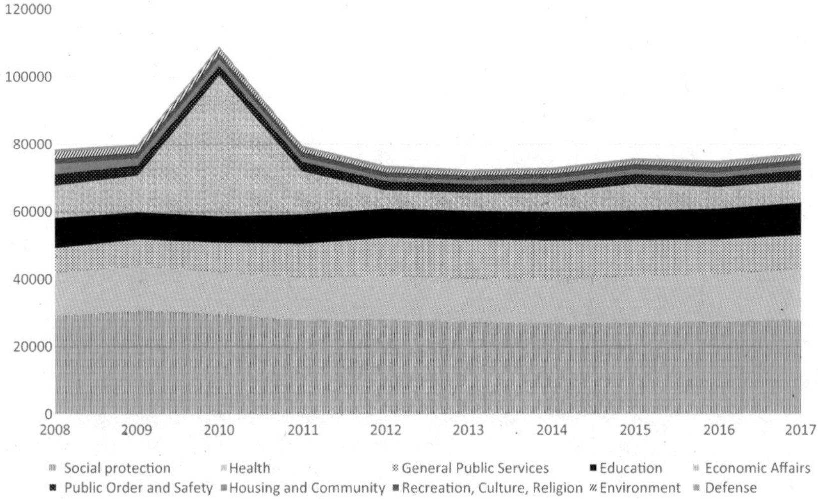

Source: Eurostat (2019)

In 2012, expenditure in economic affairs was severely reduced by almost 50 per cent in comparison to 2008, which indicates less engagement of the Irish government with economic coordination.

Second, reduction of expenditure in social protection needs to be critically acknowledged (see figure 6.3). Despite increasing unemployment numbers, especially from the collapse of the Irish construction and banking sectors, social protection spending decreased slightly. As highlighted above, the retrenchment of unemployment support systems was a central aspect of labour market changes throughout the program (see 6.2.1.3), which is also visible in terms of expenditure. Furthermore, emigration during the crisis, especially of young Irish citizens who previously worked in the construction sector, reduced unemployment numbers and thus contributed to stable social expenditure (Kinsella 2017, 42).

The total Irish government expenditure declined until 2013. Ireland left its financial assistance program in December of that year. Shortly afterward, the Irish economy started to recover from its recession and the government started to increase its spending again, albeit at smaller rates. The biggest increase of government expenditure occurred in 2018. Total government expenditure reached its nominal precrisis level in 2017 and was slightly above precrisis levels in 2018.

The presented data on government expenditure illustrates how strongly Irish fiscal policy reacted to the crisis. While government expenditure remained comparatively stable in nominal terms, in relation to GDP it was reduced by over 10 per cent, which marks a qualitative change of the government's role in economic affairs. In addition, COFOG data highlighted qualitative shifts in the government expenditure: despite high levels of unemployment from 2008 to 2015 (see table 6.1), total social protection spending was reduced (see figure 6.3), illustrating a qualitative shift in risk protection and further inclusions of market-based coordination mechanisms.

6.2.2.2 GOVERNMENT REVENUE DEVELOPMENTS

Decreasing government revenue was a central sign of the severe crisis that hit the Irish economy. After years of balanced or surplus budgets in the 1990s and early 2000s, Irish revenue started to decrease very notably within a short amount of time. Ireland's tax revenue was at its highest in 2007 with approximately 74 billion euro. As figure 6.2 illustrates, government revenue decreased from 65.39 billion euro in 2008 to its lowest point in 2010, when the Irish government collected 55.38 billion in revenue, as revenue from capital gains and acquisition taxes collapsed. In its National Plan for Recovery and the subsequent Memorandum of Understanding with the European institutions and the IMF, Ireland focused on partially increasing revenue (Republic of Ireland 2010; European Commission 2011e). Irish revenue increased in smaller steps after 2010, reaching precrisis levels only after Ireland had left the financial assistance program in 2013 (see figure 6.2). In 2018, the Irish government's revenue reached a new level, the government collecting 86 billion euro, 20 billion more than precrisis (see figure 6.2). Furthermore, as figure 6.2 highlights, the Irish government produced a budget surplus in 2018 for the first time in recent years (see figure 6.2).

The sharp decrease in revenue primarily resulted from the contraction of the construction sector, increased unemployment, and thus decreased income and corporate tax revenue in combination with a stronger reliance on property-related taxation (Walsh 2015, 4). As Kinsella has argued, Irish taxation sources also played a role in the strong decrease. Between 2002 and 2007, Ireland implemented fiscal policy decisions that shifted revenue away from income taxation to capital gains taxes, as well as taxation based on property acquisition (Kinsella 2017, 42). Property transaction taxes in combination with rising property prices were a powerful source of revenue for the Irish government until 2007 (Mody 2018, 268). As soon as the Irish banking and construction sectors contracted, capital and property taxation sharply decreased. Even after the first fiscal consolidation measures, the 2009 Irish budget struggled with a budgetary deficit of almost 10 per cent of GDP (Mody 2018, 268).

A central objective of the Irish MoU thus was broadening and diversifying of the Irish tax base (European Commission 2011e, 21) in order to correct this shift in taxation. In 2007, capital gains and acquisitions taxation made up 16 per cent of all government revenue, while income tax only accounted for 27 per cent of total revenue (Kinsella 2017, 43). Revenue sources shifted again throughout the program. Revenue from income taxation had already increased from 27 to 36 per cent from 2007 to 2009. The income tax share of the entire budget further increased to 42 per cent (Kinsella 2017, 43). In this regard, income tax increases did play a major role in closing the gap between government expenditure and revenue, especially since revenue from capital gains and real estate, as well as value added taxes, decreased in importance (Kinsella 2017, 43). Irish government revenue thus saw a broad shift away from capital gains and stamp duties to income taxation.

6.2.2.3 FISCAL RULES, BUDGETARY OVERSIGHT, AND THE REDUCTION OF GOVERNMENT DISCRETION

During the Irish crisis, additional emphasis was put on strengthening the fiscal framework of Ireland to prevent and be better prepared for future scenarios of severe fiscal stress. Ireland had already implemented several adjustments to its fiscal and budgetary frameworks as it entered EMU. These reforms focused on strengthening the position of the finance minister to block expenditure approved by the parliament if it undermined fiscal goals. Ireland extended the budgetary procedure to a three-year medium-term fiscal strategy (Enderlein 2004, 144–50). However, after the implementation of the euro, neither did the Irish fiscal framework include specific provisions for unforeseen deficits (Enderlein 2004, 148), nor were all aspects of government expenditure included in the medium-term fiscal strategy (European Commission 2011e, 35). Hence, "[s]ignificant reforms to the medium-term budgetary framework [were] to be introduced" (European Commission 2011d, 35).

Three developments stand out, developments that have been put in place as a condition of the financial assistance program and strengthened fiscal governance rules at the EU level (European Commission 2011e, 35; Kopits 2014, 135–6). First, Ireland established the Irish Fiscal Advisory Council (IFAC) in 2011. Functioning on an interim basis at first, it was further institutionalized by the implementation of the Fiscal Responsibility Act in December 2012. The IFAC is an independent statutory body that is responsible for providing economic analysis on the Irish fiscal stance, assessing Ireland's compliance with EU fiscal rules, especially the Fiscal Compact, and preparing official financial fore-casts.[11] It includes five experts as council members, who are appointed by the minister for finance.[12]

Second, the Irish fiscal policy framework was enhanced with a multi-annual expenditure framework including three-year expenditure ceil-ings (Department of Public Expenditure and Reform 2013, 1). The expend-iture ceilings were first provided on an administrative basis. However, with the Ministers and Secretaries (Amendment) Act of 2013, they re-ceived a statutory basis. The framework thus marks a shift from annual budgeting to three-year financial plans (Department of Public Expendi-ture and Reform 2013, 1), which were a central fiscal policy conditionality of the Irish MoU (European Commission 2011e, 35). Expenditure ceilings are set by the government and can only be changed in specified scenarios (Department of Public Expenditure and Reform 2013, 2–3). The fiscal rule concerning multi-annual expenditure frameworks is supposed to be su-pervised by an independent body (European Commission 2022a). IFAC took over this task. Complementing the expenditure ceilings, the Irish government legislated a medium-term budgetary framework in 2013, which includes further budgetary aspects in the medium-term planning. Last, the MoU stipulated that unplanned government revenue had to be used for sovereign debt reduction (European Commission 2011e, 35).

The EC's fiscal governance database[13] underlines this development, as the Irish fiscal policy framework has been adjusted with several fiscal rules (see table 5.5). In 2008, Ireland started with a comparatively low score in terms of fiscal rules. In 2017, however, Ireland's implementa-tion of fiscal rules was visibly increased by almost two data points. The Republic of Ireland mostly implemented fiscal rules on sovereign debt in relation to GDP in line with the reform of the Stability and Growth Pact (European Commission 2022a). Irish fiscal policy now includes stronger fiscal rules and strengthened fiscal frameworks. Most of the reforms were included in the MoU, which underlines the influence of policy conditionality in this field.

6.2.2.4 PRIVATIZATION

Privatization only played a minor role in the Irish strategy of fiscal con-solidation. The government assembled the Review Group on State As-sets and Liabilities in July 2010, which in turn put forward a report "on how commercial state assets can be better deployed or disposed of to support economic recovery" (Review Group on State Assets and Liabil-ities 2011, 1) in April 2011.[14] The group reviewed sixteen state commer-cial bodies, as well as a list of intangible assets (Review Group of State Assets and Liabilities 2011, 2). It recommended setting up a program to privatize state assets including immaterial assets to support fiscal consolidation, as well as increasing competitiveness of state assets (Review Group of State Assets and Liabilities 2011, 3, 128–34).

The MoU included privatization from two perspectives. First, privatization is predominantly mentioned in terms of competitive gains in network industries (European Commission 2011e, 37). Although Ireland's economy was already primarily structured on market-based coordination, the government had valuable influence in network industries via semi-state companies and state-owned enterprises (see table 6.5). Second, the Memorandum of Understanding underlines that privatization of state assets might have a positive effect on Ireland's debt sustainability. Building upon the Review Group's report, quarterly reviews of the MoU highlighted the commitment of the Irish government "to an ambitious programme of state asset disposals designed to enhance the efficiency and competitiveness of the economy, reduce sovereign financing needs, and provide additional resources for reinvestment in the economy" (European Commission 2012c, 44).

The Irish Fine Gael-Labour coalition government elected in 2011 included a plan in its Programme for Government to raise 2 billion euro from the sale of non-strategic state assets, based on the Review Group's report (Irish Government 2011, 14–15). As table 6.5 and subsequent program reviews underlined, privatizing state assets did occur, albeit at a slower rate than the institutions envisioned (European Commission 2012b, 32). In total, public ownership has decreased, as did the government's role in network sectors (see table 6.6). Some disposals of state assets were successful, such as in the energy and gas sector in which the Irish government realized privatizations worth 3 billion euro.[15] Others, for instance the introduction of water charges and privatization of water supply, sparked strong public opposition and were ultimately unsuccessful (Fletcher, van Heelsum, and Roggeband 2018, 242).

6.2.2.5 EFFECTS ON THE GOVERNMENT'S ROLE IN THE ECONOMY
The government's role in the economy has been the subject of severe institutional change, as table 6.6 highlights. Fiscal policy had less influence on economic activity in Ireland than in similar-sized countries. According to the MoU's spring review, this has to do with the openness of the Irish economy, in view of which the government already has less of an influence on economic affairs (European Commission 2012a, 26). Fiscal multipliers – that is, the effect that government expenditure reduction has on economic growth – are comparatively lower for countries such as Ireland, as aggregate demand is less dependent on the government. This is a typical aspect of LMEs (see 2.1.2).

Table 6.6. Ireland, OECD indicators on economic state controls

	2003	2008	2013
State control (1)	2.50	1.84	2.12
Public ownership (2)	2.62	2.54	3.05
Scope of state-owned Enterprises (3)	2.30	1.80	2.20
Government Involvement in Network Sectors (4)	4.58	3.88	3.85
Involvement in Business Operation (5)	2.39	1.14	1.20
Command & Control Regulation (6)	2.29	1.21	1.21

Source: OECD (2018a)

Traditionally, Ireland can be characterized as a liberal market economy, as not only does the state play a less important role in the economy's aggregate demand, but the state and non-market cooperation are also less important to Ireland's general economic governance. As the fiscal consolidation strategy further reduced government spending in economic affairs (see 6.2.2.1), and either put SOEs up for privatization or included more competition-focused mechanisms in the way they operated (see 6.2.2.4), market-based coordination was included in more spheres of the economy, as table 6.6 highlights. State control of the economy was already comparatively low within the OECD (OECD 2018a). However, in terms of OECD indicators, it further reduced from 2.50 in 2003 to 2.12 in 2013. Public ownership increased from 2003 to 2013 (see table 6.6). Data from 2018 suggests a strong reduction, but due to a changed methodology, the data is not comparable (OECD 2018a).

While the government was involved in network sectors before the adjustment process started, it continuously reduced its involvement from 2003 to 2013 (see table 6.6). The lowest government control on the economy can be measured in terms of direct government involvement in business operations and the influence of command and control regulation for enterprises. Already at a comparatively low level in 2003, the influence in both areas further decreased from 2003 to 2013 (see table 6.6). One indicator illustrates a contrary development. SOEs were part of the privatization plan presented in 2011 (6.2.2.4). The scope of SOEs first declined until 2008 but then increased again until 2013 (see table 6.6). It is also noticeable that most indicators illustrate increases from 2008 to 2013. This is the case for state control of the economy, public ownership, involvement in business operations, as well as command and control regulation (see table 6.6). Central to this development was the guarantee to the Irish financial market and subsequent capital injections, which increased public ownership and hence increased state control. As the economy recovered, the influence of the government in economic affairs subsequently decreased again.

In sum, while the Irish government already had comparatively less regulatory and direct influence on the economy, typical for market-based economic coordination in liberal market economies, the fiscal consolidation strategy further reduced its influence. A key consequence of the reduced fiscal and regulatory engagement of the government with the economy is a stronger emphasis on market-based coordination in the economic and institutional setting of Ireland.

6.3 Labour Market Reforms

Labour market reforms are a central aspect of the Irish structural adjustment to the crisis. Some central reforms to the Irish labour markets were put forward before the financial assistance program. Others were an explicit requirement of the program itself (see table 5.7). Two labour market policies stand out in this context: reforms to the wage structure including wage-setting institutions, as well as reforms and retrenchment of social welfare including the implementation of activation policies (European Commission 2011d, 21; see also 6.2.1). Wide-ranging institutional labour market changes are thus a key socio-economic development (see 6.2.1). While the direction of labour market adjustments points to a stronger decentralization of industrial relations (see 6.2.1.1), a continuance of limited employment protection legislation (see 6.2.1.2), and a re-commodification of labour through a combination of the retrenchment of unemployment support and the implementation of activation policies (see 6.2.1.3), the direction of policy reforms by itself does not explain how institutional change in Irish labour markets occurred.

To explain institutional change in Irish labour markets, ideational processes and policy paradigms on labour market developments are a promising analytical starting point. Actor constellations and political incentive structures can also illustrate how institutional change in Irish labour markets occurred. Lastly, the influence of policy traditions and previous institutional settings on the direction of structural adjustment offers a strong factor for study. All three aspects are analysed in the following sections.

6.3.1 Labour Market Paradigms and Ideational Processes

Ideas and ideational processes can influence policy processes to a considerable degree. As the data shows, ideas and ideational processes also influenced reforms of Irish labour markets before, during, and after the Irish financial assistance program. Ideational processes concerning Irish labour markets revolve mostly around two central topics:

Table 6.7. Document analysis, labour markets, Ireland

	MoU (2010–13)	Post-MoU (2014–18)
Wage-setting mechanisms		
State-led coordination	3	4
Sectoral coordination	6	0
Liberalization	42	7
Employment protection legislation		
Liberalization	1	0
Stricter protection	0	0
Unemployment and activation		
Retrenchment	49	8
Social investment	146	43
Public employment		
Reduction	50	6
Preservation	3	0
Increase	0	5

Source: author's compilation

First, wage-setting institutions are a central topic within the documents. Although the central institutional change and the end of the social partnership occurred before the MoU was signed, other aspects of wage setting are key topics in the documents related to the Irish program. Passages concerning wage-setting mechanisms can be identified primarily during the financial assistance program and considerably less often as a topic of the post-program surveillance (see table 6.7).

Second, unemployment support and activation policies are the labour-market-related topics most often addressed in the documents. The central topic identified in the documents is social investment, which is more common than passages including aspects of social retrenchment (see table 6.7). Nevertheless, retrenchment plays a central role during the financial assistance program. During post-program surveillance, social investment still is a regular labour-market-related issue, while welfare retrenchment is discussed less frequently (see table 6.7). In addition, the documents frequently include public employment as an important labour market issue. Most of the identified passages are focused on reducing either the number of workers in public employment, or reducing public sector pay. After Ireland left the financial assistance program at the end of 2013, public employment was discussed considerably less (see table 6.7). Employment protection legislation and employment regulation are topics that are rarely discussed in the program documents (see table 6.7).

The quantitative perspective thus underlines the importance of issues included in the documents related to the Irish financial assistance program. A qualitative analysis, however, sheds light on ideas behind reform initiatives in the areas of wage setting and unemployment support.

Implementing unemployment activation is put forward in the program documents on a regular basis. Activation policy, which the Irish MoU predominantly links to reductions in replacement rates, sanctions (European Commission 2011e, 65), and, as the program progressed, additional training, are generally discussed as key instruments to reduce unemployment. The passive character of unemployment support, previously highlighted by an OECD report in 2009 (see below), thus is a recurring theme in the discussion of unemployment support reforms: As the MoU highlights, unemployment support will be reformed "in such a way as to provide incentives for an early exit from unemployment" (European Commission 2011e, 65). The program will be "[t]aking steps to tackle unemployment and poverty traps including through reducing replacement rates" (European Commission 2011e, 67) and introducing "greater incentives to take up employment" (European Commission 2011e, 57).

In terms of ideational processes concerning active labour market policy, several interview partners mentioned the centrality of an OECD report about Irish labour markets. According to Murphy and Mercille, the report "was cited in successive government and quasi-government publications focusing on activation programmes" (Murphy and Mercille 2019, 28). The report, which was published in 2009 (Grubb, Singh, and Tergeist 2009), highlighted that Ireland's unemployment support system had a passive character (Interview 13, 12 April 2018; Interview 15, 13 April 2018; Interview 22, 19 April 2018). It had a lasting effect on Irish unemployment policy as it changed perspectives on a variety of issues of the Irish unemployment support system. Some actors certainly were always interested in ALMP, however activation only became part of the wider political agenda after the OECD report was published. As an interview partner argued,

> I suppose some of [those] sentiments [of the OECD report] are in these documents. They are reflected in the Memorandum of Understand and I suppose they drove policy over that period of five years and there were series of policy frameworks adopted onto the name of Pathways to Work and those policy frameworks, I suppose, set out a very much more engaged and active approach to labour market policy. So, quite a significant shift in labour market policy over that period. (Interview 22, 19 April 2018)

In this regard, the MoU portrays the idea that the increase in unemployment is at least partially caused by generous replacement rates. In this line of thought, unemployment is partially caused by negative incentives of unemployment support rather than the severe economic recession. The program documents thus link ideas of social retrenchment with ideas of social investment to change the perception of social welfare and unemployment support. In addition to arguing that the unemployment support system and minimum wage setting provide strong negative incentives to accepting work, the MoU links reductions in social protection expenditure to the fiscal adjustment strategy (European Commission 2011e, 62).

An ideational paradigm concerning labour market developments is thus clearly visible in the program. It predominantly focuses on the decentralization of wage bargaining, further liberalization of the Irish labour market, and the recommodification of labour. In that regard, the proposed policies mark a qualitative shift. However, they generally fit the policy legacy of previous labour market coordination mechanisms. The reform initiatives were, as Dukelow argues, driven by the idea that the Irish welfare system "was no longer 'fit for purpose'" (Dukelow 2018, 197) and thus needed a gradual change in its policy direction (Dukelow 2018, 197).

Such ideas were supported by domestic and international actors (Dukelow 2018, 197). Data from interviews conducted for this project supports this as well. Interviews highlight that the program includes specific ideas that focused on the need for activating a passive welfare system (e.g., Interview 13, 12 April 2018; Interview 15, 13 April 2018). However, as one interview partner argued, before the severe economic contraction, a more proactive approach was already discussed. The crisis as well as the Troika gave momentum to these debates and enabled their implementation (Interview 13, 12 April 2018).

Hence, strong ideational processes to reform unemployment support were already in place before the crisis. Ideas to include stronger activation measures materialized in concrete policy reforms only after the MoU was signed and implemented. The international institutions included in the process can be described as policy entrepreneurs (see 2.3.3; see also Schmidt and Radaelli 2004, 195–7).[16] They articulated and persisted on policy proposals that were already discussed within Irish policy communities. As an interview partner argued,

> What the Troika did, and its my belief, in Ireland the Troika didn't come
> in with a high powered engine of microeconomic analysis. They went to

some guys in the relevant departments and said: "What plans have you got in your desk drawers that you knew would be politically unacceptable?" And they took them away and read them and said: "Do that, do that, do that." (Interview 14, 12 April 2018)

Furthermore, the European Commission was described by interview partners as especially focused on labour market reforms. The Commission put forward reform ideas of its own (e.g., Interview 17, 16 April 2018; Interview 22, 19 April 2018): "[…] some of the people involved were extremely ideological, who came from, maybe, quite a doctrinaire neoliberal kind of background. And that they saw this as an opportunity to kind of, let's say, remake the Irish kind of socially economic model" (Interview 17, 16 April 2018). Dukelow and Considine have highlighted that the economic strategy was pursued by different coalition governments: "[s]trategies of welfare retrenchment became inextricably linked with prudent economic management, both by the Fianna Fáil/Green Party government in power when the crisis emerged, and by its replacement in 2011 by a Fine Gael/Labour Party coalition" (Dukelow and Considine 2014, 59). Trade unions took a pragmatic approach to labour market reforms. They perceived some reforms as positive but strongly opposed parts of the reforms, such as the promotion of unpaid internships (Interview 16, 16 April 2018). Despite disputes about specific aspects of social welfare reforms, there was a general consensus among Irish policymakers and social partners on implementing activation policies.

The pragmatic approach to unemployment support legislation can also be identified in terms of the somewhat reluctant implementation of sanctions for non-compliance. Sanctions, such as cuts to benefits for failing to apply for jobs, were a central piece of legislation for the institutions, and especially for the Commission. They are frequently mentioned in the quarterly reviews as a central piece of legislation during 2011 and 2012 (European Commission 2011f, 34; 2012a, 56; 2012b, 31; 2012c, 44). Their implementation, which started in 2011, is highly appreciated in the final review of the Irish MoU in December 2013:

A key achievement of the programme has been to establish such a system with on-going reforms to strengthen training and re-skilling opportunities for the unemployed, increase capacity to deliver activation support, including by contracting out some services, and improve the incentive structure by establishing sanctions for non-engagement. (European Commission 2013b, 10)

Similar ideational processes can be identified regarding wage-setting mechanisms, the second key issue of Irish labour market reforms. The central institutional change of Irish wage-setting mechanisms – the end of the social partnership and the subsequent decentralization of wage setting – was implemented before the Irish financial assistance program crisis and marks a key institutional change of Irish labour market policy (e.g., Interview 13, 12 April 2018; Interview 14, 12 April 2018). The Irish MoU and subsequent program documents include ideas and policy proposals to further decentralize wage setting and sector-wide agreements in order to enable inter-sectoral adjustments (European Commission 2011e, 37). According to the MoU, "[a] reduction in the minimum wage and a review of the framework for other regulated wages will exert downward pressure on wages both directly and through spill-over effects" (European Commission 2011e, 37), which is a recurring topic regarding wage-setting mechanisms in the documents. Improving Irish price competitiveness through wage adjustments is a central aspect of this strategy:

> Although price competitiveness has improved, a sustainable economic growth path from 2011 onwards requires further relative price and wage adjustment and shifts of production capacity across sectors. Structural reform measures to boost competition and avoid unemployment traps are an important part of this strategy. (European Commission 2011e, 7)

Concerning wage-setting mechanisms, divergent positions are visible in Irish politics and among social partners. Among government departments and social partners for the private sector, there is a broad consensus that the end of the national social partnership was a good development as it led to the development of new bargaining strategies for trade union (e.g., Interview 16, 16 April 2018) and gave businesses more possibilities to adjust wages to the economic context (e.g., Interview 19, 17 April 2018). However, a different development can be identified for public sector bargaining. Trade unions portrayed unilateral wage reductions for public sector employees as a negative development and strongly argued for collective bargaining at the national level, which they reinstated through several agreements with the government (e.g., Interview 17, 16 April 2018).

No ideational convergence is visible in terms of sectoral standards (EROs and REAs). The program documents articulate the necessity of reforming sectoral employment standards to enable inter-sectoral adjustments (European Commission 2011e, 37) and to increase labour market flexibility (European Commission 2012b, 30). In addition the MoU includes an independent review process of sectoral wage arrangements to be conducted in early 2011[17] (European Commission 2011e, 65). The Irish government agreed with the MoU's direction of further decentralizing wage bargaining. In the summer review of 2011, the institutions welcomed

> [t]he authorities' commitment to seek a radical reform, going even beyond what [was] recommended by the recent independent review of the EROs/REAs [...] as eliminating any impediments to job creation/reallocation, while safeguarding basic workers' rights, is essential to ensure that the emerging recovery benefits all. (European Commission 2011h, 34)

The reform pursued by the Irish government was perceived by the institutions to follow the objectives of the MoU: "The draft law reforming the sectoral wage setting arrangements was seen as broadly in line with the programme objectives, i.e. making wage-setting systems [...] more flexible" (European Commission 2012c, 27). This ideational convergence concerning sectoral wage mechanisms between the government and the institutions lasted until the general election of 2011. The Labour Party campaigned for and effectively put in power new sectoral employment standard mechanisms to replace EROs and REAs and reversed the reductions of the minimum wage. This was regarded as a positive development by trade unions (e.g., Interview 14, 12 April 2018; Interview 21, 18 April 2018).

The MoU thus included specific ideas concerning labour market developments. It mainly focused on decentralizing the wage-setting process to the firm level as it not only welcomed the end of the national social partnership, but also included further initiatives to decentralize wage-setting mechanisms. Labour market flexibilization was the central goal of these reforms. In addition, the MoU included ideas to further recommodify labour by reforming social welfare in a combination of welfare retrenchments and the inclusion of activation measures. Together, both aspects form a coherent reform approach that opts for stronger market-based coordination of Irish labour markets. Except for wage-setting decentralization below the national level in the public sector and sectoral minimum standards in the private sector (see above), these ideas gained strong support not only by the institutions but also among government representatives and, to some degree, social partners. Hence, the MoU and the implementation process could produce and build upon a broad ideational consensus for the reform initiatives that was only partially disrupted after a change in government in 2011.

6.3.2 Actor Preferences and Incentive Structures

Actor preferences and strategic interaction are potential explanatory factors for institutional changes to Irish labour markets, as rational choice institutionalism highlights (Hall and Taylor 1996, 942–6; for an overview, see 2.3.1). The political economic context of the Irish crisis, its intensifying balance-of-payments problem, and the loss of market access in late 2010, indicate a strong incentive for the Irish government to accept an MoU that included unpopular structural adjustments to prevent a sovereign default. The conditionality approach to financial assistance in the euro area sets additional incentives to engage in reform processes (see 2.2). In this regard, the Irish financial assistance program can be analysed as a strong incentive structure for political actors to engage in institutional changes to Irish labour markets, despite their possible support for contrary policy proposals.

In the Irish case, however, incentive structures not only put Irish governments in a situation to implement policy reforms put forward by the institutions. Rather, as MacCarthaigh and Hardiman have shown for public sector reforms, the Irish administration partially used the conditionality approach to implement reforms that had been discussed in the Irish administration before the crisis and present them as a part of the MoU's conditionality (Hardiman and MacCarthaigh 2017). Key reforms of the Irish labour market, for instance the decentralization of wage-setting mechanisms and implementation of activation measures, gained support from key political parties. As shown above, the Irish program was accompanied by a comparatively strong ideational convergence on the necessity of these reforms (see 6.3.1).

The Irish Fianna Fáil-Green Party government prepared a four-year adjustment plan that the MoU was based on. As Dukelow argued, "[a] close fit therefore prevailed between the dominant domestic policy paradigm and the paradigm underpinning the EU response to the Eurozone crisis" (Dukelow 2015, 95). The National Plan for Recovery already included central labour market reforms of the Irish MoU, namely a review of sectoral agreements and the implementation of activation policies (Republic of Ireland 2010, 10). The Fine Gael-Labour government, which took office in February 2011, included gradual changes in the direction of labour market policy.[18] However, the new government generally took over the obligations of the program (Hardiman et al. 2017, 21). In this regard, the quarterly review of the MoU saw a "strong ownership of the goals of the EU-IMF programme" by the new government (European Commission 2011g, 5).

The Irish program did not have problems with delayed implementation or severe frictions between the Irish government and the institutions. There have been differences of opinion in terms of certain policies, but the program was not subjected to open, public disputes. There was a common understanding on both sides of the objectives of the program (e.g., Interview 18, 17 April 2018; Interview 25, 9 July 2018). As Cardiff argued, the Irish administration aimed at a full implementation of the MoU (Cardiff 2020, 107). In this regard, the conditionality approach to financial assistance supported reform projects agreed to by the institutions and the Irish government. The high level of political support for the program remained stable despite changes in government (Hardiman et al. 2017, 21). The Irish government maintained a strategy focused on strong program implementation while renegotiating with the institutions (Cardiff 2020, 107).

In order to pursue this strategy, the Fine Gael-Labour government made severe changes to the way Irish economic policy was run by establishing the Economic Management Council (EMC). Including the Taoiseach, the Tánaiste, and the ministers for finance and public expenditure and reform, the government established this subcommittee that effectively governed the Irish adjustment process and met on a regular basis (2012 saw forty-seven meetings of the EMC) (Laffan 2013). An equally distributed membership in the EMC enabled the council to create consensus among coalition partners. Brigid Laffan described the EMC as "the equivalent of a war cabinet, and Ireland has been facing an economic war for the last five years" (Laffan 2013, para. 8).

In some instances, the Irish government implemented labour market reforms that went beyond the reform proposals included in the MoU (see 6.2.1.1). This was the case with sectoral minimum standards, which the MoU flagged for review (see 6.2.1.1). In other instances, the Irish administration used the policy conditionality to implement structural adjustments that had been discussed in Ireland before the crisis but were harder to implement. According to interview partners, this was the case for welfare reforms and the implementation of active labour market policies. Others were structural issues the institutions were less concerned with due to the overall good performance of Irish economic institutions (Cardiff 2020, 113). Interview partners did not recall a great difference in emphasis between the institutions, but described the European Commission as being somewhat more interested in labour market reforms than the IMF and the ECB:

> I think the European Commission were the ones who were most interested
> and the IMF, the ECB, I suppose, weren't that interested in the labour mar-
> ket policy. But I think both the Commission and the IMF were, I think, saw
> the imposition of sanctions maybe as a proof of the implementation of the
> system. (Interview 22, 19 April 2018)

The initial ideational change from a predominantly passive unemployment support system to an active labour market policy started with
an OECD report published shortly before the crisis (see 6.3.1). In this
regard, Ireland was able to make use of the presence of the institutions
in order to implement wide-ranging institutional change in unemployment support in 2011: "[t]he fact that there was a program in place made
it somewhat easier for us to get the decisions from government that we
required to what we needed to do to get our structures reorganised and
in place" (Interview 15, 13 April 2018). The program thus set an incentive to engage in policy reforms that were thought of as necessary but
were regarded as politically unacceptable.

In sum, the Irish program set incentives for political actors and strategic interaction in three ways: First, a strategy of Irish policymakers
to include politically difficult reforms in the program is clearly visible.
A case in point is the implementation of activation measures in the
unemployment system. They had been discussed before the crisis but
were implemented as a part of the policy conditionality. Wide-ranging
reorganizations of departmental institutions, such as FÁS or the implementation of one-stop-shops for social security and unemployment
support, were costly reforms. A strategy of blame-shifting and including such reforms in the conditionality of the program made their implementation easier. Providing a four-year plan that fit with the Europe
2020 strategy (Wickham 2014) supported this approach.

Second, the financial assistance program offered the Irish administration a possibility to prevent a sovereign default. As Cardiff has argued,
government sector revenue only partially covered Irish government
expenditure (Cardiff 2020, 103). As Ireland's fiscal position deteriorated
from 2007 to 2010, a strong political consensus among central parties to
prevent a default became visible. A case in point is the general persistence of the consolidation strategy despite a change in government in
2011. In the Irish case, the existence of financial assistance set strong incentives to engage in strong program implementation, especially since
the MoU was based on the National Plan for Recovery, and to engage
in renegotiations based on this strong implementation.

Last, the existence of a financial assistance program allowed the European Commission to engage in structural adjustments in Ireland that

went beyond a balance-of-payments problem. As several interview partners highlighted, the European Commission was engaged in implementing labour market adjustments. The IMF and the ECB were less interested in these issues (e.g., Interview 15, 13 April 2018; Interview 20, 18 April 2018; Interview 22, 19 April 2018).

6.3.3 The Crisis as a Critical Juncture in Irish Labour Markets

The crisis of the euro area has been analysed as a critical juncture for the institutional development of EMU by scholars such as Verdun or Gocaj and Meunier (Verdun 2015; Gocaj and Meunier 2013). In a similar way, as the analysis of the Irish case shows, the economic crisis had a strong effect on Ireland's political economy in general and Irish labour markets in particular (see 6.2.1). The strong contraction of the Irish construction sector in combination with a deep economic recession and growing imbalances between economic sectors increasingly affected formal and informal labour market procedures, especially wage-setting mechanisms (Doherty 2011, 372) and unemployment support (Dukelow 2018). The imbalances between economic sectors increasingly had effects on the sustainability of collective bargaining at the national level. The crisis thus punctured the equilibrium of Irish labour market institutions and opened the possibility of institutional change (see also 2.3.2).

Despite Ireland's general character as an LME, the institutional setting of Irish labour markets included several corporatist elements (Cardiff 2020, 95). Hence, institutional change in Irish labour markets predominantly focused on the implementation of stronger market-based coordination mechanisms (see 6.2.1). A key institutional decision took place before the Irish MoU was negotiated and signed (see 6.1): "The events of the past couple of years following the financial and social crisis that has gripped most of the Western world have brought the Irish social partnership juggernaut crashing to a halt" (Doherty 2011, 372). The national social partnership, which was an influential tripartite governance mechanism based on national wage agreements, ended in 2009 (Maccarrone, Erne, and Regan 2019, 316). Its collapse fundamentally decentralized wage-setting processes in Ireland (see 6.2.1.1 and table 6.3). What is more, under what is generally described as a voluntarist wage-bargaining system (Maccarone, Erne, and Regan 2019, 315), the end of the social partnership effectively meant that fewer employees in Ireland were covered by collective agreements (see table 6.3).

In addition, the negotiations of the Irish MoU proved to be a time of severe crisis as formal and informal labour market institutions became fluid. In addition, Ireland had critical problems refinancing its sovereign debt starting in 2009 (Mody 2018, 268–9) and lost market access in October 2010 (Guscina, Malik, and Papaioannou 2017, 18–19). The MoU certainly reduced the risk of a sovereign default, but it included further adjustments to Irish labour markets, especially in terms of activation policy and unemployment support to adjust to the economic recession (see 6.2.1). The reforms included in the MoU furthermore led to institutional reorganization of unemployment support and activation in Ireland (O'Connell 2017; see also 6.2.1.3). The crisis and the MoU thus proved to be critical junctures as they ultimately enabled institutional change and the implementation of further market-based economic coordination in Irish labour markets. The MoU played a significant role in stabilizing these institutional changes and further advancing them. With the decision to end the national social partnership, a key change in Irish industrial relations and labour market regulation was made. These reforms were further advanced by the financial assistance program as it included reviews of other sectoral employment arrangements (Maccarrone, Erne, and Regan 2019, 320).

Despite the role of the economic crisis and the MoU as critical junctures in Irish labour market institutions, the reforms of its institutional setting certainly were guided by the previous formal and informal labour market settings. As Cardiff has shown, centralized wage setting, despite being considered important in Ireland's positive economic development by several interview partners (e.g., Interview 16, 16 April 2018; Interview 13, 12 April 2018), can be described as an anomaly in the predominant market-based forms of coordination (Cardiff 2020, 95). The decentralization of wage setting consolidated the dominant LME path of the Irish economy. Reforms of unemployment support illustrate a similar development. The economic crisis and the subsequent MoU thus are critical junctures, which led to institutional redesigns of the unemployment support system. Ireland was already characterized as a liberal welfare state with minimal financial transfers and a focus on poverty prevention rather than income security (Dukelow and Considine 2014, 62). The reforms implemented during the program advanced the liberal character of the Irish welfare state.

In sum, the global financial crisis of 2007–8 and the subsequent crisis of the euro area can be analysed as a key critical juncture in Irish labour market policy. Several formal and informal procedures were abolished, reformed, or newly implemented. In this process, the financial assistance program had two functions: First, the negotiation period at the end of 2010 is a central point in the history of the Irish crisis. The program was negotiated in a time of severe economic pressure as the Irish recession had not yet ended and the country had lost access to financial markets (O'Connell 2019, 178). It included policies the Irish administration had not been able to implement previously, such as activation instruments (see 6.2.1.3). Nonetheless, key changes were either implemented before the program (e.g., the end of the social partnership), or were proposed by the Irish government in its National Plan for Recovery (see 6.1). In this regard, the MoU primarily reproduced processes of institutional change in the Irish labour market. While Irish labour markets have undergone severe institutional changes because of the global financial crisis and the subsequent financial assistance program, the institutional reforms did not change the predominant form of economic coordination in Ireland. Instead, they reinforced the predominant market-based forms of coordination and transferred them to areas that previously functioned via non-market coordination, such as wage bargaining and unemployment support. The financial assistance program thus effectively strengthened the liberal market character of Ireland's socio-economic model.

6.4 Fiscal Policy

Fiscal policy has played a key role in the Irish financial assistance program. While other socio-economic problems were important factors in Ireland's MoU, its budgetary deficit and loss of market access were the central influential factors in its application for financial support (Keane 2015, 479). Restoring financial stability was a key objective of the Irish MoU (European Commission 2011e, 38–46) and of its previous National Plan for Recovery: "Restoring stability to the public finances is the centrepiece of this Plan" (Republic of Ireland 2010, 53). The program aimed at bringing down the Irish deficit below 3 per cent of GDP by 2014 (Republic of Ireland 2010, 53; European Commission 2011e, 7). The strategy also aimed at restoring the confidence of investors in the sustainability of Irish bonds (European Commission 2011e, 28). Key aspects of the Irish strategy were fiscal consolidation based on expenditure reductions, as well as reforming the Irish fiscal governance framework (see tables 6.5 and 6.8).

In the Irish case, a strong link between the financial sector and Ireland's public finances was created when the Irish government announced a bailout of its crisis-ridden banks (European Commission 2011e, 17). In addition, the crisis disclosed problems with the Irish tax base. During the Celtic Tiger era, the tax base narrowed (Republic of Ireland 2010, 91) and shifted from income to property transaction taxation (European Commission 2011e, 17). As Keane argued, "[t]he pre-crisis structure of taxes is key to understanding the sharp increase in the government deficit" (Keane 2015, 485). As the Irish construction sector went into a recession, Ireland's tax reliance on this sector led to a pro-cyclical fiscal development which severely increased the deficit (Keane 2015, 485).

The following sections provide ideational, rational choice, and historical-institutional analyses of institutional change in Irish fiscal policy. First, an analysis of fiscal policy paradigms and ideational processes within Ireland's MoU is provided (see 6.4.1). Second, preferences of key political and institutional actors are analysed to assess the role of their interests in the adjustment process (see 6.4.2). Last, Ireland's policy legacy and the influence of its precrisis institutional setting in fiscal policy on the reforms are analysed (see 6.4.3).

6.4.1 Fiscal Policy Paradigms and Ideational Processes

Fiscal policy is a central cornerstone of the Irish financial assistance program. As illustrated above, institutional changes in the tax base, government expenditure, revenue, and rules of Irish fiscal policy are clearly visible (see 6.2.2). The analysed data shows that considerable ideational processes were at play, which promoted institutional changes. As a quantitative analysis highlights, the program documents point in a cohesive direction. The discussion of the reform of Ireland's budgetary framework clearly focuses on restraining budgetary freedoms of the government by implementing new fiscal rules, binding medium-term fiscal frameworks, and independent budgetary oversight (see table 6.8). This is the case for the time of the actual program and its post-program surveillance, although the quantity of passages is decreasing in the latter. No passages to increase budgetary flexibility can be identified (see table 6.8). The direction of fiscal policy is the topic discussed most within the program documents (see table 6.8). During the program, most passages identified as such argued in favour of restricting fiscal policy (e.g., via reducing public expenditure). During the post-program surveillance, this impression changes to a certain degree. While restricting fiscal policy is still the dominant argumentation in the program documents, the share of passages that argue for expansionary fiscal measures increases over time (see table 6.8).

The qualitative analysis of the program documents mirrors the importance of fiscal policy reforms identified in the quantitative analysis. The program documents include three central ideas that guide the reform of fiscal governance in the Irish case. First, Ireland's rule-based fiscal framework is described as weak (European Commission 2011e, 35). It is repeatedly described as lacking credibility, which the program

Table 6.8. Document analysis, fiscal policy, Ireland

	MoU (2010–13)	Post-MoU (2014–18)
Budgetary process		
Restrained	101	32
Flexible	0	0
Fiscal policy direction		
Restrictive fiscal policy	455	180
Expansionary fiscal policy	8	41
Government discretion		
Less government discretion	58	6
More government discretion	0	2

Source: author's compilation

aims at reinforcing (European Commission 2011e, 35, 68, 70; 2011g, 5, 64; 2011h, 55, 2011f, 73; 2012b, 54, 67; 2013a, 27; 2013d, 62). Second, in order to safeguard fiscal discipline, the program documents highlight the necessity of introducing new fiscal rules, especially in earlier reviews of the program (European Commission 2011g, 24, 49). Third, the program documents focus extensively on expenditure. While broadening the tax base is a relevant topic within the documents, the medium-term fiscal strategy strongly focuses on expenditure as well (European Commission 2011e, 35; 2011g, 47; 2011h, 54; 2012c, 18, 39; 2012a, 61, 74; 2012b, 21; 2013a, 27, 30; 2013d, 21).

In terms of concrete policy proposals, the program documents highlight two central reform projects: First, the program documents discuss the implementation of an independent budgetary advisory council "to provide an independent assessment of the budgetary position and the underlying forecasts" (European Commission 2011e, 35). Whereas the Fiscal Advisory Council was first established on a provisional basis (European Commission 2011h, 27), the program documents highlight the need to "further underpin the Council's independence in the context of the Fiscal Responsibility Law" (European Commission 2011g, 27). Strengthening the Council's influence and independence within Irish fiscal governance is a central policy idea that is transported throughout the program. Giving the Fiscal Advisory Council a statutory basis is a key goal pursued by the Irish government (European Commission 2012b, 67–8; Interview 18, 17 April 2018). Its statutory base was set with the Fiscal Responsibility Act. The act was later amended to "increase the functions of the Council, because the independence of the Council is extremely important" (Interview 18, 17 April 2018). In this regard, an ideational convergence concerning the role of the Financial Advisory Council among the institutions and the Irish authorities is clearly visible.

A second key idea is that Ireland found itself in a crisis because of problems with fiscal discipline.[19] Not only do fiscal measures try "to reinforce fiscal discipline and facilitate a more strategic allocation of spending" (European Commission 2011g, 47), a central approach of the program's fiscal governance reforms is to "[introduce] a Fiscal Responsibility Bill [...] including provisions for a medium-term expenditure framework with binding multi-annual ceilings on expenditure in each area" (European Commission 2011e, 35). Legislation for multi-annual expenditure ceilings has been described as a central fiscal policy reform (European Commission 2013a, 30; Interview 18, 17 April 2018; Interview 20, 18 April 2018). Initially set until 2014, expenditure reviews were planned on a three-year basis in order to set expenditure ceilings according to Ireland's socio-economic context (European Commission 2012c, 18). During a later review, the government put forward plans to "anchor our already-operational multi-annual expenditure limits in appropriate legislation" (European Commission 2012b, 74). Indeed, the institutions reminded the Irish authorities in the 2012 autumn review that "[f]urther improvements are necessary to the legislation on expenditure ceilings to ensure that the framework constitutes a credible anchor for fiscal policy" (European Commission 2013a, 27).

In the ex-post evaluation of the financial assistance program, published in 2015, the institutions argue that these reforms "give Ireland one of the strongest fiscal governance frameworks in the EA in principle" (European Commission 2015a, 14). In the post-program surveillance reports, however, the institutions continuously argue that Ireland's "medium-term fiscal strategy still needs to be fully developed" (European Commission 2015d, 7), that "[a]lthough the domestic fiscal framework has improved considerably, weaknesses remain" (European Commission 2015d, 29), and that the mission teams have witnessed increased expenditure and revisions to set expenditure ceilings (European Commission 2015d, 29; 2015c, 25; 2016b, 29). A key critique of the institutions is that, during the post-program period, "[s]hort-term, year-to-year budgeting at department level has not yet given way to multi-annual expenditure plans" (European Commission 2017a, 23).

Similar trends are visible in terms of the direction of fiscal consolidation. As Hardiman et al. argued, the fiscal consolidation strategy required by the program "fitted the ideational framework shared by the dominant policy community in Ireland" (Hardiman et al. 2017, 21). Dukelow adds, "[a] close fit therefore prevailed between the dominant domestic policy paradigm and the paradigm underpinning the EU response to the Eurozone crisis" (Dukelow 2015, 94–5). Even the trade unions generally accepted the idea of fiscal adjustment while putting forward different policy proposals associated with this strategy (Doherty 2011, 381). Within the program documents, a clear consolidation paradigm is identifiable. Fiscal consolidation in the Irish case builds on "broad-based expenditure restraint" (European Commission 2011e, 21), which is described as "a typical characteristic of successful and sustainable fiscal consolidation episodes"[20] (European Commission 2011e, 21).

While the fiscal consolidation strategy includes broadening the tax base and some revenue increases (European Commission 2011e, 28), it predominantly focuses on expenditure reductions (see table 6.8). According to an interview partner, "[i]t was agreed that it would be two-to-one expenditure/taxation consolidation because that was believed to be the most growth-friendly, based on the IMF's experience over previous decades" (Interview 20, 18 April 2018). A key issue of contestation was corporation taxes: Maintaining comparatively low corporate taxes appears to be a central ideational cornerstone of taxation in Ireland, despite arguments from the institutions to increase corporate taxes to broaden the tax base. Approaches to increase corporate taxes did not gain political support (Dukelow 2015, 104).

The program identifies central fields for reducing expenditure: public employment, pensions of public employees, and welfare spending (European Commission 2011e, 28). In addition, the program documents carry the idea of consolidating the Irish deficit by front-loading fiscal adjustments, meaning that they would engage in larger expenditure reductions at the beginning (European Commission 2011e, 7). A central reason for this given in the MoU was that "[f]rontloading a 3.8% of GDP adjusted package in 2011 should help strengthen the consolidation strategy's credibility" (European Commission 2011e, 29).

The ideas for fiscal consolidation are broadly shared between the institutions and the Irish government. Ideational convergence is visible in the program documents and the expert interviews conducted for this project. The MoU states that "[p]hasing and composition of the fiscal measures is based on the Irish 'National Recovery Plan' released by the authorities on 21 November 2010" (European Commission 2011e, 28) and that "[t]he authorities plan an expenditure heavy consolidation" (European Commission 2011e, 28). The importance of the National Plan for Recovery for the fiscal adjustment strategy has been underlined by several interview partners (e.g., Interview 18, 17 April 2018; Interview 20, 18 April 2018; Interview 31, 30 July 2018).

According to Hardiman, this ideational convergence remained strong after the change in government: "The return to government of a Fine Gael-Labour coalition in February 2011 involved minimal changes to overall policy priorities" (Hardiman 2014, 148). Even though the Labour Party campaigned with the central slogan "Frankfurt's way or Labour's way" (Laffan 2017, 185), the analysis of the program documents supports Hardiman's assessment: according to the institutions, "[t]he new government is fully committed to the programme's fiscal targets and overall objectives" (European Commission 2011c, 5) and is regularly praised for engaging in difficult fiscal decisions and keeping the consolidation path on track (e.g., European Commission 2011g, 12, 18; 2011h, 5, 23; 2011f, 7, 15, 32; 2012c, 5, 17; 2012a, 5, 18; 2012b, 4, 20). The ideational convergence between the institutions and the Irish administrations remained strong throughout the program. However, in later reviews of the program and during post-program surveillance, the institutions regularly reminded the authorities that they had created expenditure overruns, especially in terms of health care and welfare payments, which they needed to address (European Commission 2012a, 18; 2012b, 4, 8, 36; 2013a, 5; 2013c, 5; 2013b, 5). As the crisis became less urgent, government expenditure became slightly more expansionary over time (see 6.2.2.2).

In addition to the fiscal framework and the general direction of fiscal policy, the Irish program maintains the idea of reducing the government's discretion in the economy. The MoU states that "Ireland maintains a notable level of state ownership in the economy, including large stakes in the transport, energy, broadcasting and forestry sectors" (European Commission 2011e, 40). While there was some ideational convergence between the institutions and the Fianna Fáil-Green Party coalition on privatizing public assets, the Fine Gael-Labour government later abstained from large-scale privatization plans: "One of the things that we are particularly proud of is the fact that we resisted the original Troika demand that there would be a wholesale sell-off of state assets" (Interview 21, 18 April 2018), as an interview partner argued.

In sum, the program contains a clear fiscal policy paradigm. It focuses on the reduction of government expenditure while increasing revenue only to a smaller degree. Possible reductions of expenditure are primarily identified in the public pay bill and welfare spending. In addition, the MoU includes ambitious reforms of the budgetary process and envisions less fiscal influence of the Irish government in the economy. In key fiscal policy issues, there is a common understanding and ideational convergence between the Irish authorities and the institutions included in the process, which only partially opened in later states of the program.

6.4.2 Actor Preferences and Incentive Structures

The Irish crisis is characterized by a common understanding of the nature of the crisis and a consolidation paradigm broadly shared between the institutions and the Irish government (see 6.4.1). In addition, the specific character of Ireland's socio-economic crisis and the institutional setting of Ireland set similar incentive structures and thus common preferences for the Irish authorities and the institutions at the beginning of the program. At the peak of the Irish fiscal crisis in 2010, the possibility of a sovereign default set a strong incentive to engage in negotiations and to apply for a financial assistance program, despite its combination with strict policy conditionality. In addition to the incentive to prevent a sovereign default, the Irish government tried to shape the financial assistance program according to its political preferences. The National Plan for Recovery, which served as an ideational blueprint for the fiscal adjustment (see 6.4.1), was a strategic advantage, according to an interview partner. The National Plan for Recovery made the MoU negotiations less difficult, as key targets were already included in the plan, which served as a blueprint for the MoU (Interview 18, 17 April 2018).

In addition to its strategic advantage, the National Plan for Recovery also fit the general direction of socio-economic adjustment preferred by the institutions (see 6.4.1).[21] This made the negotiations easier and allowed the Irish government to pursue its own adjustment strategy. The fiscal adjustment strategy itself was heavily influenced by interests of the Irish government and structural constraints. According to Kinsella, changing and broadening the tax base was a policy strategy "born out of sheer necessity" (Kinsella 2017, 44). Changing the tax base was influenced by the bank guarantee the Irish administration set out, increased costs due to higher unemployment, and reduced revenue due to the contraction of the construction sector. In addition, the Irish government's goal to maintain a 12.5 per cent corporate tax influenced the broadening of the tax base (Kinsella 2017, 44). Interview partners argued in a similar direction, highlighting that the sharp decline in tax revenue revealed the narrow tax base (Interview 18, 17 April 2018).

The preference of the Irish authorities to prevent a sovereign default was met by the preference of the institutions to prevent further contagion of the crisis of the euro area. In addition, the institutions aimed at reducing the time required to bring the Irish deficit below 3 per cent of GDP. In the beginning of the adjustment process, there were clear incentives to frontload most fiscal adjustments, as some interview partners highlighted (Interview 18, 17 April 2018; Interview 20, 18 April 2020; Interview 31, 30 July 2018). The importance of this strategy was further underlined by the high rank of personnel sent to Ireland for the first review missions, and the reliance on the MoU as the central plan for fiscal adjustments. This progress relaxed to a certain degree as the institutions witnessed that the Irish authorities engaged in ambitious fiscal adjustments, even after a change in government (see 6.4.1). Over time, less senior personnel joined the mission:

> in – if I can call it – the real heat of the crisis, they [Department of Public Expenture and Reform] were dealing with really senior people from the Troika. A year later they were dealing with much more junior people that were just there ticking the boxes, making sure that everything was okay. (Interview 17, 16 April 2018).

In addition, despite a selection of central issues that some of the institutions focused on,[22] the institutions were less interested in the details of fiscal adjustments if the government met the fiscal targets. As an interview partner highlighted, Ireland gained some policy space within the fiscal consolidation strategy because of its strong record of program implementation: "And that was important in itself, and it also bought some space to have a discussion, okay, to say, to be able to substitute one policy proposal for another. [...] There was some credibility there, there was some level of trust there" (Interview 20, 18 April 2018).

As the implementation progressed, the program process and a change in government changed the strategy of the Irish authorities. However, the change in government in 2011 did not change Irish policy preferences overnight. There was a common understanding on the principles of the program among almost all major political parties. The Fine Gael-Labour government committed itself to further engage in fiscal adjustment. In this regard, the preferences and strategic interaction possibilities of the new government only led to small changes in the direction of fiscal policy (Holmes 2019).

However, the Fine Gael-Labour coalition engaged in regular renegotiations of the program and were able to gain concessions from the institutions, which allowed them to further advance their own adjustment strategy (Laffan 2017, 186–7). They engaged in those negotiations by creating two central governing bodies that structured the program implementation in the country and centralized the engagement with the institutions: the Department of Finance discussed the progress of the program with the institutions with the help of the External Programme Compliance Unit (Laffan 2017, 189). In addition, the Fine Gael-Labour government created a subcommittee in the prime minister's department, the EMC, "which was the key institutional device to manage relations with the Troika, deliver the MoU, and manage the coalition" (Laffan 2017, 189-90) and was described by Laffan as the economic equivalent to a war cabinet (Laffan 2013, para. 8).

In sum, the fiscal crisis, the Irish institutional setting, and the financial assistance program guided strategic interaction within Irish politics. The Irish government's fiscal policy preferences and strategies to achieve them were broadly influenced by the financial assistance program and the policy constraints included in it. These constraints were upheld even after a change in government. As the Fine Gael-Labour coalition shows, the financial assistance program even influenced Ireland's institutional architecture and the coalition strategies to negotiate fiscal policy with the European and international partners.

6.4.3 The Crisis as a Critical Juncture in Irish Fiscal Policy

The global financial crisis of 2007–8 as well as the subsequent deterioration of public finances in Ireland can be analysed as critical junctures in Irish fiscal policy. The severe fiscal pressure, which rapidly built up in 2007 as a consequence of a magnitude of political, economic, and financial problems (O'Connell 2019, 177), punctured Ireland's institutional equilibrium in fiscal policy. Previous institutional settings, policy legacies, and formal and informal practices lost influence on Irish fiscal policy as fiscal pressure and the risk of a sovereign default increased. The severity of Ireland's socio-economic crisis and the omnipresent risk of a sovereign default reduced the binding effect of path dependencies and institutional feedback loops in Irish fiscal policy.

A key aspect of Ireland's initial reaction was expenditure reductions (Hardiman 2014, 149–51; see 6.1). Central institutional changes to fiscal policy, however, were implemented as part of the policy conditionality attached to the financial assistance program (see 6.2.2.3). Thus, the financial assistance program continued and deepened Ireland's path of fiscal adjustment. It also upheld the reform pressure as Ireland's fiscal position improved, especially after 2012. Furthermore, it included reforms of Ireland's fiscal framework, which underlines the character of the crisis as a critical juncture. The EFSF[23] (see 6.2.2), as the central financing facility next to the IMF and the Commission-based EFSM, played a key role in this process. It added a new political dimension to the Irish adjustment process, as it included the European Commission, the IMF, and the ECB in the review and adjustment process, which was guided by central decisions of the Eurogroup (see 6.3.2). Paying out tranches after successful review missions put in an additional feedback loop for the reforms.

In this regard, the loan criteria of the EFSF and later the ESM structured the reform process and enabled the institutions to influence institutional changes in Irish fiscal policy. The reforms, however, were guided to a considerable degree by the country's institutional legacy and path dependence. Ireland's fiscal framework before the onset of its socio-economic crisis was fundamentally shaped by two historical episodes: first, by a period of economic crisis that lasted from 1980 to 1987, and second, by the Celtic Tiger years from the mid-1990s until the crisis of the Irish construction sector in 2007. The 1980s were characterized by a persistent socio-economic crisis, a growing government deficit, and prominent political debates about fiscal spending. Discussions of a fiscal squeeze started as early as 1981 (Hardiman 2014, 140–1). After a period of taxation increases to reduce the deficit in the early 1980s, a change in government in 1987 resulted in severe spending cuts legislated by the Fianna Fáil government (Hardiman 2014, 142–6).

In addition, the Celtic Tiger years, which saw strong economic and tax revenue growth, strengthened the reforms taken in the late 1980s. As revenue increased and the government's overall debt decreased, the stability of Ireland's fiscal setting improved. Path dependence kept the government's role in the economy small and strengthened the LME character of Ireland. In addition, Ireland's strategy to attract foreign direct investments through low corporate taxes was discussed as a comparative advantage during this period. Ireland's continued narrow tax base (see 6.1) was a consequence of this period. Both periods supported the political legacy of Ireland as a liberal market economy with a focus on market-based coordination, comparatively low taxation, and lower levels of government expenditure.

Nonetheless, institutional change in Irish fiscal policy is clearly visible (see 6.2.2). Ireland's expenditure and revenue structures were severely affected by the financial assistance program (see 6.2.2.1 and 6.2.2.2). Not only did the Irish government considerably reduce its expenditure, the structure of expenditure also changed noticeably (see 6.2.2.1). In addition, the budgetary process and Irish fiscal rules were reformed considerably during this period (see 6.2.2.3). This process put in place new institutional feedback loops to support the institutional stability of these reforms. As EMU's fiscal rules were strengthened and the EU was granted stronger instruments to influence national fiscal policy (Verdun 2018), the institutional setting of Ireland gained additional feedback loops through European legislation. In addition, the EFSF and the EFSM continue with post-program reviews of the Irish adjustment process. However, as interview partners argued, the post-program reviews were a relatively frictionless process without major debates about the general direction of policy (Interview 18, 17 April 2018; Interview 22; 19 April 2018).

In sum, the severe socio-economic crisis of Ireland in 2007–8 and the subsequent financial assistance program were a critical juncture in Irish fiscal policy. Not only did previous institutional settings become fluid as rapidly decreasing government revenue led to severe fiscal problems; institutional change also became visible in terms of fiscal policy as Ireland severely reduced its government expenditure, changed its revenue structure, and reformed its fiscal framework. The reforms, however, have not led to a shift in Ireland's predominant mode of economic coordination. Rather, the institutional changes have deepened Ireland's path as a liberal market economy. Fiscal policy reforms introduced during the financial assistance program strengthened Ireland's liberal market economy tradition in fiscal policy and underlined this developmental path with stricter fiscal rules. The EFSF and later the ESM thus supported the deepening of Ireland's path of socio-economic development through adding a new political dimension to its adjustment process that upheld the reform pressure through conditionality and quarterly reviews.

6.5 Interim Conclusion

Ireland was the euro area's second member to apply for financial assistance through the EFSF and the EFSM, the ESM's institutional predecessors, but it could have easily been the first country as the severity of its financial problems from 2007 onwards illustrates (see 6.1). During the height of the euro crisis, Ireland was discussed as the "poster child" of the program countries (Roche, O'Connell, and Prothero 2017a; Mackintosh 2013). Hence, the Irish program allows us to analyse financial assistance as a process in which the included institutions were satisfied with the adjustment processes. In addition, Ireland was the first country to exit a financial assistance program, and it did so with no time delay. As the first country to be granted financial assistance through the temporary EFSF (in combination with EFSM and IMF funding, see 4.2.2 and 4.4.2), the Irish case allows us to analyse the institutional development from the newly established, temporary EFSF to the permanent ESM, which effectively took over its operations.

Institutional change in central socio-economic spheres is clearly visible (see 6.2.1 and 6.2.2). The Irish socio-economic model was characterized by market-based coordination. However, despite being classified as an LME, Ireland's economic governance did include some non-market coordination mechanisms prior to the crisis (see 6.2.1 and 6.2.2). Despite having some tripartite mechanisms, the key economic role of the state was reduced to enabling market structures and recruiting foreign direct investments by providing business-friendly investment environments. The government played only a minor role in the Irish economy's aggregate demand. As a small, open economy, Ireland depended on international trade.

The Irish financial assistance program addressed and included central policy reforms to Ireland's socio-economic governance. It identified fiscal policy, especially Ireland's expenditure structure, tax base, and fiscal framework, as well as remaining parts of non-market modes of labour market governance and Ireland's welfare system as areas of structural problems. While the Irish government engaged in reforms from 2007 onwards, the MoU included central reform objectives for these areas. An Irish four-year plan for fiscal and economic reform was used as a blueprint for this program (see 6.3.1 and 6.4.1). As the analysis of Irish labour market and fiscal policy reforms shows, the program deepened the Irish path as a liberal market economy by reducing the government's fiscal opportunities to govern economic development and by further including market-based governance of labour markets and recommodification of labour through welfare reforms (see 6.2.1 and 6.2.2).

These institutional changes in the political economy were made possible by three central aspects: First, as analysed above, the Irish MoU included ideas that focused on stronger market-based and market-enhancing modes of governance in fiscal and labour market policy (see 6.3.1 and 6.4.1). In both policy spheres, a policy paradigm is visible that focuses on reducing the state's influence on economic governance, reducing national or sectoral governance mechanisms, and enhancing markets as key modes of economic coordination. The analysis also highlights that this is an ideational process that is characterized by a strong degree of ideational convergence between the institutions and the Irish government, which put up a similar policy program shortly before the MoU (see 6.3.1 and 6.4.1). This ideational consensus was to a large degree also shared by social partner organizations.

Second, the analysis highlights that the Irish MoU allowed the Irish government to proceed with policies that would have been hard to implement due to a lack of popular support or due to exceptional political capital required for such reforms. Some of the reforms included in the financial adjustment program were discussed in Ireland prior to the crisis, such as welfare or public sector reforms. The crisis and the financial assistance program proved to be a key opportunity to engage in these reforms and put them forward as part of the program's conditionality (see 6.3.2 and 6.4.2). The financial assistance program thus provided the Irish government with strategic interaction advantages to engage in such reforms.

Last, the crisis was a critical juncture in Ireland's political economy and thus enabled institutional changes in fiscal and labour market policy. The severe crisis of Irish financial sectors and the construction industry effectively posed a strong risk of a sovereign default in 2010 and thereafter, which made such wide-ranging reforms possible. However, while Ireland's political economy experienced institutional changes, the reforms were guided to a large degree by the Irish historical legacy as an LME. In effect, the critical juncture of the Irish crisis deepened Ireland's predominant market-based coordination mechanisms and removed previous non-market governance mechanisms (see 6.3.3 and 6.4.3).

The EFSF and EFSM, as the ESM's institutional predecessors, are key financial sources of the Irish program next to the IMF. They enabled the policy conditionality attached to the program and thus enforced key program decisions to deepen market-based governance mechanisms in Ireland. However, the EFSF and later the ESM were not involved in day-to-day operations at first. Rather, they supported the Eurogroup's central decision-making while joining review missions at later stages of the program.

Chapter Seven

Comparing Greece and Ireland

This chapter will present a synopsis of the empirical analysis of this book with a focus on the overall research objective. The chapter will proceed as follows: First, the chapter will present a comparison of the two cases, focusing on general directions and objective of the MoUs, the origins of the reforms, the reform results, and the role of post-program surveillance (see 7.1). Second, the role of the ESM in both programs will be examined (see 7.2). An interim conclusion will discuss the role of the ESM in both programs (see 7.3).

7.1 Comparison of Adjustment Processes

In political, journalistic, and popular discourses, Ireland and Greece were often discussed as antipodes of the European efforts to stabilize the euro area. Whereas Ireland was portrayed as the poster child for European financial assistance programs (see 6.1 for a critical assessment of this narrative), Greece's adjustment process was a great concern for the euro area at several critical periods throughout the euro crisis (see 5.1). The cases are characterized by distinct differences in their institutional settings and the dynamics of their socio-economic crises. However, a comparison between the two is worthwhile as it allows us to uncover common developments, policies, and adjustments, as well as divergent developments between the two financial assistance programs.

As both case studies highlight, there are interesting, shared developments between the Irish and Greek adjustment processes. The Greek and Irish financial assistance programs show strong similarities in their policy direction: As a part of the structural labour market adjustments, both programs focus on the decentralization of wage bargaining, reductions of the minimum wage, reductions of EPL, the retrenchment of social welfare, and the recommodification of labour through the implementation of ALMPs (see 5.2.1, 6.2.1, and table 7.1). Both programs focused extensively on including new or strengthening already existing market-based mechanisms to coordinate their labour markets. Despite differing political legacies as MMEs (Greece) and LMEs (Ireland) prior to the crisis of the euro area, both countries included tripartite governing mechanisms for wage-setting. In both cases, the decentralization of collective bargaining was a central adjustment to the crisis. Greece and Ireland show severely reduced coverage of collective agreements, a new centrality of firms for wage setting, and a stronger influence of market mechanisms in wage setting (see 5.2.1.1 and 6.2.1.1). In Greece and Ireland, tripartite governance mechanisms for labour markets either lost their binding effect or were removed from economic governance. A second, key similarity in their structural adjustments is a strong focus on welfare retrenchment, despite different policy legacies (see 5.2.1.3 and 6.2.1.3). In addition, both programs included the recommodification of labour through the implementation of activation measures in unemployment support systems based on negative incentives to take up work, albeit at varying degrees (see 5.2.1.3 and 6.2.1.3). Thus, both programs included stronger market-based coordination mechanisms in the institutional settings of their labour markets.

Strong similarities are visible in their fiscal adjustments as well. Both programs relied primarily on expenditure reductions and only partly included revenue increases to reduce the countries' respective deficits (see 5.2.2 and 6.2.2). In both cases, a proportion of two-to-one was proclaimed as a key factor in successful fiscal adjustments (see 5.4.1 and 6.4.1). However, both programs effectively accentuated expenditure reductions as key reform objectives. Fiscal adjustments were front-loaded to a considerable degree and did change the structure of government expenditure (see 5.2.2.1 an 6.2.2.1). Both Ireland and Greece considerably reduced their government expenditure for economic affairs and kept their welfare spending stable despite sharply increased unemployment numbers (see figures 5.2 and 6.3). In addition, both programs implemented stricter fiscal rules, medium-term budgetary planning procedures, and independent oversight of the government's fiscal conduct (see 5.2.2.3 and 6.2.2.3). The fiscal policy reforms had a lasting effect on both governments' roles in the economy, which was considerably reduced (see 5.2.2.5 and 6.2.2.5). While privatization was considered as a key component of fiscal adjustments in both programs, it only played a considerable role in the Greek program (see 5.2.2.4 and 6.2.2.4).

Hence, both programs included reforms that focused on measures to promote market-based coordination mechanisms. In the Greek case, typically classified as a mixed-market economy (see 5.1), the reforms initiated and accomplished a change of the country's path of economic development. While Greece certainly did not fully change into a typical liberal market economy, it took strong steps in this direction (see table 7.1; see also chapter 5). Ireland, on the other hand, already was a liberal market economy, despite some non-market coordination characteristics, particularly the Social Partnership (see 6.1). Policy decisions prior to the financial assistance, in combination with structural adjustments during the phase of the MoU, removed key non-market governance mechanisms and effectively deepened Ireland's path of socio-economic development as an LME. Cases in point are the end of the Social Partnership and the strong focus on activation measures in unemployment support (see table 7.1 and chapter 6).

Nonetheless, despite similarities of the MoUs and the direction of structural adjustment throughout the programs, the Irish and Greek cases are characterized by distinct differences. The strongest factor of difference between the programs is the origin of the reforms included in the MoU's policy conditionality (see table 7.1).

In the Greek case, most of the reforms included in the program came from the institutions involved, namely the European Commission, the ECB, the IMF, and the Eurogroup as a key decision-making body during the euro crisis. As the ESM expanded its capacities, it joined the institutions in the program operations. Drawing up and implementing MoUs was, for a considerable amount of time, a conflictual process between the institutions and the Greek government. The program ownership of the Greek government came into considerable question throughout the three programs. It was already visible during the first MoU (e.g., European Commission 2012e, 1). The PASOK-led government came under scrutiny for a lag of implementation and criticism of some of the structural adjustments to Greece's socio-economic model. During the New Democracy government from 2012 to 2015 under Prime Minster Samaras, the situation with the Greek administration became better. The New Democracy government implemented several reforms that enabled institutional change in the Greek labour market towards a model that was based more on governance through markets (see 5.2.1). However, as the second program entered its final stage, a lack of compliance with policy obligations was a key point of debate between the government and the institutions involved in the monitoring process.

The conflictual situation intensified during the last months of the second MoU and throughout the third when the SYRIZA coalition came into power in January 2015. SYRIZA actively challenged the institutions on key components of the MoU and initiated a referendum on the loan conditions. Nonetheless, after months of negotiation, the Greek

Table 7.1. Experiences with European financial assistance

	Greece	Ireland
Direction of reforms	Changing MME path, including more LME aspects	Deepening LME path
Examples in labour market policy	Decentralization of wage bargaining, reduction in EPL, retrenchment of social welfare, recommodification of labour (ALMPs), reduction of the state's role in economic coordination	Decentralization of wage bargaining, recommodification of labour (ALMPs), reduction of the state's role in economic coordination
Examples in fiscal policy	Consolidation focused on expenditure reduction, independent fiscal council, medium-term fiscal strategies, privatization	Consolidation focused on expenditure reduction, independent fiscal council, medium-term fiscal strategies, privatization
Origins of reform	European institutions, fewer (successful) initiatives by Greek governments	Irish government, some initiatives by the institutions
Post-program surveillance	Policy conditionality (debt relief measures, Securities Market Programme profits, further incentives)	No conditionality, no policy proposals, except privatization and water charges
Role of EFSF/ESM	Structural adjustment enabler, provision of funds, policy conditionality, special role in privatization	Structural adjustment enabler, provision of funds, providing legitimacy for the reforms
Post-program debate	Taking back labour market reforms (2018–19) Retaining labour market reforms (2019–20)	Reducing government expenditure, rainy day fund

Source: author's compilation

government accepted a third MoU in August 2015. Afterwards, the SYRIZA-led government engaged in strong program implementation even while arguing that they did not agree to the measures included in the MoU. By becoming a strong implementer, the Greek government tried to gain policy space within the MoU framework (see 5.3.2 and 5.4.2). The analysis of ideational processes concerning the reforms of Greek fiscal and labour market policy also underlines that the reforms came primarily from the institutions. That is not to say that Greek governments were unable to make some policy choices of their own. However, in terms of the financial assistance programs, the institutions set the tone. Throughout the Greek programs, strong ideational differences between the Greek authorities and the Eurogroup, ESM, European Commission, ECB, and IMF are visible in the data (see 5.3.1 and 5.4.1). The lack of Greek influence on the program was underlined by the Greek discussion on reversing some of the reforms after Greece entered post-program surveillance (see table 7.1).[1]

In contrast, structural adjustments included in the Irish MoU were strongly influenced by the Irish government. As highlighted above, the Fianna Fáil-Green Party coalition created the National Plan for Recovery, a four-year adjustment plan, shortly prior to its application for financial assistance. The National Plan for Recovery was effectively used as the basis for the Irish MoU (European Commission 2011e, 19). Not only did the Irish plan include fiscal policy goals; it also put forward structural adjustments to the Irish economy, which the MoU picked up. It was certainly the case that the institutions included in the program put forward policy reforms for the Irish government to implement. However, this process was considerably less conflictual than in the Greek case (see 6.3.2 and 6.4.2). Ireland's ownership of the program never came into serious question. After a change in government, the newly elected coalition committed itself to uphold the general reform strategy while including its own reform proposals in the strategy. During the program period, the Irish government was able make policy proposals to the institutions if the government was able to achieve structural goals set out in the program. According to interview partners, it was more important that the Irish administration met consolidation aggregates instead of specific policy implementations: "And once that was agreed broadly, the nature of the measures was left to the Irish authorities" (Interview 20, 18 April 2018).

The Irish administration was able to use the MoU process strategically to implement policies and reforms which were discussed among Irish policymakers but were less likely to be implemented prior to the crisis. ALMP are a key example for this development, as were reforms to public sector employment (see 6.3.1). The strong ideational congruence between Irish policymakers and the institutions is also highlighted in the post-program surveillance of the Irish MoU. First, the post-program period can be described as non-conflictual and a gradual return to policymaking prior to the crisis. Second, throughout most of the post-program surveillance, there were no strong initiatives to revert key reforms of the MoU. Rather, the structural adjustments were accepted as necessary. Post-crisis fiscal policy discussions were to a large part guided by the adjustments implemented during the financial assistance program (see 6.2.2 and table 7.1). While the Irish administration has been criticized in post-program reports for increasing government expenditure, the Irish public debate on fiscal policy focused strongly on the notion of fiscal space, meaning the amount of money that would be available in the budget without increasing the deficit (see 6.4.1).

In addition to political and ideational differences between both cases, their respective socio-economic crises certainly influenced their program processes. As table 6.1 highlights, the recession in Ireland only lasted from 2007 to 2009 as the Irish economy started to grow again shortly before and during the financial assistance program. Ireland experienced strong economic growth after it exited its financial assistance program (see table 6.1). Since 2011, Ireland's economic growth has exceeded the aggregate EU growth rate (Brazys and Regan 2017, 412). While Ireland experienced severe problems due to sharply increased sovereign deficits, its financial situation quickly reversed (see table 6.1). The institutions included in the program highlight the importance of the program for the Irish economy. However, it might not have been the key driver of its strong recovery. A strong if not the key factor in Ireland's economic recovery was Irish participation in the American business cycle and thus FDI-led growth (Roche, O'Connell, and Prothero 2017b; Brazys and Regan 2017; Regan 2014).

Greece, on the other hand, started to experience an economic recession in 2008 and only began to recover in early 2014 (see table 5.1). In comparison, its cumulative recession during this period exceeded the Irish economic downfall by over 10 per cent. In addition, the Greek economy grew at lower rates during the financial assistance program and post-program surveillance in comparison to the Irish economy (see table 5.1 and table 6.1). At the time of writing, the Greek economy has not reached its precrisis level whereas Ireland has exceeded its precrisis economic development.

In sum, the Irish and Greek financial assistance programs share strong similarities in the substance of the policy reforms included in their programs. As the empirical analysis highlights, the MoUs and their reform processes initiated institutional changes that extended market-based economic governance structures in the political economies. In the Irish case, this deepened its character as a liberal market economy. The Greek economy also was brought closer to being a liberal market economy. However, the institutional settings of both countries' economies are still characterized by strong differences. Both countries experienced the financial assistance programs differently. Whereas in the Irish case, a lot of the reforms were proposed by the Irish administration, the Greek administration had comparatively less policy space. In addition, their respective socio-economic crises had different effects on the implementation processes. The Irish economy began growing again quickly after the program started. Greece, on the other hand, went through a seven-year economic recession, which made structural adjustments harder to implement.

7.2 Role of the ESM

As the analysis of the Greek and Irish financial assistance programs underlines, the role of the ESM changed throughout the euro area crisis, as did the role of its temporary predecessor, the EFSF. The institution's influence and area of responsibility expanded over the years as the ESM developed its institutional capacities and gained more importance as the IMF started to phase out its European commitments. Its areas of responsibility within financial assistance programs focus on two central aspects.

First and foremost, the ESM and EFSF are key instruments for the provision of funding for financial support. The ESM, as a permanent institution, manages 80 billion euro of capital that was paid in by its shareholders. Their share is set according to the euro area members' ECB share (table 4.3). By managing the paid-in capital, the ESM secures its high creditworthiness, which is expressed by being awarded best credit ratings by international rating agencies (European Stability Mechanism 2019c, 251–4). The paid-in money is used to secure its operations on financial markets, borrowing money at low interest rates that is later used for paying out loan tranches of the programs (see 4.2.4). As shown above, the EFSF operated similarly but was not provided paid-in capital, which undermined its creditworthiness as more of its shareholders lost their top credit ratings. Eventually, the member states' guarantees had to be increased for the EFSF to keep the best possible ratings from rating agencies (see 4.2.2). The way the EFSF and the ESM provided funding certainly changed throughout the programs: the EFSF at first engaged in ad hoc borrowing on financial markets to provide funding for the programs' loan tranches. In contrast, the ESM is operating on a long-term investment strategy, according to its investment guidelines in line with article 22 of the ESM Treaty (European Stability Mechanism 2019b).

Second, as the institutional capacities of the EFSF and later the ESM increased, the institutions took over some administrative tasks concerning the policy conditionality of European financial assistance programs. At first, the EFSF was considered to be more of a "financing facility than an institution with a broader crisis resolution mandate" (European Stability Mechanism 2017a, 71). Nonetheless, the temporary facility soon started to be more involved in the administration of financial assistance programs, which was the case for both the Irish and the Greek case. Its involvement took a qualitative shift when the ESM was established. A central reason for this is that the ESM, as a permanent institution, has a stronger mandate that is laid out more clearly in the ESM Treaty (European Stability Mechanism 2017a, 71). Based on its mandate and stronger administrative capacities, the ESM expanded its operations beyond the provision of funding. As a report commissioned by the ESM argued,

> [t]he EFSF/ESM participated through the Eurogroup Working Group and Eurogroup policy discussions, and through decisions of their respective Boards. This greater involvement enabled it to assess the implementation risks and prepare disbursements. (European Stability Mechanism 2017a, 71).

Expanding competences of the temporary EFSF and the permanent ESM not only changed their own roles, they also had implications for the institutional structure of the Troika. The ad hoc GLF-solution for the first Greek financial assistance program pooled necessary funding at the European Commission (see 4.2.1). Once the EFSF was established, central decision-making processes concerning the criteria of loan payments were transferred to the Eurogroup as the central decision-making body of the financial assistance procedures (see 4.2.2 and 4.3.2). The "polarised debate on whether the Council or the Commission would lead the new mechanism" (Gocaj and Meunier 2013, 245), which was looming at the beginning of the crisis, has thus been resolved (Gocaj and Meunier 2013, 245). The ESM and its institutional predecessors underline the intergovernmental character of European financial assistance and the key responsibility of the member states for the programs.

The EFSF thus started out as a special purpose vehicle providing loan payments as a part of the financial assistance agreements (see 4.2.2). Over time, its institutional role in the European financial assistance architecture expanded. While the ESM is effectively governed by the Eurogroup and the Eurogroup Working Group (see 4.3.2) and has thus given additional weight to the voice of the Eurogroup within European financial assistance programs, it has taken up tasks and an institutional character of its own, beyond the administration of loan payments and engaging with financial investors. The ESM reform, which at the time of writing culminated in an amending agreement to the ESM Treaty in 2021 (see 8.1) reflects this expanded role of the ESM.

Given the changing institutional architecture of the Troika, relationships between the ESM and other institutions changed as well. Cases in point are its relationship with the European Commission and the IMF. As argued above, the EFSF and the ESM strengthened the relative position of the Eurogroup against the European Commission in crisis management (see 4.3.2). As an institution de facto governed by the Eurogroup, the ESM gained weight on the euro area crisis management and created a formal working relationship with the European Commission on these issues. Their working relationship was codified in a Memorandum of Understanding between the two institutions (European Commission 2018a), which was later endorsed by the Euro Summit (see table 8.1).

While respecting the Commission's competences as set out in the TFEU, the ESM and the Commission engage in close cooperation in central program processes. The European Commission includes the ESM in the preparation and carrying out of program missions, as well as preparation of policy briefs concerning financial assistance programs, and consults the ESM prior to program negotiations, drafting MoUs, and issuing compliance reports (European Commission 2018a, 3). The ESM contributes to the debt sustainability analysis of the European Commission by providing data from its Early Warning System, works on the overall financing needs for financial assistance programs with the European Commission, and collaborates with the European Commission in monitoring program compliance (European Commission 2018a, 3). Both institutions engage in timely exchange of data and information relevant for their common operations (European Commission 2018a, 4). The ESM reform reflects these vertices of their working relationship (see 8.1).

The ESM and the European Commission meet informally to exchange perspectives and analyses of macro-financial risks. The Commission may also invite ESM staff to join missions for economic policy coordination and enhance the Commission's task of budget surveillance. In addition, the ESM managing director meets twice a year with members of the European Commission tasked with financial stability as well as economic and financial affairs to discuss current socio-economic issues (European Commission 2018a, 2; European Stability Mechanism 2019a). These meetings take place irrespective of current crisis dynamics. Working at eye-level with the European Commission in providing stability for the monetary union is thus a central goal of the ESM. A clear mandate from its member states to achieve this stability has been issued to the ESM, as its previous managing director argued in an interview with the Frankfurter Allgemeine Zeitung (2018).

Despite this strong cooperation, both institutions are careful not to duplicate each other's competences and to respect their institutional mandates (Interview 31, 30 July 2018). The ESM has thus taken over tasks in certain policy areas but respects the competences of the European Commission in other fields, a division of responsibilities that first developed during the financial assistance programs and was formalized in the ESM reform process (see 8.1). The ESM is particularly engaged in financial sector policy as its ongoing long-term investment strategy has given it key knowledge in the operations of financial markets. Privatization measures were a key focus of the ESM in program surveillance, especially in the Greek program (Interview 32, 1 August 2018; see also 5.2.2.4). On the other hand, the ESM is mindful of respecting the European Commission's mandate. A key example is the coordination of labour market policy, as an interview partner argued:

> For us it [labour markets] is not our piece of cake, so we don't have any labour economists and we are following the discussions in all the meetings with the minster of labour […], but institutionally this was mainly for the Commission and the other institutions to discuss. (Interview 32, 1 August 2018)

The ESM's role has also changed in light of a decreasing IMF influence. The ESM Treaty states that the ESM will work closely with the IMF. In its original form, member states seeking financial support from the ESM should also apply for support from the IMF (European Stability Mechanism 2012, 5). However, as the financial assistance programs progressed and the ESM gained further competences, this passage of the ESM Treaty became less influential. The amending agreement requires IMF involvement "wherever appropriate and possible" (European Stability Mechanism 2021, 10). In the third Greek program, the IMF still joined review missions but did not participate financially (Thomsen 2019). The ESM became the sole financing institution of the third Greek MoU. There were two reasons: First, the IMF generally wanted to be less involved in Europe as supporting Western industrialized countries in times of severe fiscal stress was not the key task of the IMF. After yields for long-term bonds started to decrease in 2012 and, apart from Greece, no new financial assistance programs were expected for the foreseeable future, the IMF aimed at focusing its operations on other areas again.

Second and more importantly, the IMF disagreed with other institutions concerning the sustainability of Greece's sovereign debt and the question of official sector involvement in nominal debt relief for Greece, which the IMF regarded as necessary (Obstfeld and Thomsen 2016;

Thomsen 2019). The ESM's Early Warning System offered the euro area members a possibility to provide their own analysis on the likelihood of the program's full repayment. Hence, the ESM allowed the European institutions to neglect the IMF's perspective on debt sustainability and prevent official sector involvement from being a central condition, which gave additional weight to the ESM's role in European financial assistance.

Taking into consideration the role of the temporary EFSF and the permanent ESM in the program processes, their general role in the respective program countries should thus be analysed as *structural adjustment enablers* that are symbolic of the financial assistance architecture. Both the EFSF and the ESM were important in enabling structural adjustments (see table 7.1). They provided financial resources for the programs, which is a central aspect of their functioning. Furthermore, the EFSF and the ESM support the policy conditionality approach by being included in progress reviews and paying out tranches only after positive program reviews (see 4.4). This aspect of enabling structural adjustments increased as the ESM became more involved in program design and program missions. Nonetheless, the role of the EFSF and the ESM as *structural adjustment enablers* certainly took different forms in Ireland and Greece.

In the Greek case, the ESM and its institutional predecessors collected and provided the financing for the financial assistance programs, either by financial market borrowing or by pooling resources. Furthermore, the ESM and its predecessors played a key role in upholding the pressure to engage in structural reforms. As the Greek programs progressed and the EFSF/ESM developed additional institutional capacities, it was included in the review process and formulation of the program's policy conditionality. As discussed above, the ESM also took over the responsibility of parts of the policy conditionality. As shown in the case analysis, the program documents included policy paradigms that did not match with paradigms shared among Greek authorities (see 5.3.1 and 5.4.1). What is more, the programs – put forward at critical junctures of the Greek crisis – set Greece on a new political economic path (see 5.3.3 and 5.4.3). Actor preferences and strategic interaction had a strong influence on the implementation of institutional change in the Greek labour market and its fiscal policy (5.3.2 and 5.4.2). The EFSF and later the ESM enabled these processes by its funding facility and administrative roles (see table 7.1).

In the Irish case, the EFSF certainly has also served as a structural adjustment enabler. In its role as a financing facility, it provided the necessary funding, in combination with the EFSM and the IMF, to prevent an Irish sovereign default. The EFSF supported the conditionality approach by the institutions by only providing funding after positive evaluations of the program's progress. In addition, as its administrative capacities increased, the EFSF and later the ESM were included in program missions, as well as post-program reviews of the Irish program. As the Irish case study highlighted, Irish authorities themselves put forward an adjustment plan that was very much in line with the paradigm of the institutions (see 6.3.1 and 6.4.1). What is more, the Irish program set up during the critical juncture of the Irish crisis deepened the country's liberal market economy character instead of promoting institutional change towards a different socio-economic model (see 6.3.3 and 6.4.3). Nonetheless, the EFSF and the ESM were important in putting forward actor preferences and strategic interaction. The policy conditionality attached to paying out tranches allowed both the institutions and the Irish government to put forward reforms that would have been politically costly to implement outside of the program (see 6.3.2 and 6.4.2). In this regard, the EFSF and the ESM played key roles in enabling structural adjustments envisioned by the institutions and the Irish government.

7.3 Interim Conclusion

As shown in this chapter, the Irish and Greek programs showed strong similarities in the substance of their structural adjustments. Both programs aimed at liberalizing and including stronger market-based coordination mechanisms in their labour markets. Both programs focused on welfare retrenchments and the recommodification of labour through activation policies based on negative incentives. Fiscally, both programs pursued an adjustment strategy that focused primarily on expenditure reductions and thus reduced the government's influence on socio-economic development. In effect, the program deepened Ireland's socio-economic path as a liberal market economy. In the Greek case it transformed its typical MME socio-economic model to include stronger LME features (see 7.1).

The role of the ESM and the EFSF changed throughout the programs. At first, both mainly acted as special purpose vehicles to provide and distribute loans to program countries. In addition, both the EFSF and ESM increased the intergovernmental character of European financial assistance, as the Eurogroup and the Eurogroup Working Group constitute their central governing bodies. Their establishment strengthened the relative position of the Eurogroup and the EWG in comparison to the European Commission in these programs. As the ESM developed more institutional capacities, it became more involved in program operations, such as privatization programs and financial sector relations, while continuing to support the adjustment strategies. It became a structural adjustment enabling institution with symbolic resemblance to the entire European financial assistance architecture, despite closely working with the institutions involved in the process, particularly the European Commission (see 7.2).

Outlook: ESM Reform and COVID-19

This chapter will expand the analysis of the ESM's institutional development on events after the initial analytical timeframe for both cases. After Greece exited from its third financial assistance program in 2018, EMU engaged in a reform process that also included a reform of the ESM. Furthermore, political developments at the European level as a result of the COVID-19 pandemic had strong effects on the potential role of the ESM. The chapter will therefore proceed as follows: First, the chapter will discuss different reform proposals for the ESM and will discuss the reform results (8.1). Second, the role of the ESM during COVID-19 and the implications for future crises will be discussed (see 8.2). An interim conclusion will provide an outlook (see 8.3).

8.1 ESM Reform

As shown above, the creation of the European Economic and Monetary Union was accompanied by discussions about the necessity of a central institution to provide funding during asymmetric shocks (see 4.1). These discussions gained new momentum during the euro crisis and were soon projected onto the EFSF/ESM, despite being created outside of EU law (see 4.2.2 and 4.2.4). Its current and future role in EMU governance were central discussion points throughout the euro crisis and during EMU reform debates that started in 2018 and culminated in an amendment of the ESM Treaty in 2021. These debates focused to a large degree on whether the ESM, as a permanent institution, should be transformed into a European equivalent to the IMF. As the IMF became wary of its European commitments and the ESM took over parts of its role in European financial assistance programs (see 7.2), these discussions became more frequent. They did not primarily focus on the name, the European Monetary Fund (EMF), as such, although the idea of an

EMF was a vocal point of the reform debates. Rather, the reform discussions focused to large degree on institutional and programmatic issues of the ESM and its role in EMU governance.

The creation of an EMF has been debated since the start of the global financial crisis and sparked further interest among European policymakers throughout the crisis of the euro area. As the financial stability of European banks deteriorated after Lehman Brothers filed for bankruptcy in 2008, scholars such as Gros and Micossi (2008) or Gros and Mayer (2010)[1] proposed a European financial stability fund for the support of EMU members on the edge of sovereign defaults (Gocaj and Meunier 2013, 242). As most prominently argued by Wolfgang Schäuble in a *Financial Times* op-ed in 2010 (Schäuble 2010; see also Schwarzer 2015, 608), creating a European equivalent to the International Monetary Fund was proposed several times throughout the crisis. Schäuble argued in favour of a fund that would provide liquidity to EMU members in times of emergency, albeit with "strict conditionality and a prohibitive price tag" (Schäuble 2010, para. 9). While he did not offer a detailed plan on his proposal, talks about the creation of a European Monetary Fund intensified after his op-ed (Gocaj and Meunier 2013, 242). Initially, the idea of a European Monetary Fund had support from the European Commission and across political parties (Gocaj and Meunier 2013, 242). Angela Merkel supported Wolfgang Schäuble's plan in general but argued that such a proposal would not be possible given the Maastricht Treaty's no-bailout clause and the necessity of agreement among all member states for changes to the treaty (Gocaj and Meunier 2013, 242).

When it became clear to European policymakers that a temporary financial safety net would not be sufficient and the permanent ESM was established, transforming the permanent ESM into a European Monetary Fund became a central aspect of reform discussions for the euro area. The debates became more frequent as immediate crisis dynamics in the euro area were less threatening to the institutional integrity of the area. Especially with the foreseeable program exit of Greece in 2018 and less interest on the part of the IMF concerning involvement in European programs, discussions among European and national policymakers concerned the ESM's future role in EMU. As table 8.1 shows, the idea of an EMF has guided the ESM reform proposals to a larger degree:

Interestingly, interview data from Greece and Ireland shows that the idea of an EMF is discussed differently in program countries. Whereas in Greece, the ESM and a possible EMF were discussed as a positive development, especially regarding the possibility to replace the IMF (e.g., Interview 3, 4 March 2018; Interview 8, 9 March 2018), interview

Table 8.1. Proposals during the ESM reform discussion (selection)

Author	Date	Central Position
European Commission	28 November 2012	Bringing the ESM into EU law
Five Presidents	22 June 2015	Bringing the ESM into EU law; application of EU decision-making framework
European Parliament	16 February 2017	Transform the ESM into a European Monetary Fund; mandate to deal with asymmetric and symmetric shocks; possibility of automatic shock absorbers
European Commission	6 December 2017	Bringing the ESM into EU law; transform into a European Monetary fund; preservation of the ESM's institutional and financial structures; application of EU decision-making framework incl. EP involvement; stronger involvement in the management of financial assistance programs; development of new financial instruments
European Council	15 December 2017	Possibility of transforming the ESM into an EMF; possibility of using the ESM as the backstop for the Single Resolution Fund (SRF)
New Hanseatic League	6 March 2018	ESM/EMF as an intergovernmental institution, accountable only to its lenders; greater role in financial assistance programs
Eurogroup	12 March 2018	ESM as backstop for SRF; reform of ESM toolbox; strengthen the ESM's role in programs; the ESM and debt sustainability analysis
Euro Summit	23 March 2018	No written conclusion; reaffirmation of the priorities of ESM reform as set out by the Eurogroup in March 2018
ESM, speech by managing director	10 April 2018	Focus on substance, not the name; including the ESM in the SRF; limited fiscal capacity for macroeconomic stabilization; management of sovereign debt restructuring framework; including the ESM into EU law on the basis of the EIB
ECB	11 April 2018	Support for including the ESM into EU law; greater role for safeguarding financial stability within EU law; further reforms are essential; review of toolbox; reform of ESM governance and faster decision-making processes; ESM as backstop for SRF; maintaining the ESM name
Germany and France *Meseberg Declaration*	10 June 2018	Reform of the ESM's precautionary programs; strengthen its role in fiscal and economic surveillance and within financial assistance programs; preservation of policy conditionality as its main component; bringing the ESM into EU law; preserving the intergovernmental governance of the ESM; backstop for the SRF; possibly renaming the ESM in the future

(*Continued*)

Table 8.1. Proposals during the ESM reform discussion (selection) (*Continued*)

Author	Date	Central Position
Euro Summit	28 June 2018	ESM as the backstop for the SRF
Bullmann, Gualtieri, Berès (S&D)	28 June 2018	Transform the ESM into a European Stability Fund (ESF); integration in EU legal framework; key governance structure should be preserved; EIB model could be preferred
Eurogroup	1 October 2018	Review of the ESM's precautionary credit lines; development of the ESM's inclusion in EMU crisis management without creating overlaps with the Commission
New Hanseatic League	1 November 2018	ESM as an intergovernmental institution, accountable only to its lenders; greater role for the ESM in fiscal surveillance
Eurogroup *Term sheet on ESM reform*	4 December 2018	Reform of ESM precautionary tools; strengthen the ESM's role in debt sustainability analysis; stronger role in program establishment and monitoring; policy conditionality as its main component; ESM as SRF backstop; strengthened cooperation between ESM and the Commission
Euro Summit	14 December 2018	Endorsed the proposed changes from the Eurogroup's term sheet from 4 December 2018
Eurogroup	13 June 2019	Agreement of a revised ESM Treaty, including the ESM as a common backstop in the SRF, revising precautionary instruments of the ESM, and codifying the ESM's cooperation with the European Commission
Euro Summit	21 June 2019	Endorsement of the proposed treaty revisions
Eurogroup	4 December 2019	Agreement of expanding the ESM's role in future financial assistance programs, including the ESM in the SRF, review of the ESM's instruments

Source: adapted from European Parliament (2018, 18–19); author's additions

partners in Ireland were hesitant about a stronger role of the ESM, especially in regard to possible problems with the Commission's mandate and stronger economic governance mechanisms on the European level (e.g., Interview 20, 18 April 2018; Interview 22, 19 April 2018).

Proposals on the ESM's prospective role in EMU governance and its transformation into an EMF issued during EMU reform discussions largely focused on the same issues, albeit coming to different conclusions: There was a consensus on the idea that the EMF should not be a new institution. Rather, the EMF would be a reformed ESM. However, the proposals differed in terms of the reformed ESM's institutional setting and decision-making processes, as well as the objectives of financial assistance.

First, the proposals showed different opinions on the institutional setting of the EMF/the reformed ESM. The European Commission argued in its initial proposal to include the ESM under EU law (European Commission 2017c) and was supported by other proposals in this regard (e.g., European Parliament 2017; Presse- und Informationsamt der Bundesregierung 2018). Others, especially the New Hanseatic League[2] (Denmark et al. 2018; The Czech Republic et al. 2018), have highlighted that they would want the ESM/EMF to remain as an intergovernmental institution.

Second, and closely aligned to the question of the institutional setting, there were different positions on reforming ESM decision-making procedures. While the European Commission argued for the application of EU decision-making processes including participation of the EP (European Commission 2017b), as did an earlier proposal by the European Parliament (European Parliament 2017). The Meseberg Declaration (Presse- und Informationsamt der Bundesregierung 2018) and the New Hanseatic League, however, underlined their intention to keep the current intergovernmental decision-making process of the ESM, which relies de facto on the Eurogroup and the Eurogroup Working Group as its key decision-making bodies (Denmark et al. 2018; The Czech Republic et al. 2018).

Last, the question of the ESM's objectives in terms of financial assistance was a central topic during this period. The New Hanseatic League (Denmark et al. 2018; The Czech Republic et al. 2018) stressed that they would want the ESM to play a more prominent role in the EU's budgetary surveillance of its member states – a task that is also part of the Commission's area of competence. Adjustments to economic crises, according to their position, should primarily be implemented through reforms at the national level. Others, however, have considered using the ESM as an instrument to combat asymmetric shocks at the European level and put less emphasis on national structural adjustments to European socio-economic developments (e.g., European Parliament 2017).

Furthermore, it should be noted that the European Central Bank, albeit being supportive of including the ESM in EU law, publicly suggested abstaining from renaming the ESM as the European Monetary Fund. The ECB argued that the institution's objectives, as the *Pringle* case made clear, fall into the realm of economic instead of monetary policy, which was the sole responsibility of the ECB (European Central Bank 2018; see also chapter 4, note 1). This public intervention by the ECB essentially ended the discussions on renaming the ESM as EMF.

Taking all of this into consideration, the ESM reform process resulted in a reformed status quo with expanded responsibilities for the ESM.

The reform process refrained from establishing a fully fledged European equivalent to the IMF and mostly focused on implementing the ESM as the backstop for the Single Resolution Fund, reforming the ESM's toolbox by applying new rules on precautionary instruments, and further formalizing the ESM's working relationship with the European Commission, as the respective agreement to amend the ESM Treaty highlights (European Stability Mechanism 2021; see also European Commission 2018a).

The reform of the ESM Treaty certainly put forward a new and improved role of the ESM in EMU crisis management and debt sustainability surveillance, while respecting the Commission's economic policy mandate. Whereas past financial assistance programs have been conceptualized and supervised by the Troika (IMF, ECB, and European Commission) – and, after the creation of the ESM, by the Quadriga (IMF, ECB, European Commission, and ESM) – the institutional constellation for future financial assistance programs will change. For future programs, the board of governors can "entrust (i) the Managing Director and (ii) the European Commission in liaison with the ECB, together to negotiate the economic policy conditionality" (European Stability Mechanism 2021, 17). Both will be in charge of central assessments in case of a financial support request and monitor conditionality compliance (European Stability Mechanism 2021, 21). The ESM reform made access to precautionary instruments easier for those member states that comply with EMU's fiscal framework (European Stability Mechanism 2021, 22–5, 33–5) and enabled the ESM to work as backstop facility for the Single Resolution Fund (European Stability Mechanism 2021, 6).

These amendments trace and formalize the role of the ESM in financial assistance programs in the past (see 4.4.3 and 7.2). The amending agreement clearly states that the ESM should not engage in economic policy coordination where EU law provides frameworks and respect EU law on these matters (European Stability Mechanism 2021, 11). However, these amendments nonetheless institutionalize the new role of the ESM as a lender of last resort that participates in policy obligations attached to financial support. While strong differences between the ESM and the European Commission remain, in particular concerning their institutional capacities, the ESM has been strengthened. At the beginning of the reform discussions, an interview partner highlighted that the role of the ESM increased over time. The third financial assistance program for Greece strengthened its role in providing input to the program, for example, by providing the debt sustainability analysis. According to the interview partner, the role of the ESM is likely to increase in case new programs would be put forward in the future. However, the European Commission is expected to remain relevant in the process (Interview 25, 9 July 2018).

This is also the case in comparison to the role of the IMF in future programs. Whereas the IMF was a key non-majoritarian institution in European financial assistance during the euro crisis, it became less enthusiastic about its European commitments as the immediate crisis pressure went away. The IMF particularly did not agree with the European institutions about a lack of official sector involvement in the third Greek financial assistance program. The amending agreement reflects these developments and gives more weight to the European Stability Mechanism: Whereas the ESM Treaty foresaw that the IMF was to be included in negotiating and monitoring the programs' policy conditionality "wherever possible" (European Stability Mechanism 2012, 29), the amendments require an involvement of the IMF "wherever appropriate and possible" (European Stability Mechanism 2021, 10).

The ESM reform process therefore did not create a fully fledged European Monetary Fund. However, it formalized and strengthened its relative role in EMU's financial assistance architecture vis-à-vis the European Commission. In the same line of thought, the reform process reviewed its toolbox and gave the ESM an additional role in providing financial stability as a backstop of the Single Resolution Fund.

8.2 The ESM during the COVID-19 Crisis

After years of severe economic and political crises, particularly in the European South, the euro area seemed to steer into calm waters after the third Greek financial assistance program ended in 2018 (see above). The fact that the Eurogroup was given a mandate to negotiate reform options for the Economic and Monetary Union that, along with other reform objectives, included a reform of the ESM and its toolbox (Eurogroup 2018a; Euro Summit 2018, see also 8.1), was an expression of a calmer political and economic situation in the euro area, despite ongoing struggles coming from issues such as Brexit. The ESM reform debate highlighted different perspectives on such reform efforts (see 8.1). However, before the reforms were finalized, the European Union was exposed to severe economic and fiscal stress due to the COVID-19 pandemic.

When SARS-CoV-2 became publicly known in January 2020, after starting to spread in Wuhan in late November 2019 (Tooze 2021, 63), warnings by the WHO or the IMF of a global pandemic were first met with insufficient responses (Tooze 2021, 79–81). It only took a few weeks until the first cases were detected in the EU. Italy quickly became the first European focal point of the pandemic, with severe numbers of infections in northern regions and particularly high numbers in Lombardy and Veneto. The Italian government started lockdown measures in early March 2020. Non-essential shops were ordered to close on 11 March 2020. Soon after, on 21 March 2020, the Italian prime minister set in place lockdown measures that closed all non-essential business activities including the industrial sector. He also restricted the movement of people in Italy (Safi, Giuffrida, and Farrer 2020).

The emerging COVID-19 pandemic not only led to severe health problems. It also quickly put additional fiscal pressure on all EU member states, particularly on those with comparatively high debt-to-GDP ratios. Governments were faced with increasing health expenditures as well as economic recessions due to lockdowns and distorted supply chains. Most governments quickly reacted with financial support schemes for their industries and service sectors in order to reduce long-term negative effects on the economy. The countries hit hardest by the first wave were also countries that already had considerable sovereign debt. On average, GDP decreased by 6.1 per cent in 2020, but countries in the South experienced much stronger economic downturns (see table 8.2). Fears of a new euro crisis were voiced during this period.

The question of joint debt obligations to share fiscal burdens of the symmetric crisis was quickly brought up – particularly in an attempt to prevent higher debt ratios in the South. A group of nine EMU members, led by Italy, Spain, France, and Portugal, called for "a common debt instrument issued by a European institution to raise funds on the market" (Reuters 2020) on 25 March 2020. A common debt instrument, however, was quickly ruled out by Northern EMU members, Germany and the Netherlands in particular (Tesche 2021, 5). A video conference on 26 March 2020 resulted in heated debates without a clear decision on fiscal instruments. Instead, the Eurogroup was delegated to present their proposal in two-weeks' time (European Council 2020c, 4).

The Eurogroup came up with a support plan for countries in severe need. They proposed a fiscal safety net worth 540 billion euro that included measures to provide fiscal support not only to governments but also to workers and businesses. Central was the proposal to use the ESM for support: through its existing toolbox (Enhanced Conditions Credit Lines, see 4.4), the ESM would be enabled to provide each euro area member state 2 per cent of its 2019 GDP in loans – 240 billion euro

Table 8.2. GDP growth rate of selected Euro Area members, 2017–20

Country	2017	2018	2019	2020
Austria	2.3	2.4	1.5	–6.5
France	2.3	1.9	1.8	–7.8
Germany	2.7	1.0	1.1	–3,7
Greece	1.1	1.7	1.9	–9.0
Ireland	9.0	8.5	5.4	6.2
Italy	1.7	0.9	0.5	–9.0
Netherlands	2.9	2.4	2.0	–3.9
Portugal	3.5	2.8	2.7	–8.3
Spain	3.0	2.3	2.0	–11.3
Euro Area	2.6	1.8	1.6	–6.1

Source: Eurostat (2023d)

in total (Howarth and Spendzharova 2020, 213). The instrument was accompanied by 100 billion euro to support European short-time working allowances and a 200 billion euro liquidity support scheme for SMEs by the European Investment Bank (Eurogroup 2020). This proposal was received positively by the ESM. In an interview on 31 March 2020, the ESM managing director at that time, Klaus Regling, said: "I think that is the right approach. One has to look at the different contributions that can come from all the possible different sources. Otherwise we will not be able to handle this" (Fleming 2020).

Unlike previous financial assistance experiences in the EU, the loans for sovereigns would come with significantly less conditions: they would have to be used for health care related expenditures due to the COVID-19 pandemic (Eurogroup 2020). The instrument was approved by the European Council on 23 April 2020 (European Council 2020a) and became available on 15 May 2020 after a final decision by the ESM's board of governors. The instrument remained unused and expired at the end of 2022.

The ESM's symbolic representation of the EU's financial assistance architecture was a burden in this process. Its symbolic representation of and participation in financial assistance during the euro crisis was not beneficial to the cause of using it as the central financial support instrument. The strongest negative reaction clearly came from the Italian government. The ESM was not very popular with the Italian public and several parts of the political sphere, where, prior to the pandemic, the ESM reform debate (see 8.1) was met with strong opposition (Galli 2020). An approval for the ESM reform plans was highly contested until the last minute (Reuters 2021). In particular, it was the notion that a reformed ESM could lead to a restructuring of Italian sovereign debt that sparked a lot of political opposition. In Italy as well as in other Southern European member states, the ESM is strongly associated with negative experiences of financial assistance during the euro crisis. It became toxic, as Tesche argued (Tesche 2021, 6; see also Guttenberg, Hemker, and Tordoir 2021, 4). Greek experiences with structural adjustments were a case in point in the heated debates. The group of member states led by Italy and Spain therefore kept up their resistance towards financial support through the ESM and upheld their demand of a new common debt instrument to share the burden of the developing crisis.

On 18 May 2020, France and Germany put forward a joint proposal. While underlining the necessity for the 9 April package, including support through the ESM, they agreed that a common recovery fund was needed. Merkel and Macron proposed a 500 billion euro fund that would support member states during the COVID-19 pandemic. Their proposal would be financed through funds that the European Commission borrowed on financial markets – effectively leading to a one-off common debt instrument, as Southern European countries had requested (Fleming, Mallet, and Chazan 2020). The European Commission took up the Franco-German idea: on 27 May 2020, Ursula von der Leyen presented the Commission's proposal to the European Parliament. She argued for an instrument that would include 750 billion euro in total. 250 billion euro as loans and 500 billion euro as grants. There was a lot of opposition, in particular from Austria, Denmark, the Netherlands, and Sweden, which called themselves the Frugal Four and were later joined by Finland (Verdun 2021, 11–12). They were particularly opposed to a higher EU budget and common debt obligations to provide grants to member states, in particular with no reform obligations attached to them (Verdun 2021, 12).

The special European Council meeting in July 2020 saw heated negotiations about the size of the European budget as well as the conditions of financial assistance to EU members during the COVID-19 pandemic (Fleming, Kahn, and Brunsden 2020). The negotiations took from 17 July to 21 July, which was the longest European Council meeting to this day. The meeting took particularly long because of the Frugal Four's opposition (Verdun 2021, 12). Once a compromise was reached, it included concessions to their opposition: a majority of the financial support would be provided as loans instead of grants and the financial assistance would also come with some requirements in form of a rule of law conditionality (European Council 2020b). NextGenerationEU and the Recovery and Resilience Facility (RRF), through which grants and loans will be provided (see table 8.3), nonetheless proves to be a

Table 8.3. NextGenerationEU

Instrument	Objective	Billion
Recovery and Resilience Facility	Provides grants and loans to member states for investments and economic growth. 338.0 billion euro will be provided in grants, 385.8 in loans.	723.8
REACT-EU	Cohesion policy	50.6
Just Transition Fund	Social objectives in transition towards climate neutrality	10.9
Rural Development	Farmer support	8.1
InvestEU	Business investment support	6.1
Horizon Europe	Research funding	5.4
rescEU	EU Civil Protection Mechanism	2.0

Source: European Commission/Directorate General for the Budget (2021, 5)

new approach to financial assistance in EMU, in particular because it includes a common debt instrument that allows the European Commission to borrow funds on financial markets. Whether NextGenerationEU will lead to less or more conflicts in the future remains unclear at time of writing (e.g., Tesche 2021).

The Recovery and Resilience Fund effectively sidelined the ESM as the go-to institution to provide financial support during the COVID-19 pandemic. The ESM's resemblance to financial assistance during the euro crisis, which included far-reaching policy obligations (see above), strongly politicized and polarized the use of the ESM during the outbreak of the COVID-19 pandemic (Tesche 2021, 5). Its symbolic representation turned against the institution and its activation during the COVID-19 pandemic.

8.3 Interim Conclusion

As chapter 8 highlights, the euro crisis certainly shaped the role and tasks of the ESM. Shortly before Greece exited its third financial assistance program and the euro area came into calmer economic waters, the future role of the ESM in EMU governance became a regular discussion point between EU policymakers and a key part of an EMU reform process. As its reform process of 2017 to 2021 highlights (see 8.1), the ESM certainly was an important aspect of the European financial assistance architecture during the euro crisis. The reform process formalized its influence on financial assistance, and made clear which competences it shared with the European Commission and which fields of expertise are not part of the ESM's scope. The reform process and the variety of proposals made clear that the demands for a more active ESM certainly differ among member states. The ESM reform ultimately resulted in a reformed status quo by giving more weight and formal competences to competences the ESM already had, formalizing its relationship to the European Commission, reviewing its toolbox, and adding the role as backstop for the Single Resolution Fund to its repertoire. While the reform process made clear that the ESM will have more influence on debt sustainability analysis and play a stronger role vis-à-vis a potential IMF participation, it did not create a full equivalent of the IMF or introduced the ESM into EU law (see 8.1).

Its symbolic role in the euro crisis' financial assistance architecture polarized and politicized the ESM at the beginning of the COVID-19 pandemic, during which countries in the South requested fiscal solidarity to cope with the emerging crisis. Northern European member states quickly pointed to the ESM for financial support. However, its Pandemic Crisis Support instrument remained unused. Instead, the EU has created a new instrument that relies on a mixture of grants and loans and comes with less policy conditionality (see 8.2). It remains to be seen what the establishment of NextGenerationEU will mean for the ESM – in particular in potential future asymmetric crises.

Chapter Nine

Conclusion

The euro crisis shaped and shifted the institutional and political landscape of the European Economic and Monetary Union. A decade after the euro was established, the single currency experienced a deep crisis that almost resulted in a breakup of the euro area. To combat the crisis and to secure the euro's institutional integrity, EMU member states set up new mechanisms and institutions. The ESM, as analysed above, is the institutional embodiment of the euro area's strategy against the crisis: on an intergovernmental basis, the ESM provides loans with interest rates below market prices to euro area members in severe fiscal stress. However financial assistance programs have come with the condition of structural adjustments in fiscal, financial, and socio-economic policy areas. The policy conditionality is drawn up by non-majoritarian institutions that work closely with the ESM. Drawing on the centrality of the ESM and its predecessors, this book pursued the research objective of exploring whether the ESM, as a permanent financing institution for European financial assistance programs, is enabling the convergence of different socio-economic models in the euro area. The research objective was further specified in three research questions that relate to the overall research objective: (1) How were the current political economic varieties in EMU affected by the establishment of the ESM? (2) What is the role played by ideas of political economic development in the single currency to explain convergence? (3) What was the impact of path dependence to explain persisting divergence between European economies affected by the ESM?

Drawing on the varieties of capitalism framework and new institutionalism, the book theorized that the ESM, based on financial assistance programs, would enable institutional change in member states of the euro area that apply for financial assistance. The project hypothesized that the ESM would shape political economic reform processes and institutional changes in program countries. According to the central hypothesis, program countries would focus on similar reforms, which would lead to a (partial) convergence of their socio-economic models. Based on the analysis, *the central hypothesis on the direction of socio-economic reforms and the role of the ESM can be verified.* However, some points have to be added. Financial assistance in the euro area did lead to similar developments in different program countries. As the case studies of Ireland and Greece underline, financial assistance programs in the euro area focus on similar program objectives and policy developments, which primarily support market-based governance mechanisms.

The Greek and Irish MoUs included several institutional changes in the countries' economic governance of their labour markets. The reforms focused on decentralization of labour markets, especially in terms of wage-setting mechanism. Both countries included tripartite wage-setting mechanisms on the national level in their socio-economic models but have since decentralized wage setting primarily to the firm level. This development had severe repercussions on the coverage of collective agreements (see 5.2.1 and 6.2.1). Both countries reduced their employment protection legislation (see 5.2.1.2 and 6.2.1.2) and implemented labour market reforms in combination with welfare retrenchments that focused on the reduction of replacement rates for unemployed workers and the implementation of ALMPs, which focus on negative incentives to accept employment offers (see 5.2.1.3 and 6.2.1.3). Both countries' labour markets include more market-based governance mechanisms than before the crisis.

Similar developments are visible in fiscal policy. Both programs primarily focused on expenditure reduction as their key strategy to reduce the budgetary deficits of Greece and Ireland and regain access to financial markets (see 5.2.2.1 and 6.2.2.1). Increasing government revenue played only a minor role in both programs, as the institutions included in the program argued that higher taxation would harm economic growth (see 5.2.2.2 and 6.2.2.2). Greece and Ireland reformed their fiscal frameworks in similar ways: including independent supervision of fiscal developments was a key development in both programs. In addition, both countries' fiscal frameworks now include medium-term budgetary plans and medium-term budgetary ceilings. These reforms were further enhanced by new fiscal rules on the European level (see 5.2.2.3 and 6.2.2.3). Reducing the government's influence on the economy by including privatization in the fiscal consolidation strategy played a key role in both MoUs but was only implemented on a large scale in Greece (see 5.2.2.4 and 6.2.2.4). These fiscal reforms resulted in weaker governmental influence on the economy in both cases (see 5.2.2.5 and 6.2.2.5). Fiscal policy reforms thus deepened Ireland's institutional character as an LME and caused a shift in Greece's socio-economic model to include more market-based governance mechanisms.

The ESM, however, did not produce these results alone. It played an important role as it enabled financial assistance programs. The ESM furthermore had strong symbolic power in the programs and focused on some parts of the policy conditionality. Nonetheless, by itself, the ESM was not able to put forward such wide-ranging programs. The European Commission, the European Central Bank, and, when requested, the International Monetary Fund, played central roles in the adjustment process.

The general hypothesis of this research project was further diversified into three hypotheses on the theoretical assumptions underlying institutional change enabled by financial assistance associated with the ESM. These hypotheses focus on incentive structures (H1), ideational influences by the ESM (H2), and the influence of political legacies on adjustment processes (H3) (see 2.4).

Based on the empirical evidence, Hypothesis 1 can be verified. As derived from rational choice institutionalism (see 2.3.1 and 2.4), the ESM and its institutional predecessor clearly put in place a new incentive structure for countries that apply for financial assistance. The analysis highlights that the conditionality approach of the ESM was an effective instrument in enabling institutional change. In the Greek case, policy conditionality set an incentive to engage in reforms that several governments and key social partners generally rejected. However, due to the program's combination of providing funding below market prices to prevent sovereign default and strict policy conditionality, political agents were able to calculate the risk of a sovereign default against the risk of implementing said reforms. This became particularly visible after SYRIZA came into office. While the left-wing government rejected the MoU completely at first, the risk of a Greek default increased over the summer of 2015. In the end, they became strong program implementers despite their continuous argument that they rejected the MoU in general (see 5.3.2 and 5.4.2). In this regard, the EFSF and later the ESM set incentive structures that influenced policymakers to implement institutional changes despite rejecting them in the first place.

In the Irish case, the risk of a sovereign default certainly influenced the government to comply with the conditionality at first. However, as the analysis highlights, Ireland soon started to use the conditionality approach to implement policies that the government was unable to implement prior to the program and in some cases even went beyond the reform objectives of the institutions (see 6.3.2 and 6.4.2). In the Irish case, the EFSF set the incentive for the government to use the program to engage in reforms it had postponed due to political and financial costs. Nonetheless, it was the EFSF's focus on policy conditionality that allowed such strategies to be developed.

According to the analysis, Hypothesis 2 has to be partly rejected. The ESM certainly promotes a specific perspective on socio-economic development which resembles the Brussels-Frankfurt Consensus (for a description see Jones 2013), which was underlined by qualitative data collected for this project. The EFSF and ESM's strong institutional link to the Eurogroup and the Eurogroup Working Group linked them to ideas and ideational processes in both decision-making bodies. In this regard, the EFSF and ESM certainly had an influence on ideational processes in the program countries (see 5.3.1, 5.4.1, 6.3.1, and 6.4.1). However, the ideational processes concerning the financial assistance programs appeared to be more complex. In the Irish case, ideas concerning socio-economic reform mostly came from Irish policy debates or had their origin in OECD reports (such as ALMP) (see 6.3.1 and 6.4.1). During the first stages of the Irish program, the EFSF was primarily concerned with providing financial resources and building up its institutional capacities. However, there was a general ideational consensus among Irish and European policymakers on the reforms they regarded as necessary. In the Greek case, most ideas concerning socio-economic reform had their origin in the institutions and, within the third program, to some degree in the ESM (see 5.3.1 and 5.4.1). There was, in comparison to Ireland, considerably less influence on the program from the Greek authorities. No general ideational convergence between Greek and European policymakers could be identified in the analysis. A strong case in point are discussions about reversing the program to some degree after Greece exited from the financial assistance program in 2018 (see table 7.1).

Based on the empirical findings in this research project, Hypothesis 3 can be verified. The crisis and the respective MoUs can be analysed as critical junctures in Greece and Ireland, in which their existing paths of socio-economic development became fluid (see 5.3.3, 5.4.3, 6.3.3, and 6.4.3). There is a common path of adjustment within both countries focusing on market-based economic coordination (see above). However, both countries come from very different political economic traditions, which is reflected in the program results. While the Irish program deepened the country's path as a liberal market economy (see 6.5), Greece has taken strong steps toward more marked-based coordination but without completely leaving its path as a mixed-market economy (see 5.5). In both cases, existing historical legacies clearly guided the adjustment process.

The role of the ESM and its predecessors within the financial assistance programs can therefore be described as a *structural adjustment enabler* (see 7.2). The institution has been engaging in reform talks and became more active during the third Greek program. As the programs progressed, the ESM gained areas of expertise, such as privatization or engagement with financial markets. While its main function still is to provide funds in exchange for reforms and thus secure its member states' interests concerning debt sustainability in program countries, the ESM has developed somewhat of an institutional character. Its managing director is invited to informal talks with the ECON committee of the EP and joins the Eurogroup press conferences. In addition, the ESM joins country missions and engages in central aspects of the programs and socio-economic governance of EMU with the European Commission (see 7.2). Hence, in its role as a reform-enabling institution, it is able to set its own priorities (in consultation with its member states).

In the Irish case, the financial assistance program was often described as being helpful in allowing the Irish government to implement unpopular policies and to stay on its reform path. In this case, the EFSF/ESM clearly enabled structural reforms that were in the interest of the institutions and the government (see chapter 6). In the Greek case, the financial assistance program was predominantly a tool to implement a reform program based on external organizations, with comparatively less influence by the Greek government. Here, the EFSF/ESM enabled reforms that were predominantly in the interest of its member states, whereas the interest of the successive Greek governments would have suggested a reform path adjusted to the country's specific socio-economic context (see chapter 5). Hence, the ESM's role as a structural adjustment enabler has certainly depended on the political and economic circumstances of financial assistance.

The crisis of the euro area is a key research topic in political economic research. Its influence on institutional, political, and economic developments of EMU and the European Union has been the focus of attention for several scholars. However, as the state of research discussed in the introduction highlights, the ESM, as a new institution, has only been included in a small number of articles and research projects. In addition, political economic research on the euro crisis has highlighted the differences between EMU's socio-economic models, but focused less on changes to existing varieties of capitalism in the member states. The book thus contributes to two central fields in political economic research.

First, it provided a thorough analysis of the establishment, development, and future perspectives of the European Stability Mechanism.

The book assessed the influence of the ESM on financial assistance in the euro area during the euro crisis and provided insights into its future role. In concluding that the establishment of the EFSF and the ESM strengthened the role of the Eurogroup in EMU's economic governance and thus provided the ESM with influence on central program operations, we are able to put further focus on the ESM beyond the prevailing analysis regarding it solely as an instrument for providing financial resources. The analysis here has shown that the ESM has significant effects on economic governance in the euro area at times of crisis. It is reasonable to predict that there will be new socio-economic crises in the euro area. The analysis provided in this book contributes to our understanding of the ESM's role in such processes and offers a rationale for why countries like Italy might be hesitant to apply for financial support from the ESM.

Second, the book adds to our understanding of socio-economic diversity in the euro area. As argued above, the state of research primarily focuses on the influence of socio-economic differences between member states in the emergence of the euro crisis (Scharpf 2018; Streeck 2013a). Furthermore, political economists have argued to great length whether the euro area can combine different varieties of capitalism (Johnston 2016; Johnston and Regan 2016; Regan 2017). Institutional change as a consequence of the euro crisis, however, has remained underexposed by political economists. This is understandable given that a key assumption of the varieties of capitalism approach is the stability of socio-economic models (Hall and Soskice 2001; Schmidt 2002). However, as the analysis provided in this book highlights, financial assistance in the euro area can enable institutional change and thereby change member states' socio-economic models. Policy conditionality, as supported by the ESM, thus proves to be a powerful instrument. Future research on socio-economic diversity should therefore put additional emphasis on institutional changes of key economic institutions.

Nonetheless, more research should be conducted to advance the empirical analysis provided by this research project. To keep the analysis manageable, it had to focus on two program countries and two central policy fields. Research on the influence of the EFSF/ESM on other program countries should be conducted in order to generalize the project's results. Portugal and Cyprus would be very interesting cases, as their socio-economic institutional settings prior to the crisis were closer to the Greek model. However, both countries experienced different developments than Greece did. In addition, including more policy fields in the analysis would be worthwhile in order to assess if institutional change in the countries' socio-economic models is taking place in other policy fields as well. As the euro area is currently experiencing a health crisis, research on the program's influence on health sectors would be very interesting indeed.

The analysis points to a number of perspectives for future research projects. Researching the ESM's developing working relationship with the European Commission on central aspects of financial assistance programs would be a worthwhile project after the current EMU reform has been concluded (see 8.1). Furthermore, one could conduct research on how the Eurogroup discusses ESM matters and executes its central position in the ESM's governing bodies. While both of these aspects were not central to the research objective of this book, they would certainly pick up on central results of this analysis.

In addition, it should be very interesting to analyse the ESM's role in the current COVID-19 pandemic, the effects of NextGenerationEU on its competences, and its future influence on socio-economic governance in times of severe asymmetric fiscal stress (see 8.2). Lastly, the ESM's conduct and influence on financial markets would prove to be a worthwhile future research project. As argued in the analysis above, the ESM manages almost 80 billion euro of paid-in contributions and engages with financial markets in order to leverage contributions of up to 500 billion. Finally, the ESM will be included in the Single Resolution Fund as a common backstop, which should garner it additional attention on the part of financial institutions.

List of Interviews

No.	Interview partner	Place	Date
1	Business association official	Skype call	12 October 2017
2	Policy advisor	Skype call	20 February 2018
3	Civil servant	Athens	4 March 2018
4	Policy advisor	Athens	5 March 2018
5	Former member of the Greek cabinet	Athens	7 March 2018
6	Policy advisor	Athens	7 March 2018
7	Trade union official	Athens	8 March 2018
8	Trade union official	Athens	9 March 2018
9	Member of the Hellenic Parliament	Skype call	9 March 2018
10	Former member of the Greek cabinet	Athens	12 March 2018
11	Business association official	Athens	12 March 2018
12	Party official	Athens	12 March 2018
13	Policy advisor	Dublin	12 April 2018
14	Trade union official	Dublin	12 April 2018
15	Civil servant	Dublin	13 April 2018
16	Trade union official	Dublin	16 April 2018
17	Trade union official	Dublin	16 April 2018
18	Civil servant	Dublin	17 April 2018
19	Business association official	Dublin	17 April 2018
20	Civil servant	Dublin	18 April 2018
21	Irish senator	Dublin	18 April 2018
22	Civil servant	Dublin	19 April 2018
25	European Commission official	Brussels	9 July 2018
26	Member of European Parliament	Brussels	10 July 2018
30	European Stability Mechanism official	Luxembourg	24 July 2018
31	European Stability Mechanism official	Skype call	29 July 2018
32	European Stability Mechanism official	Skype call	1 August 2018

List of Documents, Greek Case

Title	Date	Published by
The Economic Adjustment Programme for Greece	May 2010	European Commission
The Economic Adjustment Programme for Greece, First Review – Summer 2010	August 2010	European Commission
The Economic Adjustment Programme for Greece, Second Review – Autumn 2010	December 2010	European Commission
The Economic Adjustment Programme for Greece, Third Review – Winter 2011	February 2011	European Commission
The Economic Adjustment Programme for Greece, Fourth Review – Spring 2011	July 2011	European Commission
The Economic Adjustment Programme for Greece, Fifth Review – October 2011	October 2011	European Commission
The Second Economic Adjustment Programme for Greece	March 2012	European Commission
The Second Economic Adjustment Programme for Greece, First Review – December 2012	December 2012	European Commission
The Second Economic Adjustment Programme for Greece, Second Review – May 2013	May 2013	European Commission
The Second Economic Adjustment Programme for Greece, Third Review – July 2013	July 2013	European Commission
The Second Economic Adjustment Programme for Greece, Fourth Review – April 2014	April 2014	European Commission
Memorandum of Understanding between the European Commission acting on behalf of the European Stability Mechanism and the Hellenic Republic and the Bank of Greece	August 2015	European Commission
Financial Assistance Facility Agreement	August 2015	European Commission
Compliance Report: The Third Economic Adjustment Programme for Greece, First Review – June 2016	June 2016	European Commission

(*Continued*)

Title	Date	Published by
Compliance Report: The Third Economic Adjustment Programme for Greece, Second Review – June 2017	June 2017	European Commission
Supplemental Memorandum of Understanding: Greece. Third Review of the ESM Programme, 18 January 2018	January 2018	European Commission
Compliance Report: The Third Economic Adjustment Programme for Greece, Third Review – March 2018	March 2018	European Commission
Greece: Technical Memorandum of Understanding: Accompanying the MoU of the ESM programme	January 2018	European Commission
Compliance Report: The Third Economic Adjustment Programme for Greece, Fourth Review – July 2018	July 2018	European Commission
Commission Implementing Decision on the activation of enhanced surveillance for Greece	July 2018	European Commission

List of Documents, Irish Case

Title	Date	Published by
The National Plan for Recovery	November 2010	Republic of Ireland
Letter of Intent, Memorandum of Economic and Financial Policies, and Technical Memorandum of Understanding	December 2010	Republic of Ireland
The Economic Adjustment Programme for Ireland	February 2011	European Commission
The Economic Adjustment Programme for Ireland, Spring 2011 Review	May 2011	European Commission
Economic Adjustment Programme for Ireland, Summer 2011 Review	September 2011	European Commission
Economic Adjustment Programme for Ireland, Autumn 2011 Review	December 2011	European Commission
Economic Adjustment Programme for Ireland, Winter 2011 Review	March 2012	European Commission
Economic Adjustment Programme for Ireland, Spring 2012 Review	June 2012	European Commission
Economic Adjustment Programme for Ireland, Summer 2012 Review	September 2012	European Commission
Economic Adjustment Programme for Ireland, Autumn 2012 Review	January 2013	European Commission
Economic Adjustment Programme for Ireland, Winter 2012 Review	April 2013	European Commission
Economic Adjustment Programme for Ireland, Spring 2013 Review	July 2013	European Commission
Economic Adjustment Programme for Ireland, Summer 2013 Review	October 2013	European Commission
Economic Adjustment Programme for Ireland, Autumn 2013 Review	December 2013	European Commission

(Continued)

Title	Date	Published by
Post-Programme Surveillance for Ireland, Spring 2014 Report	June 2014	European Commission
Post-Programme Surveillance for Ireland, Autumn 2014 Report	January 2015	European Commission
Post-Programme Surveillance for Ireland, Spring 2015 Report	July 2015	European Commission
Ex post Evaluation of the Economic Adjustment Programme Ireland, 2010–2013	July 2015	European Commission
Post-Programme Surveillance for Ireland, Autumn 2015 Report	January 2016	European Commission
Post-Programme Surveillance for Ireland, Spring 2016 Report	September 2016	European Commission
Post-Programme Surveillance for Ireland, Autumn 2016 Report	March 2017	European Commission
Post-Programme Surveillance for Ireland, Spring 2017 Report	July 2017	European Commission

Notes

Epigraph

1 *Rocky II*, dir. Sylvester Stallone (Los Angeles: Chartoff-Winkler Productions, 1979).

Chapter 1

1 For an overview of how a narrative developed around the euro crisis being caused by fiscal profligacy in the periphery, see Matthijs and McNamara (2015).

Chapter 2

1 This is further mirrored by empirical research, such as Schneider and Panescu (2012).
2 Schmidt (2002) did not use coordinated market economies, liberal market economies, or mixed-market economies as names for her ideal-types. Instead Schmidt refered to managed capitalism, market capitalism, and state capitalism. However, she refers to similar cases as other scholars. Table 2.1 therefore includes the names of Schmidt's typology.
3 While the ESM was created outside of EU law, financial assistance is restricted to members of EMU (see also chapter 4).

Chapter 3

1 The 232 variables include central data on 11 issues: "Rights (6); Wage Setting (21); Social Pacts, Agreements and Social Dialogue (29), Works Councils and employee representation in the enterprise (4); Sectoral institutions and employer organization (4); Number, names and membership

of confederations and unions (31); Union density and bargaining coverage (19); membership shares and divisions between/within confederations (15); activities and statutory powers of confederation and unions (20); indicators of union concentration and centralization (6); membership composition and union density by categories (79)" (Visser 2019a, 1–2).

2 LABREF includes data on (1) labour taxation, (2) unemployment benefits, (3) other welfare-related benefits, (4) active labour market policies, (5) job protection legislation, (6) disability and early retirement schemes, (7) wage bargaining, (8) working time organization, (9) immigration, and (10) mobility (European Commission 2022b).

3 COFOG data separates government expenditure into 10 functions: (1) general public services, (2) defence, (3) public order and safety, (4) economic affairs, (5) environmental protection, (6) housing and community amenities, (7) health, (8) recreation, culture and religion, (9) education, and (10) social protection (Eurostat 2019).

4 The OECD's Indicators on Product Market Regulation include several variables indicating the government's role in economic governance and market regulation. For this project, variables related to public ownership, such as (1) scope of state-owned enterprises, (2) government involvement in network sectors, (3) command and control regulation, and (4) involvement in business administration (OECD 2018a), have been chosen for analysis of the state's role in economic affairs.

5 SPSS is an acronym that stands for sammeln, prüfen, sortieren, subsumieren, which is German for collect, check, sort by, and subsume (Helfferich 2011).

6 During the selection process, a decision between the different EMU cases had to be made to make the comparative case analysis manageable. Of the five countries, three were particularly interesting: Ireland, Portugal, and Greece. Spain's financial assistance program is different from the other cases as it used the indirect bank recapitalization instrument, which did not come with a full structural adjustment program. Therefore, using Spain as a case for institutional change in the dependent variable (socio-economic models) is not a fruitful option. Cyprus is an interesting case of a mixed-market economy developing severe balance of payment problems during the euro crisis. However, the Cypriot case is less prominent and includes developmental aspects that give less fruitful material to answer the research question of this study. Lastly, Portugal would have been a perfect case for this study, either in a comparative case study with Ireland or with Greece. However, to make a comparative case study between two different VoCs in order to analyse converging trends, Ireland as the only LME case had to be included. Furthermore, the Greek case was selected because of its empirical richness as an MME receiving

European financial assistance over a long period of time. Thus, Portugal was not included in the comparative case analysis although it is an interesting case nonetheless.

7 For a critical analysis of the Irish recovery, see Regan (2014), Brazys and Regan (2017), and Roche, O'Connell, and Prothero (2017b).

Chapter 4

1 Despite being located outside of EU law, the ESM's legality under EU law has been discussed in EU and national case law. In *Pringle v. the Government of Ireland*, the European Court of Justice ruled that providing financial assistance is compatible with Article 125 of the Treaty on the Functioning of the EU (TFEU) (Court of Justice of the European Union 2012). The German Constitutional Court ruled in 2014 that the ESM does not affect the German budgetary autonomy (European Parliament 2018, 1).

2 As Verdun (2002, 58) argues, in the 1970s there were already discussions between economists and monetarists concerning EMU. Hence, there is no clear dichotomy between the 1970s and 1990s in terms of economic thought. Rather, the description of the 1970s as Keynesian and the 1990s as monetarist describe the predominant economic schools of the time.

3 The Werner Group included "Central Banks Governors, the chairmen of the Short and Medium-Term Economic Policy, Monetary and Budgetary Policy Committees, as well as a representative of the European Commission" (Verdun 2002, 57).

4 While there is a small passage in the appendix which argues that monetary unions generally have centralized budgets (written by Alexandre Lamfalussy, according to Mody [2018, 84]), creating large fiscal instruments for the single currency is deliberately not an objective of the Delors Report (Committee for the Study of Economic and Monetary Union 1989).

5 The IMF did not publicly announce this participation. However, the IMF managing director (at that time Dominique Strauß-Kahn) argued that the IMF's participation, on a country-by-country basis, would be in proportion to its previous European engagements, where the IMF participated with one third of the costs (International Monetary Fund 2010). Since the EU put up 500 billion euro in total, the IMF's participation in the safety net was assumed to be 250 billion euro (European Stability Mechanism 2019c, 53).

6 The Single Resolution Fund is an essential part of the European Single Resolution Mechanism, one of the key components of the European Banking Union. The Single Resolution Fund is supposed to provide

financial support for financial institutions in times of severe crisis. The Single Resolution Fund, however, is only supposed to be used for financial institutions that are under resolution. Its funding comes from the financial sector itself and has been paid in from 2016 to 2023. Each institution's contribution depends on the size of and potential risks to the financial institution (Single Resolution Board 2021). The backstop, which the ESM is supposed to provide – a role that the ESM itself argued for (e.g., European Stability Mechanism 2020) – is an additional fund which can be activated in times of severe crisis of the financial sector. If activated, the backstop would provide additional funding to support the tasks of the Single Resolution Fund (Single Resolution Board 2021).

7 For more detailed accounts of the participation of parliaments in ESM governance, see Kreilinger (2019) and Höing (2015).

8 In total, the ESM's lending toolbox includes six instruments: (1) loans within a macroeconomic adjustment program; (2) indirect bank recapitalization; (3) direct bank recapitalization; (4) primary market purchases of bonds and debt securities; (5) secondary market purchases of bonds and debt securities; and (6) precautionary credit lines, of which two versions are available, Precautionary Conditioned Credit Lines and Enhanced Conditions Credit Lines (European Stability Mechanism 2012). Of the six instruments, only two have been used: loans within a macroeconomic adjustment program for Greece, Ireland, Portugal, and Cyprus; and indirect bank recapitalization for Spain. The other instruments remain unused and were subjects of the ESM reform debates in 2017 and 2018 (Eurogroup 2018b).

9 The ESM Treaty does not include criteria for sustainable sovereign debt (European Stability Mechanism 2012). After the ESM was formally established, it started to develop its own debt sustainability assessment, which differs from the criteria of the IMF. The differences of their debt sustainability assessment became visible in the third Greek financial assistance program (2015–18). The IMF argued for a haircut of Greek debt because from the IMF's perspective, Greek sovereign debt was not sustainable. The ESM, however, argued that Greek sovereign debt was sustainable, and no haircut was needed. In the end, the EU focused on the ESM's assessment. As a consequence, the IMF did not participate financially in the third Greek program.

Chapter 5

1 For a theoretical perspective on mixed-market economies, see 2.1.3.

2 Signing and ratifying the Fiscal Compact and thus implementing EMU's new fiscal framework is a central precondition of the application for an ESM program (see 5.4.1).

3 Health sector expenditure reductions were an issue of international criticism within the financial assistance to Greece because they had an immediate negative effect on public health (Stuckler and Basu 2013, 77–94).

4 The fiscal governance database is an index provided by the European Commission, which includes several fiscal rules, e.g., rules on expenditure and revenue, as well as debt and the budgetary process at different levels of government (European Commission 2022a).

5 As Hadjimichalis argued, "The experience of Treuhand has inspired the founding and the operation of the HRADF in Greece" (Hadjimichalis 2014, 504). The Treuhandanstalt was a trust agency created in Germany in 1990 in order to privatize publicly owned enterprises in the former German Democratic Republic.

6 The third MoU stipulated that the previous objective of achieving 50 billion euro via privatizing state assets, state-owned enterprises, and economic participation stayed intact. However, only the first 25 billion euro had to be exclusively used for loan repayments. Of the second 25 billion euro, 50 per cent could be used for investment (12.5 billion euro), while the second 50 per cent was to be used to reduce sovereign debt (European Commission 2015e, 29).

7 An unnamed PASOK minister was quoted by Papadopoulos in the newspaper *To Vima*, saying: "We have not made any kind of preparatory work. Just at the last minute we have copied and pasted isolated segments from earlier Letters of Intent to the IMF by Turkey, Mexico or Hungary and hastily adapted them to synthesize the Greek Memorandum. […]. It's a bad compilation, a Frankenstein Memorandum" (Papadopoulos 2011, cited in Katrougalos 2013, 97).

8 Greece's traditionally adversarial industrial relations and class conflicts came into effect here as well. As an interview partner argued, public sector trade unions would not engage with the institutions, especially the IMF, as they regarded them as their "enemy" (Interview 7, 9 March 2018). Other interview partners argued that they did not have an influence on the MoUs but attested to the privileged influence of the industrialists' organization (SEV, Hellenic Federation of Enterprises) on the institutions (e.g., Interview 2, 20 February 2018; Interview 8, 9 March 2018; Interview 11, 12 March 2018).

9 The expert group agreed on twelve recommendations that focused on strengthening institutional settings of collective actions, making stricter rules for collective dismissals and short-time work regulations, setting minimum wages, and organizing collective bargaining (Expert Group for the Review of Greek Labour Market Institutions 2016, 4–5). The group, however, was unable to agree on all recommendations and thus drew up two recommendation reports, including a minority vote against parts

of the recommendations (Expert Group for the Review of Greek Labour Market Institutions 2016, 45–58).

10 In the summer of 2015, at the height of the political turmoil between the newly elected Greek government on the one side and the other euro area members on the other side, 65 per cent of Greek citizens agreed that the euro was a good thing for their country, while only 25 per cent agreed that the euro was a bad thing (European Commission 2015b, 8).

11 The continuous existence of the EGSEE despite it having less political influence is a prime example.

12 The report includes recommendations for collective action, collective bargaining, collective dismissal rules, and minimum wages (Expert Group for the Review of Greek Labour Market Institutions 2016, 4–5).

13 According to Jones, the Frankfurt-Brussels Consensus commits euro area members to fiscal discipline, low inflation, competitiveness, and little governmental economic activity. These principles have been shaping the EU since Maastricht and appear to define the current EMU paradigm (Jones 2013).

14 The policy measures have been widely criticized for being one-sided and for not taking the Greek socio-economic foundations into consideration. IMF economists, according to Mody, were convinced that early debt relief and fiscal consolidation less focused on expenditure reductions would have led to better program results in Greece (Mody 2018, 262) The IMF argued that there were mistakes made in the Greek financial assistance program (International Monetary Fund 2013, 1; see also Spanou 2020, 143), which, from perspectives within the IMF, largely revolved around questions of growth forecasts and wrong fiscal multipliers for the Greek case (e.g., Blanchard and Leigh 2013). However, as Spanou argued, "the 'policy mix' was never really questioned" (Spanou 2020, 143). Differences among the institutions, at least at the beginning of providing financial assistance for Greece, was more of degree, rather than of kind.

Chapter 6

1 For a critical analysis of the poster child image of Ireland see Roche, O'Connell, and Prothero 2017b; Donovan and Murphy 2013; Brazys and Regan 2017.

2 According to Kinsella, the Irish economy was overly dependent on the construction sector. In 2006, it represented 24 per cent of GDP. The EU average was 12 per cent. Thirteen per cent of all workers worked in the

construction sector. Furthermore, the construction sector accounted for 18 per cent of Irish tax revenues (Kinsella 2012, 225).

3 If the Irish government had not paid 64 billion euro in order to bailout its banking sector, the deficit of the Irish government would have been considerably lower. As McArdle has analysed, the deficit would have developed as follows: 2009: 11 per cent; 2010: 11 per cent; 2011: 9 per cent (McArdle 2012, 3).

4 The national tripartite negotiations included Ibec on the employers' side and ICTU for the trade unions (Wallace et al. 2013, 284–95). Negotiations of the social pacts furthermore included civil society organizations (O'Connell 2019, 179). Leading business organizations for small and medium enterprises, such as ISME, generally were not included in the negotiations and criticized them as negative for small businesses (Wallace et al. 2013, 78, 289).

5 The first national social pact in 1987 was created to preserve the Irish economy's cost competitiveness. It included wage moderation in an exchange for income tax reductions. In the subsequent national social pacts, more policy fields were included. The national social pacts thus became central socio-economic plans which were supported by key social partners (O'Connell 2019, 179).

6 Regan argues that the Irish labour market is divided in four parts: (1) the public sector and semi-state economy, which is highly organized by trade unions; (2) Irish industrial, banking, and manufacturing spheres, which are covered by sectoral agreements and have higher unionization rates; (3) the multinational firm sector, which is non-unionized and covers approximately 15 per cent of the Irish labour force; and (4) small and medium enterprises reliant on domestic demand, which are non-unionized and predominantly without sectoral agreements or specific minimum standards above the legal minimum (Regan 2012b, 13–14).

7 In 2010, the Irish government and the public sector trade unions concluded the Public Service Agreement (2010–14, "Croke Park Agreement"). It was followed by the Public Service Stability Agreement (2013–20, "Haddington Road Agreement"/"Landsdowne Road Agreement") (O'Connell 2019, 180).

8 Agricultural workers, catering, contract cleaning, hairdressing, hotels, retail and groceries, security (Citizen Information Board 2019).

9 *Pathways to Work* is a broad strategy that is based on several activation programs implemented during the Memorandum of Understanding, including JobBridge, Jobpath, Job Initiative, and Tus (Murphy and Mercille 2019, 30).

10 In December 2010, Ireland had injected 29.3 billion euro in total into the Anglo Irish Bank, 7.3 billion euro in total into the Allied Irish Bank, 3.5 billion euro in total into the Bank of Ireland, 5.4 billion euro in total into

the Irish Nationwide Building Society, as well as 0.9 billion euro into the
EBS Building Society (European Commission 2011e, 15).

11 The IFAC's central publication is the Fiscal Assessment Report, which
is published twice per year: in the autumn after the Irish budget is presented and in spring in line with the Stability Programme update (Irish
Fiscal Advisory Council 2019a). In addition, the IFAC published state-
ments before the budget and budgetary role compliance reports and provides a set of analytical reports (Irish Fiscal Advisory Council 2019b).

12 As Kopits has argued, the IFAC can be seen as a positive development
in creating a sustainable fiscal environment in Ireland. However, its resources are limited: "By any standard, the annual funding of €800.000 is
inadequate for this purpose" (Kopits 2014, 144).

13 The fiscal governance database is an index provided by the European
Commission, which includes diverse fiscal rules, e.g., rules on expenditure and revenue, as well as debt and the budgetary process on different
levels of government (European Commission 2022a).

14 The Review Group included Colm McCarthy (School of Economics,
University College Dublin, chair of the Review Group), Donal McNally
(Department of Finance), and Alan Mathews (Department of Economics,
Trinity College). The group received forty-five submissions by government departments, commercial state bodies, and interested parties, and
met with a diverse group of experts, stakeholders, and delegations (Review Group on State Assets and Liabilities 2011, 1, 176–7).

15 In line with the program, the Irish government announced in February
2012 that it would privatise Bord Gáis, a central energy provider, as well
as non-strategic parts of the predominantly state-owned Electric Supply
Board. In addition, the Irish government privatized its 20 per cent shares
of Aer Lingus (McGee 2012).

16 As an interview partner highlighted, the implementation of sanctions on
unemployed workers was a topic that was regularly brought up by the
institutions, especially the European Commission, during mission meetings with the Irish government (Interview 22, 19 April 2018).

17 The "Report of Independent Review of Employment Regulation Orders and
Registered Employment Agreement Wage Setting Mechanisms" was published in 2011 (Duffy and Walsh 2011). Publicly known as the Duffy/Walsh
Report, it concluded that sectoral wage-setting arrangements needed a
strong overhaul in order to facilitate adjustments to economic circumstances.

18 The Fine Gael-Labour government from 2011 to 2016 did enable gradual
changes to the direction of labour market reforms. A lot of the changes in
direction had their origin in Labour's election campaign, which focused
on the slogan "Frankfurt's way or Labour's way" (Laffan 2017, 185).
Labour campaigned to renegotiate the financial assistance program with

the EU and the IMF, but only in changes of degree and not of kind. The Fine Gael-Labour government reversed the cut to the national minimum wage and implemented new legislation for sectoral minimum standards (see 7.2.1.1). However, as Fine Gael campaigned to further accelerate structural adjustments in labour markets and activation policy (Fine Gael 2011, 55–6), the Irish Labour Party saw it as a success to be able to tone down the reform agenda, according to an interview partner (Interview 21, 18 April 2018).

19 In the 2012 autumn review of the program, the institutions underline the centrality of expenditure in their approach: "The programme [...] targeted a very significant reduction in nominal expenditure relative to their 2010 level as a key component of the fiscal consolidation. This was underpinned by the multi-annual expenditure ceilings for gross voted expenditure introduced on administrative levels" (European Commission 2013a, 30).

20 The documents do not provide strong empirical cases to support this claim.

21 It is speculative to argue whether the outcome might have been different if the Irish National Plan for Recovery had differed from the dominant adjustment paradigm. However, based on the data analysed for this project, it appears to be unlikely that the negotiations between the Irish government and the institutions would have resulted in a program that was largely based on the Irish proposal.

22 Interview partners described the ECB to be a driving force of fiscal adjustments. Whereas the IMF was described as interested in meeting the fiscal targets and the European Commission was focused on achieving the goals set by a council recommendation, the ECB pushed for stronger fiscal adjustments and quicker implementations (Interview 18, 17 April 2018).

23 Ireland was the first country to receive financial support through the temporary EFSF in 2010–11. Although the ESM effectively took over the operations of the EFSF after it was established, Ireland received an EFSF program, to be precise.

Chapter 7

1 After the Greek legislative elections in July 2019, New Democracy won a majority in the Hellenic Parliament. The newly elected ND government did not push for reversing labour market reforms put forward as part of the financial assistance programs during the period analysed in this book.

Chapter 8

1 In the early discussions of an EMF, institutional support for market mechanisms, market discipline, and the possibility of a structured sovereign default were key aspects of the proposals.
2 The New Hanseatic League is a group of EU member states, led particularly by the Netherlands, which came together after Brexit to coordinate their positions concerning European economic and fiscal policy coordination, particularly concerning EMU (Verdun 2021, 4). While their individual positions certainly differ, a common denominator of their policy preferences is a rejection of deeper economic and fiscal integration as well as a reluctance to give the European Commission additional competences. The New Hanseatic League was particularly vocal from 2018 to early 2020 during the EMU reform debate (see also 8.1).

Works Cited

Abels, Joscha. 2018a. "Ein Europa der Finanzministerien? Die Eurogruppe im Projekt der Restrukturierung der Eurozone." *PROKLA*, no. 192: 399–416. https://doi.org/10.32387/prokla.v48i192.905.

– 2018b. "Power behind the Curtain: The Eurogroup's Role in the Crisis and the Value of Informality in Economic Governance." *European Politics and Society* 20, no. 5: 519–34. https://doi.org/10.1080/23745118.2018. 1542774.

– 2019. "Machtzentrum hinter dem Vorhang: Die informelle Eurogruppe und ihre erneuerte Rolle im Euroregime." In *Neue Segel, alter Kurs?*, edited by Hans-Jürgen Bieling and Simon Guntrum, 83–108. Wiesbaden: Springer Fachmedien Wiesbaden.

Altvater, Elmar. 2013. "Der politische Euro: Eine Gemeinschaftswährung ohne Gemeinschaft hat keine Zukunft." *Blätter für deutsche und internationale Politik* (May): 71–9.

Amable, Bruno. 2003. *The Diversity of Modern Capitalism*. Oxford: Oxford University Press.

Amable, Bruno, Aidan Regan, Sabina Avdagic, Lucio Baccaro, Jonas Pontusson, and Natascha Van der Zwan. 2019. "New Approaches to Political Economy." *Socio-Economic Review* 17, no. 2 (April): 433–59. https://doi.org/10.1093/ser /mwz002.

Armingeon, K., and L. Baccaro. 2012. "Political Economy of the Sovereign Debt Crisis: The Limits of Internal Devaluation." *Industrial Law Journal* 41, no. 3: 254–75. https://doi.org/10.1093/indlaw/dws029.

Armingeon, Klaus, Kai Guthmann, and David Weisstanner. 2016. "Choosing the Path of Austerity: How Parties and Policy Coalitions Influence Welfare State Retrenchment in Periods of Fiscal Consolidation." *West European Politics* 39, no. 4: 628–47. https://doi.org/10.1080/01402382.2015.1111072.

Armstrong, Kenneth A. 2013. "The New Governance of EU Fiscal Discipline." The Jean Monnet Center of the NYU School of Law, Working Paper Series,

no. 29. https://jeanmonnetprogram.org/wp-content/uploads/2014/12
/Armstrong.pdf.

Baccaro, Lucio, and Chris Howell. 2011. "A Common Neoliberal Trajectory:
The Transformation of Industrial Relations in Advanced Capitalism." *Politics
& Society* 39, no. 4: 521–63. https://doi.org/10.1177/0032329211420082.

Baccaro, Lucio, and Chris Howell. 2017a. *Trajectories of Neoliberal Transformation:
European Industrial Relations since the 1970s.* Cambridge: Cambridge
University Press.

– 2017b. "Unhinged: Industrial Relations Liberalization and Capitalist Instability."
MPIfG Discussion Paper, no. 19. https://econpapers.repec.org/paper
/zbwmpifgd/1719.htm.

Baccaro, Lucio, and Jonas Pontusson. 2016. "Rethinking Comparative Political
Economy: The Growth Model Perspective." *Politics & Society* 44, no. 2: 175–207.
https://doi.org/10.1177/0032329216638053.

Ban, Cornel. 2020. "Ben Clift's *The IMF and the Politics of Austerity.*" *Comparative
European Politics* 18: 78–84. https://doi.org/10.1057/s41295-018-0151-0.

Ban, Cornel, and Leonard Seabrooke. 2017. "From Crisis to Stability: How to Make
the European Stability Mechanism Transparent and Accountable?" Transparency
International. https://transparency.eu/wp-content/uploads/2017/03/ESM_
Report_DIGITAL-version.pdf.

Beach, Derek, and Rasmus Brun Pedersen. 2013. *Process-Tracing Methods: Foundations
and Guidelines.* Ann Arbor: University of Michigan Press.

Bearce, David H. 2009. "EMU: The Last Stand for the Policy Convergence
Hypothesis?" *Journal of European Public Policy* 16, no. 4: 582–600. https://doi
.org/10.1080/13501760902872700.

Becker, Uwe. 2009. *Open Varieties of Capitalism: Continuity, Change and Performance.*
New York: Palgrave Macmillan.

– 2014. "The Heterogeneity of Capitalism in Crisis-Ridden Europe." *Journal
of Contemporary European Studies* 22, no. 3: 261–75. https://doi.org/10.1080
/14782804.2014.937407.

Béland, Daniel. 2009. "Ideas, Institutions, and Policy Change." *Journal of European
Public Policy* 16, no. 5: 701–18. https://doi.org/10.1080/13501760902983382.

Béland, Daniel, and Alex Waddan. 2015. "Breaking Down Ideas and Institutions:
The Politics of Tax Policy in the U.S. and the U.K." *Policy Studies* 36, no. 2:
176–95. https://doi.org/10.1080/01442872.2014.1000845.

Beramendi, Pablo, Silja Häusermann, Herbert Kitschelt, and Hanspeter Kriesi,
eds. 2015. *The Politics of Advanced Capitalism.* Cambridge: Cambridge University
Press.

Bieling, Hans-Jürgen. 2011. "Vom Krisenmanagement zur neuen
Konsolidierungsagenda der EU." *PROKLA*, no. 161: 173–94. https://doi.org
/10.32387/prokla.v41i163.348.

– 2013. "Das Projekt der Euro-Rettung und die Widersprüche des europäischen Krisenkonstitutionalismus." *Zeitschrift für Internationale Beziehungen* 20, no. 1: 89–103. https://doi.org/10.5771/0946-7165-2013-1-89.

Bieling, Hans-Jürgen, and Daniel Buhr, eds. 2015. *Europäische Welten in der Krise: Arbeitsbeziehungen und Wohlfahrtsstaaten im Vergleich.* Frankfurt am Main: Campus.

Bieling, Hans-Jürgen, and Simon Guntrum, eds. 2019. *Neue Segel, alter Kurs? Die Eurokrise und ihre Folgen für das europäische Wirtschaftsregieren.* Wiesbaden: Springer VS.

Blanchard, Olivier, and Daniel Leigh. 2013. *Growth Forecast Errors and Fiscal Multipliers.* Washington: Internatonal Monetary Fund. https://www.imf.org/~/media/Websites/IMF/imported-full-text-pdf/external/pubs/ft/wp/2013/_wp1301.ashx.

Blyth, Mark. 2013. *Austerity: The History of a Dangerous Idea.* Oxford: Oxford University Press.

Bofinger, Peter. 2015. "German Wage Moderation and the EZ Crisis." VoxEU Column, CEPR. 30 November 2015. https://voxeu.org/article/german-wage-moderation-and-ez-crisis.

Brazys, Samuel, and Aidan Regan. 2017. "The Politics of Capitalist Diversity in Europe: Explaining Ireland's Divergent Recovery from the Euro Crisis." *Perspectives on Politics* 15, no. 2: 411–27. https://doi.org/10.1017/S1537592717000093.

Bruff, Ian. 2011. "What about the Elephant in the Room? Varieties of Capitalism, Varieties in Capitalism." *New Political Economy* 16, no. 4: 481–500. https://doi.org/10.1080/13563467.2011.519022.

Brunnermeier, Markus Konrad, Harold James, and Jean-Pierre Landau. 2016. *The Euro and the Battle of Ideas.* Princeton: Princeton University Press.

Buiter, Willem, and Ebrahim Rahbari. 2010. "Greece and the Fiscal Crisis in the Eurozone." VoxEU Column, CEPR, 12 October 2010. https://cepr.org/voxeu/columns/greece-and-fiscal-crisis-eurozone.

Busch, Klaus, Christoph Hermann, Karl Hinrichs, and Thorsten Schulten. 2012. "Eurokrise, Austeritätspolitik und das Europäische Sozialmodell: Wie die Krisenpolitik in Südeuropa die soziale Dimension der EU bedroht." FES Internationale Politikanalyse. https://library.fes.de/pdf-files/id/ipa/09444.pdf.

Buti, Marco, and Nicolas Carnot. 2012. "The EMU Debt Crisis: Early Lessons and Reforms: The EMU Debt Crisis." *JCMS: Journal of Common Market Studies* 50, no. 6: 899–911. https://doi.org/10.1111/j.1468-5965.2012.02288.x.

Cardiff, Kevin. 2020. "Ireland: Back to a Different Normal." In *The Political Economy of Adjustment throughout and beyond the Eurozone Crisis: What Have We Learned?*, edited by Francisco Torres García, Michele Chang, and Federico Steinberg, 94–121. London: Routledge, Taylor & Francis.

Carswell, Simon. 2015. "Lagarde Interview: Lessons Learned from Ireland's Crash." *Irish Times*, Dublin, 19 January 2015. https://www.irishtimes.com /business/economy/lagarde-interview-lessons-learned-from-ireland-s -crash-1.2068907.

Chasoglou, Jannis. 2015. "Griechenland: Umbau oder Abriss des Wohlfahrtsstaates?" In *Europäische Welten in der Krise: Arbeitsbeziehungen und Wohlfahrtsstaaten im Vergleich*, edited by Hans-Jürgen Bieling and Daniel Buhr, 243–72. Frankfurt am Main: Campus.

Citizen Information Board. 2019. "Joint Labour Committees." Last updated 23 November 2021. https://www.citizensinformation.ie/en/employment /employment_rights_and_conditions/industrial_relations_and_trade_unions /joint_labour_committees.html.

Clift, Ben. 2014. *Comparative Political Economy: States, Markets and Global Capitalism.* Basingstoke, UK: Palgrave Macmillan.

– 2018 *The IMF and the Politics of Austerity in the Wake of the Global Financial Crisis.* Oxford: Oxford University Press.

– 2020. "The IMF, the Eurozone and Global Financial Crises, and the Politics of Economic Ideas." *Comparative European Politics* 18, no. 1: 99–108. https:// doi.org/10.1057/s41295-018-0146-x.

Colasanti, Fabio. 2016. "Financial Assistance to Greece: Three Programmes." European Policy Centre Discussion Paper. 26 February 2016. https://www .epc.eu/en/Publications/Financial-assistance-to-Greece~2579c0.

Committee for the Study of Economic and Monetary Union. 1989. "Report on Economic and Monetary Union in the European Community." 17 April 1989. http://aei.pitt.edu/1007/1/monetary_delors.pdf.

Council of the European Union. 2015. "Council Implementing Decision on Granting Short-Term Union Financial Assistance to Greece." 17 July 2015. http://data.consilium.europa.eu/doc/document/ST-10991-2015-INIT/en/pdf.

Court of Justice of the European Union. 2012. Judgment in Case C-370/12 Thomas Pringle v Government of Ireland, Ireland, The Attorney General. http://curia.europa.eu/juris/document/document.jsf?docid=130381 &doclang=EN.

Crespy, Amandine, and Vivien A. Schmidt. 2017. "The EU's Economic Governance in 2016: Beyond Austerity?" In *Social Policy in the European Union: State of Play 2017*, edited by Bart Vanhercke, Sebastiano Sabato, and Denis Bouget, 99–114. Brussels: ETUI.

Crouch, Colin. 2005. *Capitalist Diversity and Change.* Oxford: Oxford University Press.

Culpepper, Pepper D., and Aidan Regan. 2014. "Why Don't Governments Need Trade Unions Anymore? The Death of Social Pacts in Ireland and Italy." *Socio-Economic Review* 12, no. 4: 723–45. https://doi.org/10.1093/ser /mwt028.

Darvas, Zsolt, and Olga Tschekassin. 2015. "Poor and under Pressure: The Social Impact of Europe's Fiscal Consolidation." Bruegel. 4 March 2015. http://bruegel.org/wp-content/uploads/imported/publications/Poor_and_under_pressure.pdf.

De Grauwe, Paul. 2012. "In Search of Symmetry in the Eurozone." CEPS Policy Brief, 268. https://papers.ssrn.com/sol3/papers.cfm?abstract_id=2060116.

De Grauwe, Paul, and Yuemei Ji. 2015. "Correcting for the Eurozone Design Failures: The Role of the ECB." *Journal of European Integration* 37, no. 7: 739–54. https://doi.org/10.1080/07036337.2015.1079370

Denmark/Estonia/Finland/Ireland/Latvia/Lithuania/The Netherlands/Sweden. 2018. "Finance ministers from Denmark, Estonia, Finland, Ireland, Latvia, Lithuania, the Netherlands and Sweden underline their shared views and values in the discussion on the architecture of the EMU." https://vm.fi/documents/10623/6305483/Position+EMU+Denmark+Estonia+Finland+Ireland+Latvia+Lithuania+the+Netherlands+and+Sweden.pdf.

Department of Finance. 2018. "Presentation at the Department of Finance." 18 April 2018. Department of Finance, Dublin, 2018.

Department of Public Expenditure and Reform. 2013. "Medium-Term Expenditure Framework: Application to Current Expenditure." Government of Ireland. 30 September 2013. https://circulars.gov.ie/pdf/circular/per/2013/15.pdf.

D'Erman, Valerie J., Daniel F. Schulz, Amy Verdun, and Dennis Zagermann. 2022. "The European Semester in the North and in the South: Domestic Politics and the Salience of EU-Induced Wage Reform in Different Growth Models." *JCMS: Journal of Common Market Studies* 60, no. 1: 21–39. https://doi.org/10.1111/jcms.13274.

D'Erman, Valerie, Jörg Haas, Daniel F. Schulz, and Amy Verdun. 2019. "Measuring Economic Reform Recommendations under the European Semester: 'One Size Fits All' or Tailoring to Member States?" *Journal of Contemporary European Research* 15, no. 2: 194–211. https://doi.org/10.30950/jcer.v15i2.999.

Dimoulas, Constantine, and Vassilis K. Fouskas. 2017. "Imperial Bondage: Austerity in Greece, 2008–2018." In *Austerity: A Journey to an Unknown Territory*, edited by Tim Griebel, Roland Sturm, and Thorsten Winkelmann, 191–212. Baden-Baden: Nomos.

Doherty, Michael. 2011. "It Must Have Been Love… but It's Over Now: The Crisis and Collapse of Social Partnership in Ireland." *Transfer: European Review of Labour and Research* 17, no. 3: 371–85. https://doi.org/10.1177/1024258911410803.

– 2016. "New Morning? Irish Labour Law Post-Austerity." *Dublin University Law Journal* 39, no. 1: 104–25. https://doi.org/10.2139/ssrn.2827256.

Donnelly, Shawn. 2018. *Power Politics, Banking Union and EMU: Adjusting Europe to Germany*. London: Routledge.

Donovan, Donal. 2016. "The IMF's Role in Ireland." IMF. Independent Evaluation Office of the IMF Background Paper, BP/16-02/04. http://www .ieo-imf.org/ieo/files/completedevaluations/EAC__BP_16-02_04__The _IMF_s_Role_in_Ireland%20v5.PDF.

Donovan, Donal, and Antoin E. Murphy. 2013. *The Fall of the Celtic Tiger: Ireland and the Euro Debt Crisis*. Oxford: Oxford University Press.

Duffy, Kevin, and Frank Walsh. 2011. "Report of Independent Review of Employment Regulation Orders and Registered Employment Agreement Wage Setting Mechanisms." Department of Jobs, Enterprise and Innovation. 30 April 2011. https://researchrepository.ucd.ie/entities/publication/58a700cb-bc42-4d24 -a952-05e8fb71cdcf/details.

Dukelow, Fiona. 2015. "'Pushing against an Open Door': Reinforcing the Neo-liberal Policy Paradigm in Ireland and the Impact of EU Intrusion." *Comparative European Politics* 13, no. 1: 93–111. https://doi.org/10.1057 /cep.2014.43.

– 2018. "No Longer 'Fit for Purpose'? Consolidation and Catch-Up in Irish Labour Market Policy." In *Labour Market Policies in the Era of Pervasive Austerity*, edited by Sotiria Theodoropoulou, 197–224. Bristol: Policy Press.

Dukelow, Fiona, and Mairéad Considine. 2014. "Between Retrenchment and Recalibration. The Impact of Austerity on the Irish Social Protection System." *Journal of Sociology & Social Welfare* 41, no. 2: 55–72. https://doi.org /10.15453/0191-5096.3950.

Dullien, Sebastian, and Ulrike Guérot. 2012. "The Long Shadow of Ordoliberalism." European Council on Foreign Relations. 27 July 2012. https://www.ecfr.eu /article/commentary_the_long_shadow_of_ordoliberalism.

Enderlein, Henrik. 2004. *Nationale Wirtschaftspolitik in der europäischen Währungsunion*. Frankfurt am Main: Campus.

– 2006. "Adjusting to EMU: The Impact of Supranational Monetary Policy on Domestic Fiscal and Wage-Setting Institutions." *European Union Politics* 7, no. 1: 113–40. https://doi.org/10.1177/1465116506060914.

Enderlein, Henrik, and Amy Verdun. 2009. "EMU's Teenage Challenge: What Have We Learned and Can We Predict from Political Science?" *Journal of European Public Policy* 16, no. 4: 490–507. https://doi.org/10.1080 /13501760902872106.

Euro Summit. 2018. "Euro Summit meeting (29 June 2018) – Statement." https:// www.consilium.europa.eu/media/35999/29-euro-summit-statement-en.pdf.

Eurogroup. 2010. "Statement by the Eurogroup." Brussels, 2 May 2010. https://www.consilium.europa.eu/media/25673/20100502-eurogroup _statement_greece.pdf.

Eurogroup. 2018a. "Letter by Eurogroup President Mário Centeno to European Council President Donald Tusk ahead of the Euro Summit of 29 June 2018." Brussels, 25 June 2018. https://www.consilium.europa.eu/media/35798 /2018-06-25-letter-president-centeno-to-president-tusk.pdf.

Eurogroup. 2018b. "Term Sheet on the European Stability Mechanism Reform." https://www.consilium.europa.eu/media/37267/esm-term-sheet-041218 _final_clean.pdf.

Eurogroup. 2020. "Report on the Comprehensive Economic Policy Response to the COVID-19 Pandemic." 9 April 2020. https://www.consilium.europa .eu/en/press/press-releases/2020/04/09/report-on-the-comprehensive -economic-policy-response-to-the-covid-19-pandemic/.

European Central Bank. 2018. "Opinion of the European Central Bank of 11 April 2018 on a Proposal for a Regulation on the Establishment of the European Monetary Fund." https://eur-lex.europa.eu/legal-content/EN /TXT/PDF/?uri=CELEX:52018AB0020&from=PL.

European Commission. n.d. "EU Financial Assistance." https://economy-finance .ec.europa.eu/eu-financial-assistance_en

– 1975. "Report of the Study Group 'Economic and Monetary Union 1980.'" https://www.cvce.eu/content/publication/2010/10/27/93d25b61-6148 -453d-9fa7-9e220e874dc5/publishable_en.pdf.

– 1977. "Report of the Study Group on the Role of Public Finance in European Integration (The MacDougall Report)." Commission of the European Communities. http://ec.europa.eu/archives/emu_history/documentation /chapter8/19770401en73macdougallrepvol1.pdf.

– 2010a. "Council Regulation (EU) No 407/2010 of 11 May 2010 Establishing a European Financial Stabilisation Mechanism." *Official Journal of the European Union* 53 (May): 1–4. http://eur-lex.europa.eu/legal-content/EN/TXT /PDF/?uri=CELEX:32010R0407&from=EN.

– 2010b. *The Economic Adjustment Programme for Greece*. Brussels: European Commission. https://ec.europa.eu/economy_finance/publications /occasional_paper/2010/pdf/ocp61_en.pdf.

– 2010c. *The Economic Adjustment Programme for Greece. Second Review – Autumn 2010*. Brussels: European Commission. https://ec.europa.eu/economy _finance/publications/occasional_paper/2010/pdf/ocp72_en.pdf.

– 2011a. "EFSF Framework Agreement." https://www.esm.europa.eu/sites /default/files/20111019_efsf_framework_agreement_en.pdf.

– 2011b. *The Economic Adjustment Programme for Greece. Fifth Review – October 2011*. Brussels: European Commission. https://ec.europa.eu/economy _finance/publications/occasional_paper/2011/pdf/ocp87_en.pdf.

– 2011c. *The Economic Adjustment Programme for Greece. Fourth Review – Spring 2011*. Brussels: European Commission. https://ec.europa.eu/economy _finance/publications/occasional_paper/2011/pdf/ocp82_en.pdf.

– 2011d. *The Economic Adjustment Programme for Greece. Third Review – Winter 2011*. Brussels: European Commission. https://ec.europa.eu/economy_finance/publications/occasional_paper/2011/pdf/ocp77_en.pdf.
– 2011e. *The Economic Adjustment Programme for Ireland*. Brussels: European Commission. https://ec.europa.eu/economy_finance/publications/occasional_paper/2011/pdf/ocp76_en.pdf.
– 2011f. *Economic Adjustment Programme for Ireland, Autumn 2011 Review*. Brussels: European Commission. https://ec.europa.eu/economy_finance/publications/occasional_paper/2011/pdf/ocp88_en.pdf.
– 2011g. *The Economic Adjustment Programme for Ireland, Spring 2011 Review*. Brussels: European Commission. https://ec.europa.eu/economy_finance/publications/occasional_paper/2011/pdf/ocp78_en.pdf.
– 2011h. *Economic Adjustment Programme for Ireland, Summer 2011 Review*. Brussels: European Commission. https://ec.europa.eu/economy_finance/publications/occasional_paper/2011/pdf/ocp84_en.pdf.
– 2012a. *Economic Adjustment Programme for Ireland, Spring 2012 Review*. Brussels: European Commission. https://ec.europa.eu/economy_finance/publications/occasional_paper/2012/pdf/ocp96_en.pdf.
– 2012b. *Economic Adjustment Programme for Ireland, Summer 2012 Review*. Brussels: European Commission. https://ec.europa.eu/economy_finance/publications/occasional_paper/2012/pdf/ocp115_en.pdf.
– 2012c. *Economic Adjustment Programme for Ireland, Winter 2011 Review*. Brussels: European Commission. https://ec.europa.eu/economy_finance/publications/occasional_paper/2012/pdf/ocp93_en.pdf.
– 2012d. *The Second Economic Adjustment Programme for Greece. First Review December 2012*. Brussels: European Commission. https://ec.europa.eu/economy_finance/publications/occasional_paper/2012/pdf/ocp123_en.pdf.
– 2012e. *The Second Economic Adjustment Programme for Greece. March 2012*. Brussels: European Commission. https://ec.europa.eu/economy_finance/publications/occasional_paper/2012/pdf/ocp94_en.pdf.
– 2013a. *Economic Adjustment Programme for Ireland, Autumn 2012 Review*. Brussels: European Commission. https://ec.europa.eu/economy_finance/publications/occasional_paper/2013/pdf/ocp127_en.pdf.
– 2013b. *Economic Adjustment Programme for Ireland, Autumn 2013 Review*. Brussels: European Commission. https://ec.europa.eu/economy_finance/publications/occasional_paper/2013/pdf/ocp167_en.pdf.
– 2013c. *Economic Adjustment Programme for Ireland, Spring 2013 Review*. Brussels: European Commission. https://ec.europa.eu/economy_finance/publications/occasional_paper/2013/pdf/ocp154_en.pdf.
– 2013d. *Economic Adjustment Programme for Ireland, Winter 2012 Review*. Brussels: European Commission. https://ec.europa.eu/economy_finance/publications/occasional_paper/2013/pdf/ocp131_en.pdf.

– 2013e. *The Second Economic Adjustment Programme for Greece. Second Review – May 2013*. Brussels: European Commission. https://ec.europa.eu/economy _finance/publications/occasional_paper/2013/pdf/ocp148_en.pdf.

– 2014. *The Second Economic Adjustment Programme for Greece. Fourth Review – April 2014*. Brussels: European Commission. https://ec.europa.eu/economy _finance/publications/occasional_paper/2014/pdf/ocp192_en.pdf.

– 2015a. "Ex post Evaluation of the Economic Adjustment Programme: Ireland, 2010–2013." https://ec.europa.eu/dgs/economy_finance/evaluation/pdf /ex-post_ireland_en.pdf.

– 2015b. "Flash Eurobarometer 429: The Euro Area." https://europa.eu /eurobarometer/surveys/detail/2057.

– 2015c. "Post-Programme Surveillance Report: Ireland, Autumn 2015." https://op.europa.eu/en/publication-detail/-/publication/dcff0ea1-e1d3 -11e5-8a50-01aa75ed71a1/language-en.

– 2015d. "Post-Programme Surveillance Report: Ireland, Spring 2015." https://economy-finance.ec.europa.eu/publications/post-programme -surveillance-report-ireland-spring-2015_en.

– 2015e. "Memorandum of Understanding between the European Commission acting on behalf of the European Stability Mechanism and the Hellenic Republic and the Bank of Greece." https://economy-finance.ec .europa.eu/system/files/2017-01/01_mou_20150811_en1.pdf.

– 2016a. *Compliance Report: The Third Economic Adjustment Programme for Greece, First Review, June 2016*. Brussels: European Commission. https:// www.tweedekamer.nl/downloads/document?id=2016D24518.

– 2016b. *Post-Programme Surveillance Report: Ireland, Spring 2016*. Luxembourg: Publications Office of the European Union. https://economy-finance.ec .europa.eu/publications/post-programme-surveillance-report-ireland -spring-2016_en.

– 2017a. *Post-Programme Surveillance Report: Ireland, Autumn 2016*. Luxembourg: Publications Office of the European Union. https://economy -finance.ec.europa.eu/publications/post-programme-surveillance-report -ireland-autumn-2016_en.

– 2017b. *Proposal for a Council Regulation on the Establishment of the European Monetary Fund*. COM(2017) 827 final, 6.12.2017. https://eur-lex.europa.eu /legal-content/EN/TXT/?uri=CELEX%3A52017PC0827.

– 2017c. *Supplemental Memorandum of Understanding (Second Addendum to the Memorandum of Understanding) between the European Commission Acting on Behalf of the European Stability Mechanism and the Hellenic Republic and the Bank of Greece*. Brussels: European Commission. https://economy-finance. ec.europa.eu/system/files/2017-07/smou_final_to_esm_2017_07_05.pdf.

– 2017d. *Compliance Report, The Third Economic Adjustment Programme for Greece, Second Review – June 2017*. Brussels: European Commission. https://

economy-finance.ec.europa.eu/system/files/2017-06/compliance_report
-to_ewg_2017_06_21.pdf.

– 2018a. *Memorandum of Understanding on the Working Relations between the
Commission and the European Stability Mechanism.* https://www.esm.europa.
eu/content/memorandum-understanding-working-relations-between
-european-commission-and-european.

– 2018b. *Supplemental Memorandum of Understanding: Greece. Third Review of the ESM
Programme, 18 January 2018.* https://www.esm.europa.eu/sites/default/files
/migration_files/20180219_-_esm_bog_-_3_-_resolution_1_-_annex_-_smou.pdf.

– 2018c. *Supplemental Memorandum of Understanding: Greece. Fourth Review of the
ESM Programme, DRAFT 20 June 2018.* https://economy-finance.ec.europa.eu
/system/files/2018-06/draft_smou_4th_review_to_eg_2018.06.20.pdf.

– 2022a. "Fiscal Governance Database." Economy and Finance. https://
economy-finance.ec.europa.eu/economic-research-and-databases/economic
-databases/fiscal-governance-database_en.

– 2022b. LABREF Database. https://webgate.ec.europa.eu/labref/application.

European Commission/Directorate General for the Budget. 2021. *The
EU's 2021–2027 Long-Term Budget & NextGenerationEU: Facts and Figures.*
Luxembourg: Publications Office of the European Union. https://data
.europa.eu/doi/10.2761/808559.

European Council. 1997. "Resolution of the European Council on the Stability
and Growth Pact Amsterdam, 17 June 1997." http://eur-lex.europa.eu
/legal-content/EN/TXT/PDF/?uri=CELEX:31997Y0802(01)&from =EN.

– 2010. "Press Release, Extraordinary Council Meeting, Economic and
Financial Affairs, Brussels, 9/10 May 2010." https://www.consilium
.europa.eu/uedocs/cms_data/docs/pressdata/en/ecofin/114324.pdf.

– 2011. "Speech by Herman Van Rompuy, President of the European Council
to the Annual Conference of EU Ambassadors, Brussels, 30 November
2011." https://www.consilium.europa.eu/media/26531/126426.pdf.

– 2012. "Remarks by President of the European Council Herman Van Rompuy
at the European Parliament, Brussels, 1 February 2012." https://www
.consilium.europa.eu/media/26452/127776.pdf.

– 2018. "Euro Summit Meeting (14 December 2018) – Statement." https://www
.consilium.europa.eu/media/37563/20181214-euro-summit-statement.pdf.

– 2020a. "Conclusions of the President of the European Council following the
Video Conference of the Members of the European Council, 23 April 2020."
Press Releases. https://www.consilium.europa.eu/en/press/press
-releases/2020/04/23/conclusions-by-president-charles-michel-following
-the-video-conference-with-members-of-the-european-council-on-23-april-2020/.

– 2020b. "Special Meeting of the European Council (17, 18, 19, 20 and 21 July
2020) – Conclusions." https://www.consilium.europa.eu/media/45109
/210720-euco-final-conclusions-en.pdf.

– 2020c. "Joint Statement of the Members of the European Council." 26 March 2020. https://www.consilium.europa.eu/media/43076/26-vc-euco-statement-en.pdf.

European Investment Bank. 2010. "Limited Services Provision Role for EIB in European Financial Stability Facility." Newsroom. 21 May 2010. http://www.eib.org/en/infocentre/press/news/all/limited-services-provision-role-for-eib-in-european-financial-stability-facility.htm.

European Parliament. 2014. *The Troika and Financial Assistance in the Euro Area: Successes and Failures.* Brussels: European Parliament. https://www.europarl.europa.eu/RegData/etudes/etudes/join/2014/497764/IPOL-ECON_ET(2014)497764_EN.pdf.

– 2017. *Report on Budgetary Capacity for the Eurozone (2015/2344(INI)).* http://www.europarl.europa.eu/sides/getDoc.do?pubRef=-//EP//TEXT+REPORT+A8-2017-0038+0+DOC+XML+V0//EN&language=en.

– 2018. "In-Depth Analysis: The European Stability Mechanism (ESM): Main Features, Instruments, and Accountability." Economic Governance Support Unit. http://www.europarl.europa.eu/RegData/etudes/BRIE/2014/497755/IPOL-ECON_NT(2014)497755_EN.pdf.

European Stability Mechanism. 2012. "Treaty Establishing the ESM." https://www.esm.europa.eu/system/files/document/2023-05/05-TESM2-HR.en12.pdf.

– 2017a. *EFSF/ESM Financial Assistance Evaluation Report.* Luxembourg: Publications Office of the European Union.

– 2017b. "Presentation: European Financial Stability Facility & European Stability Mechanism." https://www.esm.europa.eu/sites/default/files/efsfesmnewinvestorpresentation11january2017.pdf.

– 2019a. "ESM Treaty Reform - Explainer." About ESM. https://www.esm.europa.eu/about-esm/esm-treaty-reform-explainer.

– 2019b. "Investment Guidelines." ESM Public. https://www.esm.europa.eu/sites/default/files/2019-05-02_investment_guidelines.pdf.

– 2019c. *Safeguarding the Euro in Times of Crisis: The Inside Story of the ESM.* Luxembourg: Publication Office of the European Union. https://www.esm.europa.eu/publications/safeguarding-euro.

– 2020. "A Backstop to the Single Resolution Fund Now!" https://www.esm.europa.eu/blog/backstop-single-resolution-fund-now.

– 2021. "Agreement Amending the Treaty Establishing the European Stability Mechanism." https://www.esm.europa.eu/sites/default/files/migration_files/esm-treaty-amending-agreement-21_en.pdf.

– 2022a. "Working at the ESM." https://www.esm.europa.eu/careers/working-esm.

– 2022b. "How We Decide." https://www.esm.europa.eu/esm-governance.

– 2022c. "Who We Are." https://www.esm.europa.eu/about-us.

– 2023. "Explainers." https://www.esm.europa.eu/about-us/explainers.

Eurostat. 2018a. "Total General Government Expenditure." European Commission. https://ec.europa.eu/eurostat/databrowser/view/TEC00023/default/table?lang=en.

– 2018b. "Total General Government Revenue." European Commission. https://ec.europa.eu/eurostat/databrowser/view/TEC00021/default/table?lang=en.

– 2019. "General Government Expenditure by Function (COFOG)." https://ec.europa.eu/eurostat/databrowser/view/GOV_10A_EXP/default/table

– 2023a. "Employment and Activity by Sex and Age – Annual Data." https://ec.europa.eu/eurostat/databrowser/view/LFSI_EMP_A/default/table.

– 2023b. "Unemployment by Sex and Age – Annual Data." https://ec.europa.eu/eurostat/databrowser/view/UNE_RT_A/default/table?lang=en.

– 2023c. "Long-Term Unemployment by Sex– Annual Data." https://ec.europa.eu/eurostat/databrowser/product/view/UNE_LTU_A.

– 2023d. "Real GDP Growth Rate – Volume." https://ec.europa.eu/eurostat/databrowser/view/TEC00115/default/table.

– 2023e. "Government Deficit/Surplus, Debt and Associated Data." https://ec.europa.eu/eurostat/databrowser/view/GOV_10DD_EDPT1/default/table.

– 2023f. "Total General Government Expenditure." https://ec.europa.eu/eurostat/databrowser/view/TEC00023/default/table.

– 2023g. "GDP and Main Components." https://ec.europa.eu/eurostat/databrowser/view/NAMA_10_GDP/default/table.

Expert Group for the Review of Greek Labour Market Institutions. 2016. "Recommendations." 27 September 2016. http://www.ieri.es/wp-content/uploads/2016/10/Final-Report-Greece-September-2016.pdf.

Featherstone, Kevin. 2011. "The Greek Sovereign Debt Crisis and EMU: A Failing State in a Skewed Regime." *JCMS: Journal of Common Market Studies* 49, no. 2: 193–217. https://doi.org/10.1111/j.1468-5965.2010.02139.x.

Featherstone, Kevin, and Dimitris Papadimitriou. 2012. "Assessing Reform Capacity in Greece: Applying Political Economy Perspectives." In *From Stagnation to Forced Adjustment: Reforms in Greece, 1974/2010*, edited by Stathis N. Kalyvas, George Pagoulatos, Haridimos Tsoukas, 31–46. New York: Columbia University Press.

– 2017. "Greece: A Crisis in Two-Level Governance." In *The European Union in Crisis*, edited by Desmond Dinan, Neill Nugent, and William E. Paterson, 233–52. London: Palgrave Macmillan.

Feldmann, M. 2006. "Emerging Varieties of Capitalism in Transition Countries: Industrial Relations and Wage Bargaining in Estonia and Slovenia." *Comparative Political Studies* 39, no. 7: 829–54. https://doi.org/10.1177/0010414006288261.

Fine Gael. 2011. "Fine Gael Manifesto." http://michaelpidgeon.com/manifestos/docs/fg/Fine%20Gael%20GE%202011.pdf.

Fink, Philipp. 2008. "Länderanalyse Irland: Ein Erfolgsmodell auf dem Prüfstand." FES Internationale Politikanalyse. https://library.fes.de /pdf-files/id/ipa/05351.pdf.

Fleming, Sam. 2020. "Euro Bailout Chief Sees Hurdles to Quick 'Coronabonds.'" *Financial Times*, 31 March 2020. https://www.ft.com /content/865ced7d-1e33-463e-a04c-6be7fd21cda7.

Fleming, Sam, Mehreen Khan, and Jim Brunsden. 2020. "EU Leaders Strike Deal on €750bn Recovery Fund after Marathon Summit." *Financial Times*, 20 July 2020. https://www.ft.com/content/713be467-ed19-4663-95ff -66f775af55cc.

Fleming, Sam, Victor Mallet, and Guy Chazan. 2020. "Germany and France Unite in Call for €500bn Europe Recovery Fund." *Financial Times*, 18 May 2020. https://www.ft.com/content/c23ebc5e-cbf3-4ad8-85aa-032b574d0562.

Fletcher, Cory, Anja van Heelsum, and Conny Roggeband. 2018. "Water Privatization, Hegemony and Civil Society: What Motivates Individuals to Protest about Water Privatization?" *Journal of Civil Society* 14, no. 3: 241–56. https://doi.org/10.1080/17448689.2018.1496308.

Frangakis, Marcia. 2014. "The 'Debt Crisis,' the Adventure of the 'Rescue': Public Debt after 2009." In *Crisis, Debt and the Development Perspective*, edited by Sotiris Koskoletos and Elena Papadopoulou, 33–46. Athens: Nissos.

Frankfurter Allgemeine Zeitung, Werner. 2018. "ESM-Chef Klaus Regling: Konflikt mit Italien ist keine Krise." *Frankfurter Allgemeine Zeitung*, 8 December 2018. https://www.faz.net/aktuell/wirtschaft/esm-chef-regling -konflikt-mit-italien-ist-keine-krise-15930275.html.

Franz, Wolfgang, Clemens Fuest, Martin Hellwig, and Hans-Werner Sinn. 2010. "A Euro Rescue Plan." *CESifo Forum* 11, no. 2: 101–4. https://www .cesifo.org/en/publications/2010/article-journal/euro-rescue-plan.

Gabor, Daniela, and Cornel Ban. 2012. "Fiscal Policy in (European) Hard Times: Financialization and Varieties of Capitalism." https://www .academia.edu/31924876/Fiscal_policy_in_European_hard_times _financialization_and_varieties_of_capitalism.

Galanoo, George, and Thomas Poufinas. 2018. "Impact of FDI in the Fiscal Adjustment Process." *International Advances in Economic Research* 24, no. 3: 265–77. https://doi.org/10.1007/s11294-018-9692-x.

Galli, Giampaolo. 2020. "The Reform of the ESM and Why It Is So Controversial in Italy." *Capital Markets Law Journal* 15, no. 3: 262–76. https:// doi.org/10.1093/cmlj/kmaa011.

Genschel, Philipp, and Markus Jachtenfuchs. 2015a. "Conclusion: The European Integration of Core State Powers. Patterns and Causes." In *Beyond the Regulatory Polity? The European Integration of Core State Powers*, edited by Philipp Genschel and Markus Jachtenfuchs, 249–70. Oxford: Oxford University Press.

— 2015b. "Introduction: Beyond Market Regulation. Analysing the European Integration of Core State Powers." In *Beyond the Regulatory Polity? The European Integration of Core State Powers*, edited by Philipp Genschel and Markus Jachtenfuchs, 1–23. Oxford: Oxford University Press.

— 2018. "From Market Integration to Core State Powers: The Eurozone Crisis, the Refugee Crisis and Integration Theory: Crises in Core State Powers." *JCMS: Journal of Common Market Studies* 56, no. 1: 178–96. https://doi.org/10.1111/jcms.12654.

George, Alexander L., and Andrew Bennett. 2005. *Case Studies and Theory Development in the Social Sciences*. Cambridge, MA: MIT Press.

Gianviti, Francois, Anne O. Krueger, Jean Pisani-Ferry, André Sapir, and Jürgen von Hagen. 2010. *A European Mechanism for Sovereign Debt Crisis Resolution: A Proposal*. Bruegel Blueprint 10. Brussels: Bruegel.

Gkasis, Pavlos. 2018. "Greece and European Monetary Union: The Road to the Demise of the Greek Economy." In *Crisis in the Eurozone Periphery: The Political Economies of Greece, Spain, Ireland and Portugal*, edited by Owen Parker and Dimitris Tsarouhas, 93–110. Basingstoke, UK: Palgrave Macmillan.

Gocaj, Ledina, and Sophia Meunier. 2013. "Time Will Tell: The EFSF, the ESM, and the Euro Crisis." *Journal of European Integration* 35, no. 3: 239–53. https://doi.org/10.1080/07036337.2013.774778.

Greer, S. 2014. "Structural Adjustment Comes to Europe: Lessons for the Eurozone from the Conditionality Debates." *Global Social Policy* 14, no. 1: 51–71. https://doi.org/10.1177/1468018113511473.

Gros, Daniel, and Thomas Mayer. 2010. "How to Deal with Sovereign Default in Europe: Create the European Monetary Fund Now!" *CEPS Policy Brief*, no. 202 (17 May 2010). https://papers.ssrn.com/sol3/papers.cfm?abstract_id=1610303.

Gros, Daniel, and Stefano Micossi. 2008. "A Call for a European Financial Stability Fund." *CEPS Commentary* (October 30, 2008). https://www.ceps.eu/ceps-publications/call-european-financial-stability-fund/.

Grubb, David, Shrunti Singh, and Peter Tergeist. 2009. "Activation Policies in Ireland." OECD Social, Employment and Migration Working Papers 75. https://doi.org/10.1787/227626803333.

Gschwend, Thomas, and Frank Schimmelfennig, eds. 2007. *Forschungsdesign in der Politikwissenschaft: Probleme - Strategien - Anwendungen*. Frankfurt am Main: Campus.

Guscina, Anastasia, Sheheryar Malik, and Michael Papaioannou. 2017. "Assessing Loss of Market Access: Conceptual and Operational Issues." IMF Working Paper WP/17/246. https://www.imf.org/~/media/Files/Publications/WP/2017/wp17246.ashx.

Guttenberg, Lucas, Johannes Hemker, and Sander Tordoir. 2021. "Everything Will Be Different: How the Pandemic Is Changing EU Economic Governance." Policy Brief, Jacques Delors Centre, Hertie School, 11 February 2021. https://hertieschool-f4e6.kxcdn.com/fileadmin /2_Research/1_About_our_research/2_Research_centres/6_Jacques _Delors_Centre/Publications/20200211_Economic_governance _Guttenberg_et_al.pdf.

Habermas, Jürgen. 2013. "Demokratie oder Kapitalismus? Vom Elend der nationalstaatlichen Fragmentierung in einer kapitalistisch integrierten Weltgesellschaft." *Blätter für deutsche und internationale Politik* (May): 59–70.

Hacker, Björn. 2018. "Deutschlands europapolitische Reformoptionen: Instrumente für eine progressive EU-Wirtschafts- und Sozialpolitik." Friedrich-Ebert-Stifung. http://library.fes.de/pdf-files/id-moe/14713.pdf.

Hadjimichalis, Costis. 2014. "Crisis and Land Dispossession in Greece as Part of the Global 'Land Fever.'" *City* 18, no. 4–5: 502–8. https://doi.org/10.1080 /13604813.2014.939470.

Hall, Peter A., and Rosemary C.R. Taylor. 1996. "Political Science and the Three New Institutionalisms." *Political Studies* 44, no. 5: 936–57. https://doi .org/10.1111/j.1467-9248.1996.tb00343.x.

Hall, Peter. A., and Kathleen Thelen. 2008. "Institutional Change in Varieties of Capitalism." *Socio-Economic Review* 7, no. 1: 7–34. https://doi.org/10.1093/ser /mwn020.

Hall, Peter A. 2003. "Aligning Ontology and Methodology in Comparative Research." In *Comparative Historical Analysis in the Social Sciences*, edited by James Mahoney and Dietrich Rueschemeyer, 373–404. Cambridge: Cambridge University Press.

– 2006. "Systematic Process Analysis: When and How to Use It." *European Management Review* 3, no.1: 24–31. https://doi.org/10.1057/palgrave .emr.1500050.

– 2007. "The Evolution of Varieties of Capitalism in Europe." In *Beyond Varieties of Capitalism: Conflict, Contradictions, and Complementarities in the European Economy*, edited by Bob Hancké, Martin Rhodes, and Mark Thatcher, 39–87. Oxford: Oxford University Press.

– 2012. "The Economics and Politics of the Euro Crisis." *German Politics* 21, no. 4: 355–71. https://doi.org/10.1080/09644008.2012.739614.

– 2014. "Varieties of Capitalism and the Euro Crisis." *West European Politics* 37, no. 6: 1223–43. https://doi.org/10.1080/01402382.2014.929352.

– 2018. "Varieties of Capitalism in Light of the Euro Crisis." *Journal of European Public Policy* 25, no. 1: 7–30. https://doi.org/10.1080/13501763.2017.1310278.

Hall, Peter A., and Daniel W. Gingerich. 2004. "Varieties of Capitalism and Institutional Complementarities in the Macroeconomy: An Empirical

Analysis." MPIfG Discussion Paper 04/5. https://econstor.eu/dspace
/bitstream/10419/19907/1/dp04-5.pdf.

Hall, Peter A., and David Soskice, eds. 2001. *Varieties of Capitalism: The Institutional Foundations of Comparative Advantage*. Oxford: Oxford University Press.

Hancké, Bob. 2013a. *Unions, Central Banks, and EMU: Labour Market Institutions and Monetary Integration in Europe*. Oxford: Oxford University Press.

– 2013b. "The Missing Link. Labour Unions, Central Banks and Monetary Integration in Europe." *Transfer: European Review of Labour and Research* 19, no. 1: 89–101. https://doi.org/10.1177/1024258912469347.

Hancké, Bob, Martin Rhodes, and Mark Thatcher, eds. 2007. *Beyond Varieties of Capitalism: Conflict, Contradictions, and Complementarities in the European Economy*. Oxford: Oxford University Press.

Hardiman, Niahm, Joaquim Filipe Araujo, Muiris MacCarthaigh, and Callicope Spanou. 2017. "The Troika's Variation on a Trio: Why the Loan Programmes Worked So Differently in Greece, Ireland, and Portugal." In UCD Heary Institute for Public Policy Discussion Paper Series, 2017/11. https://researchrepository.ucd.ie/entities/publication/8c5a20ce-79d2-47ab-b634-fc7d6333f33b/details.

Hardiman, Niamh. 2014. "Repeating History: Fiscal Squeeze in Two Recessions in Ireland." In *When the Party's Over: The Politics of Fiscal Squeeze in Perspective*, edited by Christopher Hood, David Heald, and Rozana Himaz, 139–60. Oxford: Oxford University Press.

Hardiman, Niamh, and Muiris MacCarthaigh. 2017. "State Retrenchment and Administrative Reform in Ireland: Probing Comparative Policy Paradigms." *Journal of Comparative Policy Analysis: Research and Practice* 19, no. 2: 100–18. https://doi.org/10.1080/13876988.2015.1103432.

Hassel, Anke. 2014. "Adjustments in the Eurozone: Varieties of Capitalism and the Crisis in Southern Europe." LSE Europe in Question Discussion Paper Series, 74/2014. https://lse.ac.uk/european-institute/Assets/Documents/LEQS-Discussion-Papers/LEQSPaper76.pdf.

Hassel, Anke, and Bruno Palier, eds. 2021. *Growth and Welfare in Advanced Capitalist Economies*. Oxford: Oxford University Press.

Hay, Colin. 2004. "Common Trajectories, Variable Paces, Divergent Outcomes? Models of European Capitalism under Conditions of Complex Economic Interdependence." *Review of International Political Economy* 11, no. 2: 231–62. https://doi.org/10.1080/09692290420001672796.

Heipertz, Martin, and Amy Verdun. 2004. "The Dog That Would Never Bite? What We Can Learn from the Origins of the Stability and Growth Pact." *Journal of European Public Policy* 11, no. 5: 765–80. https://doi.org/10.1080/1350176042000273522.

– 2010. *Ruling Europe: The Politics of the Stability and Growth Pact*. Cambridge: Cambridge University Press.

Helfferich, Cornelia. 2011. *Die Qualität qualitativer Daten: Manual für die Durchführung qualitativer Interviews*. 4. Aufl. Wiesbaden: VS, Verl. für Sozialwiss.

Hellenic Republic Asset Development Fund. 2015. "Asset Development Plan." 30 July 2015. http://www.sven-giegold.de/wp-content/uploads/2015/08/Privatisation-Programme.pdf.

Hellenic Republic, Ministry of Finance. 2019. "Stability Programme 2019." https://www.in.gr/wp-content/uploads/2019/05/2019-european-semester-stability-programme-greece_en.pdf.

Henning, C. Randall. 2017. *Tangled Governance: International Regime Complexity, the Troika, and the Euro Crisis*. Oxford: Oxford University Press.

Hermann, Christoph. 2014. "Structural Adjustment and Neoliberal Convergence in Labour Markets and Welfare: The Impact of the Crisis and Austerity Measures on European Economic and Social Models." *Competition & Change* 18, no. 2: 111–30. https://doi.org/10.1179/1024529414Z.00000000051.

– 2017. "Crisis, Structural Reform and the Dismantling of the European Social Model(s)." *Economic and Industrial Democracy* 38, no. 1: 51–68. https://doi.org/10.1177/0143831X14555708.

Herrmann, Andrea. 2005. "Converging Divergence: How Competitive Advantages Condition Institutional Change under EMU." *JCMS: Journal of Common Market Studies* 43, no. 2: 287–310. https://doi.org/10.1111/j.0021-9886.2005.00556.x.

Höing, Oliver. 2015. *Asymmetric Influence: National Parliaments in the European Stability Mechanism*. PhD diss., Köln: Universität zu Köln. http://kups.ub.uni-koeln.de/id/eprint/6485.

– 2016. "Weder Stabilitäts- noch Transferunion: der Europäische Stabilitätsmechanismus in einer reformierten Währungszone." *integration* 39, no. 1: 15–29. https://doi.org/10.5771/0720-5120-2016-1-15.

Holmes, Michael. 2019. "Frankfurt's Way or Labour's Way." In *The European Left and the Financial Crisis*, edited by Michael Holmes and Knut Roder, 68–85. Manchester: Manchester University Press.

Hope, David, and David Soskice. 2016. "Growth Models, Varieties of Capitalism, and Macroeconomics." *Politics & Society* 44, no. 2: 209–26. https://doi.org/10.1177/0032329216638054.

Höpner, Martin. 2013. "Ein Währungsraum und viele Lohnregime: Warum der Euro nicht zum heterogenen Unterbau der Eurozone passt." *dms - der moderne staat - Zeitschrift für Public Policy, Recht und Management* 6, no. 2: 289–309. https://doi.org/10.3224/dms.v6i2.02.

Howarth, David, and Aneta Spendzharova. 2020. "Delivering Value for Money? The Problematic Accountability of the European Stability Mechanism (ESM)." In *Financial Accountability in the European Union: Institutions, Policy and Practice*, edited by Paul Stephenson, María-Luisa Sánchez-Barrueco, and Hartmut Aden, 211–26. London: Routledge.

Illing, Falk. 2013. *Die Euro-Krise*. Wiesbaden: Springer Fachmedien Wiesbaden.

Illing, Gerhard, Sebastian Jauch, and Michael Zabel. 2012. "Die Diskussion um den Euro: Endogene Risiken und multiple Gleichgewichte." *Leviathan* 40, no. 2: 156–72. https://doi.org/10.5771/0340-0425-2012-2-156.

International Labour Office. 2011. *Report on the High Level Mission to Greece*. 19–23 September 2011. https://www.ilo.org/wcmsp5/groups/public/---ed_norm/---normes/documents/missionreport/wcms_170433.pdf.

International Labour Organisation. 2022. "Statistics on Collective Bargaining." https://ilostat.ilo.org/topics/collective-bargaining/.

International Monetary Fund. 2010. "IMF Survey: Agreed EU Support Model Boosts Confidence, Says IMF." 11 May 2010. https://www.imf.org/en/News/Articles/2015/09/28/04/53/sonew051110a.

International Monetary Fund. 2013. "Greece: Ex Post Evaluation of Exceptional Access under the 2010 Stand-By Arrangement." https://www.imf.org/external/pubs/ft/scr/2013/cr13156.pdf.

Ioannou, Demosthenes, Patrick Leblond, and Arne Niemann. 2015. "European Integration and the Crisis: Practice and Theory." *Journal of European Public Policy* 22, no. 2: 155–76. https://doi.org/10.1080/13501763.2014.994979.

Irish Fiscal Advisory Council. 2019a. "Fiscal Assessment Reports." https://www.fiscalcouncil.ie/fiscal-assessment-reports/.

– 2019b. "Publications." https://www.fiscalcouncil.ie/publications/.

Irish Government. 2011. "Programme for Government 2011–2016." https://merrionstreet.ie/en/wp-content/uploads/2010/05/Programme_for_Government_2011.pdf.

Iversen, Torben, and David Soskice. 2018. "A Structural-Institutional Explanation of the Eurozone Crisis." In *Welfare Democracies and Party Politics*, edited by Philip Manow, Bruno Palier, and Hannah Schwander, 257–80. Oxford: Oxford University Press.

Iversen, Torben, David Soskice, and David Hope. 2016. "The Eurozone and Political Economic Institutions." *Annual Review of Political Science* 19, no. 1: 163–85. https://doi.org/10.1146/annurev-polisci-022615-113243.

Jabko, Nicolas. 2015. "Contested Governance. The New Repertoire of the Eurozone Crisis." Presented at CES Conference, July 2015, Paris.

Johnston, Alison. 2016. *From Convergence to Crisis: Labor Markets and the Instability of the Euro*. Ithaca: Cornell University Press.

Johnston, Alison, and Bob Hancké. 2009. "Wage Inflation and Labour Unions in EMU." *Journal of European Public Policy* 16, no. 4: 601–22. https://doi.org/10.1080/13501760902872742.

Johnston, Alison, Bob Hancké, and Suman Pant. 2014. "Comparative Institutional Advantage in the European Sovereign Debt Crisis."

Comparative Political Studies 47, no. 13: 1771–1800. https://doi.org/10.1177
/0010414013516917

Johnston, Alison, and Aidan Regan. 2016. "European Monetary Integration
and the Incompatibility of National Varieties of Capitalism." *JCMS: Journal of
Common Market Studies*, 54, no. 2: 318–36. https://doi.org/10.1111/jcms.12289.

– 2018. "Introduction: Is the European Union Capable of Integrating Diverse
Models of Capitalism?" *New Political Economy* 23, no. 2: 145–59. https://doi
.org/10.1080/13563467.2017.1370442.

Jones, Erik. 2013. "The Collapse of the Brussels-Frankfurt Consensus and
the Future of the Euro." In *Resilient Liberalism in Europe's Political Economy*,
edited by Vivien A. Schmidt and Mark Thatcher, 145–70. Cambridge:
Cambridge University Press.

Jones, Erik, R. Daniel Kelemen, and Sophie Meunier. 2016. "Failing Forward?
The Euro Crisis and the Incomplete Nature of European Integration."
Comparative Political Studies 49, no. 7: 1010–34. https://doi.org/10.1177
/0010414015617966.

Kaplanoglou, Georgia, and Vassilis T. Rapanos. 2011. "The Greek Fiscal Crisis
and the Role of Fiscal Governance." *GreeSE*, no. 48. https://eprints.lse.ac.uk
/36432/1/GreeSE_No48_(lsero).pdf.

Karamessini, Maria. 2015. "Greece as an International Test-Case: Economic
Adjustment through a Troika/State-Induced Depression and Social
Catastrophe." In *Divisive Integration: The Triumph of Failed Ideas in Europe
– Revisited*, edited by Stefan Lehndorff, 95–126. Brussels: ETUI.

Karatzia, Anastasia, and Menelaos Markakis. 2017. "What Role for the
Commission and the ECB in the European Stability Mechanism?" *Cambridge
International Law Journal* 6, no. 2: 232–52. https://doi.org/10.4337/cilj.2017.02.07.

Kassim, Hussein, John Peterson, Michael W. Bauer, Sara Connolly, Renaud
Dehouse, Liesbet Hooghe, and Andrew Thompson. 2013. *The European
Commission of the Twenty-First Century*. Oxford: Oxford University Press.

Katrougalos, George. 2013. "'Memoranda': Greek Exceptionalism or the
Mirror of Europe's Future?" In *The Greek Crisis and European Modernity*,
edited by Anna Triandafyllidou, Ruby Gropas, and Hara Kouki, 89–109.
Basingstoke, UK: Palgrave Macmillan.

Kazákos, Pános. 2015. "Griechische Politik 2009–2014: Der Kampf um
Kredite und der mühsame Weg zu Reformen." In *Die Krise in Griechenland:
Ursprünge, Verlauf, Folgen*, edited by Ulf-Dieter Klemm and Wolfgang
Schultheiß, 35–53. Frankfurt am Main: Campus.

Keane, Claire. 2015. "Irish Public Finances through the Financial Crisis: Irish
Public Finances through the Financial Crisis." *Fiscal Studies* 36, no. 4: 475–97.
https://doi.org/10.1111/j.1475-5890.2015.12077.

Kennedy, Geoff. 2016. "Embedding Neoliberalism in Greece: The Transformation
of Collective Bargaining and Labour Market Policy in Greece during the

Eurozone Crisis." *Studies in Political Economy* 97, no. 3: 253–69. https://doi.org
/10.1080/07078552.2016.1249129.

– 2018. "From Competitive Corporatism to Embedded Austerity: Neoliberalism
and Structural Reform in Greece during the Eurozone Crisis." *E-Journal of
International and Comparative Labour Studies* 7, no. 1: 1–29. https://www
.researchgate.net/publication/322977415_From_Competitive_Corporatism
_to_Embedded_Austerity_Neoliberalism_and_Structural_Reform_in_Greece
_during_the_Eurozone_Crisis.

Kentikelenis, Alexander E. 2018. "The Social Aftermath of Economic Disaster: Karl
Polanyi, Countermovements in Action, and the Greek Crisis." *Socio-Economic
Review* 16, no. 1: 39–59. https://doi.org/10.1093/ser/mwx031.

Kinsella, Stephen. 2012. "Is Ireland Really the Role Model for Austerity?" *Cambridge
Journal of Economics* 36, no. 1: 223–35. https://doi.org/10.1093/cje/ber032.

– 2017. "Economic and Fiscal Policy." In *Austerity and Recovery in Ireland:
Europe's Poster Child and the Great Recession*, edited by William K. Roche, Philip
J. O'Connell, and Andrea Prothero, 40–61. Oxford: Oxford University Press.

Kompsopoulos, Ioannis. 2016. "Zentrale Strukturelemente des griechischen
Kapitalismusmodells." In *Griechenland im europäischen Kontext*, edited by
Aristotelis Agridopoulos and Ilias Papagiannopoulos, 91–105. Wiesbaden:
VS Springer.

Kompsopoulos, Jannis. 2015. "Irland: Alles beim Alten?" In *Europäische
Welten in der Krise: Arbeitsbeziehungen und Wohlfahrtsstaaten im Vergleich*,
edited by Hans-Jürgen Bieling and Daniel Buhr, 217–42. Frankfurt am
Main: Campus.

– 2018. "Neue Hoffnung im Süden? Erfahrungen linker Regierungspolitik in
Zeiten der Austerität." *PROKLA* 48, no. 192: 475–88. https://doi.org
/10.32387/prokla.v48i192.917.

Kopits, George. 2014. "Ireland's Fiscal Framework: Options for the Future."
The Economic and Social Review 45, no. 1: 135–58. https://www.esr.ie
/article/view/111.

Koukiadaki, Aristea, and Damian Grimshaw. 2016. "Evaluating the Effects of
the Structural Labour Market Reforms on Collective Bargaining in Greece."
INWORK Working Paper. Conditions of Work and Employment Series No.
85. International Labour Organisation. https://www.ilo.org/wcmsp5
/groups/public/---ed_protect/---protrav/---travail/documents
/publication/wcms_538161.pdf.

Kreilinger, Valentin. 2019. National Parliaments in Europe's Post-crisis
Economic Governance. PhD diss., Hertie School of Governance. https://
opus4.kobv.de/opus4-hsog/frontdoor/deliver/index/docId/2730/file
/KreilingerDissertationPUBLICATION.pdf.

Kuckartz, Udo. 2014. *Mixed Methods: Methodologie, Forschungsdesigns und
Analyseverfahren*. Wiesbaden: Springer VS.

Laffan, Brigid. 2013. "Economic Management Council Acts as a 'War Cabinet' in Ireland's Fight for Survival." *Irish Times*, 28 August 2013. https://www.irishtimes.com/news/politics/economic-management-council-acts-as-a-war-cabinet-in-ireland-s-fight-for-survival-1.1507361.

– 2017. "International Actors and Agencies." In *Austerity and Recovery in Ireland: Europe's Poster Child and the Great Recession*, edited by William K.Roche, Philip J. O'Connell, and Andrea Prothero, 177–93. Oxford: Oxford University Press.

Lallement, Michel. 2011. "Europe and the Economic Crisis: Forms of Labour Market Adjustment and Varieties of Capitalism." *Work, Employment and Society* 25, no. 4: 627–41. https://doi.org/10.1177/0950017011419717.

Lanara, Zoe. 2012. "Trade Unions in Greece and the Crisis: A Key Actor under Pressure." FES International Policy Analysis. https://library.fes.de/pdf-files/id/ipa/09012.pdf.

Lane, Christel. 2006. "Institutional Transformation and System Change: Changes in the Corporate Governance of German Corporations." In *Changing Capitalisms? Internationalization, Institutional Change, and Systems of Economic Organization*, edited by Glenn Morgan, 78–109. Oxford: Oxford University Press.

Lane, Philip R. 2012. "The European Sovereign Debt Crisis." *Journal of Economic Perspectives* 26, no. 3: 49–68. https://doi.org/10.1257/jep.26.3.49.

Lapavitsas, Costas, and Heiner Flassbeck. 2013. "The Systemic Crisis of the Euro – True Causes and Effective Therapies." RLS Studien. https://www.rosalux.de/fileadmin/rls_uploads/pdfs/Studien/Studien_The_systemic_crisis_web.pdf.

Lapavitsas, Costas, and Eustache Kouvélakis. 2012. *Crisis in the Eurozone.* London: Verso.

Lijphart, Arend. 1971. "Comparative Politics and the Comparative Method." *American Political Science Review* 65, no. 3: 682–93. https://doi.org/10.2307/1955513.

Lübker, Malte, and Thorsten Schulten. 2017. "Europäischer Tarifbericht des WSI – 2016/2017." *WSI-Mitteilungen* 70, no. 6 (January): 421–31. https://ideas.repec.org/a/nms/wsimit/10,5771-0342-300x-2017-6-421.html.

Lüggert, Max. 2017. "Die Immunisierung der Krisenverarbeitung in der Eurozone." In *Die Grenzen der Demokratie*, edited by Annette Förster and Matthias Lemke, 111–40. Wiesbaden: Springer Fachmedien Wiesbaden.

– 2019. *Die Entwicklung der hybriden Rolle der Europäischen Zentralbank im Laufe der Eurokrise*. PhD diss., University of Bonn. https://hdl.handle.net/20.500.11811/8133.

Lütz, Susanne. 2004. "Convergence within National Diversity: The Regulatory State in Finance." *Journal of Public Policy* 24, no. 2: 169–97. https://doi.org/10.1017/S0143814X04000091.

Lütz, Susanne, and Matthias Kranke. 2014. "The European Rescue of the Washington Consensus? EU and IMF Lending to Central and Eastern European Countries." *Review of International Political Economy* 21, no. 2: 310–38. https://doi.org/10.1080/09692290.2012.747104.

Lux, Julia, and Jannis Kompsopoulos. 2019. "Sozialpolitischer Interventionismus." In *Neue Segel, alter Kurs?*, edited by Hans-Jürgen Bieling and Simon Guntrum, 175–200. Wiesbaden: Springer Fachmedien Wiesbaden.

Maccarrone, Vincenzo, Roland Erne, and Aidan Regan. 2019. "Ireland: Life after Social Partnership." In *Collective Bargaining in Europe: Towards an Endgame*, edited by Torsten Müller, Kurt Vandaele, and Jeremy Waddington, 315–35. Brussels: ETUI.

MacCarthaigh, Muiris, and Niamh Hardiman. 2019. "Exploiting Conditionality: EU and International Actors and Post-NPM Reform in Ireland." *Public Policy and Administration* 35, no. 2: 179–200. https://doi.org/10.1177/0952076718796548.

Mackintosh, James. 2013. "When Irish Eyes Are Not Smiling." *Financial Times*, 4 March 2013. https://www.ft.com/content/a627f8bc-8a6d-11e2-bf79-00144feabdc0.

Majone, Giandomenico. 2014. "From Regulatory State to a Democratic Default." *Journal of Common Market Studies* 52, no. 6: 1216–23. https://doi.org/10.1111/jcms.12190.

Manow, Philip. 2018. "Die Politische Ökonomie Südeuropas." In *Mittelweg 36* (May): 78–93.

Marini, Alessandra, Michele Davide Zini, Eleni Kanavitsa, Natalia Milan, Chrysa Leventi, and Nithin Umapathi. 2019. "A Quantitative Evaluation of the Greek Social Solidarity Income." World Bank Group. http://documents.worldbank.org/curated/en/882751548273358885/A-Quantitative-Evaluation-of-the-Greek-Social-Solidarity-Income.

Matsaganis, Manos. 2014. "The Catastrophic Greek Crisis." *Curent History* 113, no. 761: 110–16. https://doi.org/10.1525/curh.2014.113.761.110.

– 2018. "Income Support Policies and Labour Market Reforms under Austerity in Greece." In *Labour Market Policies in the Era of Pervasive Austerity*, edited by Sotiria Theodoropoulou, 43–68. Bristol: Policy Press.

Matthijs, Matthias, and Kathleen McNamara. 2015. "The Euro Crisis' Theory Effect: Northern Saints, Southern Sinners, and the Demise of the Eurobond." *Journal of European Integration* 37, no. 2: 229–45. https://doi.org/10.1080/07036337.2014.990137.

Mayring, Philipp. 2010. *Qualitative Inhaltsanalyse: Grundlagen und Techniken.* Weinheim Basel: Beltz.

McArdle, Par. 2012. "The Euro Crisis: Refinancing the Irish Bailout – The Options Post the June 2012 Summit." Institute of International and

European Affairs (IIEA), Euro Crisis Working Paper no. 12. https:// historyiiea.com/product/the-euro-crisis-refinancing-the-irish-bailout-the -options-post-the-june-2012-summit/.

McGee, Harry. 2012. "Government to Dispose of up to €3bn in Assets over Two Years." *Irish Times*, Dublin, 23 February 2012. https://www.irishtimes .com/business/transport-and-tourism/government-to-dispose-of-up-to-3bn -in-assets-over-two-years-1.468356.

McLaughlin, Colm, and Chris F. Wright. 2018. "The Role of Ideas in Understanding Industrial Relations Policy Change in Liberal Market Economies." *Industrial Relations: A Journal of Economy and Society* 57, no. 4: 568–610. https://doi.org/10.1111/irel.12218.

Mitsopoulos, Michael. 2016. "Greek Export and Labor Market Performance: Facts and Myths That Can Help Devise a Useful Growth Strategy." In *Stagnation Versus Growth in Europe*, edited by Luigi Paganetto, 155–82. Cham: Springer International Publishing.

Mody, Ashoka. 2018. *Eurotragedy: A Drama in Nine Acts*. New York: Oxford University Press.

Molina, Oscar, and Martin Rhodes. 2007. "The Political Economy of Adjustment in Mixed Market Economies: A Study of Spain and Italy." In *Beyond Varieties of Capitalism: Conflict, Contradictions, and Complementarities in the European Economy*, edited by Bob Hancké, Martin Rhodes, and Mark Thatcher, 223–52. Oxford: Oxford University Press.

Moschella, Manuela. 2017. "When Some Are More Equal than Others: National Parliaments and Intergovernmental Bailout Negotiations in the Eurozone." *Government and Opposition* 52, no. 2: 239–65. https://doi .org/10.1017/gov.2016.49.

Moses, Jonathon Wayne. 2017. *Eurobondage: The Political Costs of European Monetary Union*. Colchester, United Kingdom: ECPR Press.

Moury, Catherine, Stella Ladi, Daniel Cardoso, and Angie Gado. 2021. *Capitalising on Constraint: Bailout Politics in Eurozone Countries*. Manchester: Manchester University Press.

Müller, Torsten, Thorsten Schulten, and Sepp Zuckerstätter. 2016. "Die Bedeutung der Löhne für die wirtschaftliche Entwicklung in Europa." In *Lohnpolitik unter europäischer Economic Governance: Alternative Strategien für inklusives Wachsum*, edited by Thorsten Schulten, Torsten Müller, and Guy Van Gyes, 188–208. Hamburg: VSA-Verlag.

Murphy, Enda, and Julien Mercille. 2019. "(Re)Making Labour Markets and Economic Crises: The Case of Ireland." *The Economic and Labour Relations Review* 30, no. 1: https://doi.org/10.1177/1035304619829015.

Nölke, Andreas. 2016. "Economic Causes of the Eurozone Crisis: The Analytical Contribution of Comparative Capitalism." *Socio-Economic Review* 14, no. 1: 141–61. https://doi.org/10.1093/ser/mwv031.

Nölke, Andreas, and Arjan Vliegenthart. 2009. "Enlarging the Varieties of Capitalism: The Emergence of Dependent Market Economies in East Central Europe." *World Politics* 61, no. 4: 670–702. https://doi.org/10.1017/S0043887109990098.

North, Douglass C. 1990. *Institutions, Institutional Change, and Economic Performance*. Cambridge: Cambridge University Press.

Obstfeld, Maurice, and Poul M. Thomsen. 2016. "The IMF Is Not Asking Greece for More Austerity." International Monetary Fund. https://blogs.imf.org/2016/12/12/the-imf-is-not-asking-greece-for-more-austerity/.

Obwexer, Walter. 2012. "Das System der "Europäischen Wirtschaftsregierung" und die Rechtsnatur ihrer Teile: Sixpack – Euro-Plus-Pakt – Europäisches Semester – Rettungsschirm." *Zeitschrift für öffentliches Recht* 67, no. 2: 209–51. https://doi.org/10.1007/s00708-012-0135-5.

O'Connell, Philip J. 2017. "Unemployment and Labour Market Policy." In *Austerity and Recovery in Ireland: Europe's Poster Child and the Great Recession*, edited by William K. Roche, Philip J. O'Connell, and Andrea Prothero, 232–51. Oxford: Oxford University Press.

– 2019. "Ireland after the Great Recession: Convergence or Divergence?" In *Towards Convergence in Europe: Institutions, Labour and Industrial Relations*, edited by Daniel Vaughan-Whitehead, 175–204. Cheltenham, UK: Edward Elgar Publishing.

OECD. 2013. "OECD Indicators of Employment Protection 2013." https://www.oecd.org/employment/emp/oecdindicatorsofemploymentprotection2013.htm.

– 2015. "Economic Policy Reforms 2015: Going for Growth." OECD. https://doi.org/10.1787/growth-2015-en.

– 2018a. "Indicators of Product Market Regulation." OECD. http://www.oecd.org/economy/reform/indicators-of-product-market-regulation/.

– 2018b. "OECD Economic Surveys: Greece, April 2018." OECD. https://www.oecd.org/eco/surveys/Greece-2018-OECD-economic-survey-overview.pdf.

– 2019. "Budgeting and Public Expenditures in OECD Countries 2019." OECD. https://doi.org/10.1787/9789264307957-en.

OECD/AIAS. 2021. "OECD/AIAS ICTWSS Database." https://www.oecd.org/employment/ictwss-database.htm.

Offe, Claus. 2013. "Europa in der Falle." *Blätter für deutsche und internationale Politik* (January): 67–80. https://www.blaetter.de/ausgabe/2013/januar/europa-in-der-falle.

– 2016. *Europa in der Falle*. Berlin: Suhrkamp.

Pelagidis, Theodōros K., and Michal Mitsopoulos. 2016. *Who's to Blame for Greece? Austerity in Charge of Saving a Broken Economy*. New York: Palgrave Macmillan.

Perez, Sofia A., and Manos Matsaganis. 2018. "The Political Economy of Austerity in Southern Europe." *New Political Economy* 23, no. 2: 192–207. https://doi.org/10.1080/13563467.2017.1370445.

Pisani-Ferry, Jean, André Sapir, and Guntram B Wolff. 2013. "EU-IMF Assistance to Euro Area Countries: An Early Assessment." *Bruegel Blueprint* 19. https://www.bruegel.org/book/eu-imf-assistance-euro-area -countries-early-assessment.

Presse- und Informationsamt der Bundesregierung. 2018. "Erklärung von Meseberg." https://www.diplomatie.gouv.fr/de/frankreichs-beziehungen -zu-deutschland-osterreich-und-der-schweiz/bilaterale-beziehungen -zu-deutschland/neuigkeiten/article/europa-gemeinsame-erklarung -deutschlands-und-frankreichs-19-06-2018.

Priewe, Jan, and Philipp Stachelsky. 2015. "Griechische Depression – wenn die Chefärzte versagen." *WISO direkt* (March). https://library.fes.de/pdf-files /wiso/11271.pdf.

Prodromidou, Alexandra. 2018. "Continuity and Change in Greek Politics in an Age of Austerity." In *Crisis in the Eurozone Periphery: The Political Economies of Greece, Spain, Ireland and Portugal,* edited by Owen Parker and Dimitris Tsarouhas, 181–201. Basingstoke, UK: Palgrave Macmillan.

Puetter, Uwe. 2006. *The Eurogroup: How a Secretive Circle of Finance Ministers Shape European Economic Governance.* Manchester, UK: Manchester University Press.

– 2012. "Europe's Deliberative Intergovernmentalism: The Role of the Council and European Council in EU Economic Governance." *Journal of European Public Policy* 19, no. 2: 161–78. https://doi.org/10.1080/13501763.2011.609743.

Regan, Aidan. 2012a. "The Political Economy of Social Pacts in the EMU: Irish Liberal Market Corporatism in Crisis." *New Political Economy* 17, no. 4: 465–91. https://doi.org/10.1080/13563467.2011.613456.

– 2012b. *The Rise and Fall of Irish Social Partnership: The Political Economy of Institutional Change in European Varieties of Capitalism.* Amsterdam: Rozenberg.

– 2013. "Political Tensions in Euro-Varieties of Capitalism: The Crisis of the Democratic State in Europe." EUI Working Papers. http://cadmus.eui.eu /bitstream/handle/1814/28177/MWP_2013_24.pdf.

– 2014. "What Explains Ireland's Fragile Recovery from the Crisis? The Politics of Comparative Institutional Advantage." *CESifo Forum* 15, no. 2: 26–31. https://www.cesifo.org/en/publications/2014/article-journal /what-explains-irelands-fragile-recovery-crisis-politics.

– 2017. "The Imbalance of Capitalisms in the Eurozone: Can the North and the South of Europe Converge?" In *Comparative European Politics* 15 (October): 969–90. https://doi.org/10.1057/cep.2015.5.

Republic of Ireland. 2010. "The National Recovery Plan 2011–2014." https:// www.gov.ie/en/publication/b9ef4-the-national-recovery-plan-2011-2014/.

Reuters. 2010. "Greek PM Statement on Activating EU/IMF Aid." https://www.reuters.com/article/greece-statement/text-greek-pm-statement-on-activating-eu-imf-aid-idUSLDE63M1AJ20100423.
– 2011. "Trichet Urges Enhanced Europe Standby Fund." *Reuters*, 16 January 2011. https://www.reuters.com/article/uk-eurozone-trichet-commitments/trichet-urges-enhanced-europe-standby-fund-idUKTRE70F21O20110116.
– 2015. "EU's Dombrovskis: EFSM Is Best Option for Short-Term Greek Financing." *Reuters*, 15 July 2015. https://www.reuters.com/article/eurozone-greece-loans-dombrovskis-idINB5N0ZA00X20150715.
– 2020. "Nine EU Leaders Call for Joint Debt Issuance for Coronavirus Spending." *Reuters*, 25 March 2020. https://www.reuters.com/article/us-health-coronavirus-eu-letter-idUSKBN21C1SC.
– 2021. "Italy Senate Backs PM Conte on ESM Reform." *Reuters*, 9 December 2021. https://www.reuters.com/article/italy-politics-senate-idUKR1N2G8006.
Review Group on State Assets and Liabilities. 2011. *Report of the Review Group on State Assets and Liabilities*. https://www.socialjustice.ie/content/publications/review-state-assets-full-texts-and-recommendations-2012.
Roche, William K. 2017. "Workplaces." In *Austerity and Recovery in Ireland: Europe's Poster Child and the Great Recession*, edited by William K. Roche, Philip J. O'Connell, Andrea Prothero, 194–213. Oxford: Oxford University Press.
Roche, William K., Philip J. O'Connell, and Andrea Prothero, eds. 2017a. *Austerity and Recovery in Ireland: Europe's Poster Child and the Great Recession*. Oxford: Oxford University Press.
– 2017b. "Introduction: 'Poster Child' or 'Beautiful Freak'? Austerity and Recovery in Ireland." In *Austerity and Recovery in Ireland: Europe's Poster Child and the Great Recession*, edited by William K. Roche, Philip J. O'Connell, and Andrea Prothero, 1–22. Oxford: Oxford University Press.
Rueschemeyer, Dietrich, and John D. Stevens. 1997. "Comparing Historical Sequences: A Powerful Tool for Causal Analysis." *Comparative Social Research* 16: 55–72. https://www.researchgate.net/publication/281296944_Comparing_Historical_Sequences-A_Powerful_Tool_for_Causal_Analysis.
Sadeh, Tal. 2006. *Sustaining European Monetary Union: Confronting the Costs of Diversity*. Boulder: L. Rienner Publishers.
Safi, Michael, Angela Giuffrida, and Michael Farrer. 2020. "Coronavirus: Italy Bans Any Movement inside Country as Toll Nears 5,500." *Guardian*, 22 March 2020. https://www.theguardian.com/world/2020/mar/22/italian-pm-warns-of-worst-crisis-since-ww2-as-coronavirus-deaths-leap-by-almost-800.
Salines, Marion, Gabriel Glöckler, and Zbigniew Truchlewski. 2012. "Existential Crisis, Incremental Response: The Eurozone's Dual Institutional Evolution 2007–2011." *Journal of European Public Policy* 19, no. 5: 665–81. https://doi.org/10.1080/13501763.2011.646777.

Sawyer, Malcolm C. 2017. *Can the Euro Be Saved?* Malden, MA: Polity.

Schäfer, Armin. 2005. *Die neue Unverbindlichkeit: wirtschaftspolitische Koordinierung in Europa*. Frankfurt am Main: Campus.

Scharpf, Fritz W. 2018. "There Is an Alternative: A Two-Tier European Currency Community." MPIfG Discussion Paper, 18/7. https://pure.mpg .de/rest/items/item_2626693_13/component/file_2626695/content.

Schäuble, Wolfgang. 2010. "Why Europe's Monetary Union Faces Its Biggest Crisis." *Financial Times*, 11 March 2010. https://www.ft.com/content /2a205b88-2d41-11df-9c5b-00144feabdc0.

Schelkle, Waltraud. 2015. "Fiscal Integration by Default." In *Beyond the Regulatory Polity? The European Integration of Core State Powers*, edited by Philipp Genschel and Markus Jachtenfuchs, 105–23. Oxford: Oxford University Press.

Schlosser, Pierre. 2019. *Europe's New Fiscal Union*. Cham, Switzerland: Palgrave Macmillan.

Schmidt, Vivien A. 2002. *The Futures of European Capitalism*. Oxford: Oxford University Press.

– 2007. "Bringing the State Back into the Varieties of Capitalism and Discourse Back into the Explanation of Change." CES Germany & Europe Working Papers, no. 07.3. Center for European Studies. http://aei.pitt. edu/9281/.

– 2008. "Bringing Ideas and Discourse Back into the Explanation of Change in Varieties of Capitalism and Welfare States." Working Paper no. 2. The Centre for Global Political Economy. https://www.sussex.ac.uk/webteam /gateway/file.php?name=cgpe-wp02-vivien-a-schmidt.pdf&site=359.

– 2009. "Putting the Political Back into Political Economy by Bringing the State Back in Yet Again." *World Politics* 61, no. 3: 516–46. https://doi. org/10.1017 /S0043887109000173.

– 2010. "Taking Ideas and Discourse Seriously: Explaining Change through Discursive Institutionalism as the Fourth 'New Institutionalism.'" *European Political Science Review* 2, no. 1: 1–25. https://doi.org/10.1017 /S175577390999021X.

Schmidt, Vivien A. and Claudio M. Radaelli. 2004. "Policy Change and Discourse in Europe: Conceptual and Methodological Issues." *West European Politics* 27, no. 2: 183–210. https://doi.org/10.1080/0140238042000214874.

Schneider, Martin R., and Mihai Paunescu. 2012. "Changing Varieties of Capitalism and Revealed Comparative Advantages from 1990 to 2005: A Test of the Hall and Soskice Claims." *Socio-Economic Review* 10, no. 4: 731–53. https://doi.org/10.1093/ser/mwr038.

Schulten, Thorsten. 2015. "Chancen für einen Wiederaufbau? Die Zukunft des griechischen Tarifvertragssystems nach dem dritten Memorandum." Friedrich Ebert Stiftung. http://library.fes.de/pdf-files/id-moe/11610.pdf.

Schulten, Thorsten, and Torsten Müller. 2015. "European Economic Governance and Its Intervention in National Wage Development and Collective Bargaining." In *Divisive Integration. The Triumph of Failed Ideas in Europe – Revisited*, edited by Stefan Lehndorff, 331–63. Brussels: VSA-Verlag.

Schwarzer, Daniela. 2015. "Building the Euro Area's Debt Crisis Management Capacity with the IMF." *Review of International Political Economy* 22, no. 3: 599–625. https://doi.org/10.1080/09692290.2014.965263.

Schweiger, Christian. 2014. *The EU and the Global Financial Crisis: New Varieties of Capitalism*. Cheltenham, UK: Edward Elgar.

Seikel, Daniel. 2017. "Verrechtlichung und Entpolitisierung marktschaffender Politik als politikfeldübergreifender Trend in der EU." *Leviathan* 45, no. 3: 335–56. https://doi.org/10.5771/0340-0425-2017-3-335.

Seralidou, Rodothea. 2019. "Mindestlohn in Griechenland: 'Es zählt jeder Cent.'" Deutschlandfunk, Cologne, 2 Februrary 2019. https://www.deutschlandfunk.de/mindestlohn-in-griechenland-es-zaehlt-jeder-cent.795.de.html?dram:article_id=442031.

Shepsle, James G. 2006. "Rational Choice Institutionalism." In *The Oxford Handbook of Political Institutions*, edited by R.A.W. Rhodes, Sarah A. Binder, and Bert A. Rockman, 23–38. Oxford: Oxford University Press.

Single Resolution Board. 2021. "The Single Resolution Fund." https://www.srb.europa.eu/en/content/single-resolution-fund.

Sinn, Hans-Werner. 2014. *The Euro Trap: On Bursting Bubbles, Budgets, and Beliefs*. Oxford: Oxford University Press.

Spanou, Calliope. 2018. "EU Coordination in Greece: 'Forced' Europeanization under the MoU?" In *Managing the Euro Crisis: National EU Policy Coordination in the Debtor Countries*, edited by Sabrina Ragone, 13–38. Abingdon, Oxon: Routledge.

– 2020. "External Influence on Structural Reform: Did Policy Conditionality Strengthen Reform Capacity in Greece?" *Public Policy and Administration* 35, no. 2: 135–57. https://doi.org/10.1177/0952076718772008.

Steinmo, Sven. 2008. "Historical Institutionalism." In *Approaches and Methodologies in the Social Sciences. A Pluralist Perspective*, edited by Donatella della Porta and Michael Keating, 118–38. Cambridge: Cambridge University Press.

Steinmo, Sven, Kathleen Ann Thelen, and Frank Longstreth, eds. 1992. *Structuring Politics: Historical Institutionalism in Comparative Analysis*. Cambridge: Cambridge University Press.

Strange, Susan. 1996. *The Retreat of the State: The Diffusion of Power in the World Economy*. Cambridge: Cambridge University Press.

Streeck, Wolfgang. 2013a. Gekaufte Zeit: Die vertagte Krise des demokratischen Kapitalismus. Berlin: Suhrkamp Verlag.

— 2013b. "Vom DM-Nationalismus zum Euro-Patriotismus? Eine Replik auf Jürgen Habermas." *Blätter für deutsche und internationale Politik* (September): 75–92.

— 2013c. "Was nun, Europa? Kapitalismus ohne Demokratie oder Demokratie ohne Kapitalismus." *Blätter für deutsche und internationale Politik* (April): 57–68.

Streeck, Wolfgang, and Kathleen Thelen. 2005. "Introduction: Institutional Change in Advanced Political Economies." In *Beyond Continuity: Institutional Change in Advanced Political Economies*, edited by Wolfgang Streeck and Kathleen Thelen, 1–39. Oxford: Oxford University Press.

Stuckler, David, and Sanjay Basu. 2013. *The Body Economic: Why Austerity Kills: Recessions, Budget Battles, and the Politics of Life and Death*. New York: Basic Books.

Stützle, Ingo. 2013. *Austerität als politisches Projekt: von der monetären Integration Europas zur Eurokrise*. Münster: Westfälisches Dampfboot.

Tesche, Tobias. 2021. "Pandemic Politics: The European Union in Times of the Coronavirus Emergency." *JCMS: Journal of Common Market Studies* 60, no. 2: 480–96. https://doi.org/10.1111/jcms.13303.

The Czech Republic/Denmark/Estonia/Finland/Ireland/Latvia/Lithuania /The Netherlands/Sweden/Slovakia. 2018. "ESM Reform – Shared Views of the Finance Ministers from the Czech Republic, Denmark, Estonia, Finland, Ireland, Latvia, Lithuania, the Netherlands, Sweden and Slovakia." Department of Finance, Government of Ireland. https://www.finance.gov .ie/updates/esm-reform-shared-views-of-the-finance-ministers-from -the-czech-republic-denmark-estonia-finland-ireland-latvia-lithuania-the -netherlands-sweden-and-slovakia/.

Thelen, Kathleen. 1999. "Historical Institutionalism in Comparative Politics." *Annual Review of Political Science* 2, no. 1: 369–404. https://doi.org/10.1146 /annurev.polisci.2.1.369.

— 2009. "Institutional Change in Advanced Economies." *British Journal of Industrial Relations* 47, no. 3: 471–98. https://doi.org/10.1111/j.1467-8543 .2009.00746.x.

— 2010. "Beyond Comparative Statics: Historical-Institutional Approaches to Stability and Change in the Political Economy of Labor." In *Oxford Handbook of Comparative Institutional Analysis*, edited by Glenn Morgan, John Campbell, Colin Crouch, Ove Kaj Petersen, and Richard Whitley, 41–62. Oxford: Oxford University Press.

— 2012. "Varieties of Capitalism: Trajectories of Liberalization and the New Politics of Social Solidarity." *Annual Review of Political Science* 15, no. 1: 137–59. https://doi.org/10.1146/annurev-polisci-070110-122959.

— 2014. *Varieties of Liberalization and the New Politics of Social Solidarity*. Cambridge: Cambridge University Press.

Thelen, Kathleen, and Sven Steinmo. 1992. "Historical Institutionalism in Comparative Politics." In *Structuring Politics: Historical Institutionalism in Comparative Analysis*, edited by Kathleen Thelen and Sven Steinmo, 1–32. Cambridge: Cambridge University Press.

Theodoropoulou, Sotiria. 2015. "National Social and Labour Market Policy Reforms in the Shadow of EU Bail-Out Conditionality: The Cases of Greece and Portugal." *Comparative European Politics* 13, no. 1: 29–55. https://doi.org /10.1057/cep.2014.40.

– 2016. "Severe Pain, Very Little Gain: Internal Devalutation and Rising Unemployment in Greece." In *Unemployment, Internal Devaluation and Labour Market Deregulation in Europe*, edited by Martin Myant, Sotiria Theodoropoulou, and Agnieszka Piasna, 25–58. Brussels: ETUI.

–, ed. 2018. *Labour Market Policies in the Era of Pervasive Austerity: A European Perspective*. Bristol: Policy Press.

Thomsen, Poul M. 2019. "The IMF and the Greek Crisis: Myths and Realities." International Monetary Fund. 30 September 2019. https://www.imf.org /en/News/Articles/2019/10/01/sp093019-The-IMF-and-the-Greek-Crisis -Myths-and-Realities.

Tilly, Charles. 2001. "Mechanisms in Political Processes." *Annual Review of Political Science* 4, no. 1: 21–41. https://doi.org/10.1146/annurev.polisci.4.1.21.

Tooze, J. Adam. 2018. *Crashed: How a Decade of Financial Crises Changed the World*. New York: Viking.

– 2021. *Welt im Lockdown: die globale Krise und ihre Folgen*. München: C.H. Beck.

Troost, Axel, and Rainald Ötsch. 2019. *Umsteuern in Athen: Griechische Steuerpolitik under SYRIZA und den Memoranden*. Berlin: Rosa-Luxemburg-Stiftung.

Tugwell, Paul. 2018. "Are Greek Leftists Really 'Stepping Up' the Privatization Drive?" Bloomberg. 22 August 2018. https://www.bloomberg.com/news /articles/2018-08-22/greek-progress-on-privatizations-seen-as-key-to-post -bailout-era.

Van Gyes, Guy, Thorsten Schulten, and Torsten Müller. 2016. "Einleitung." In *Lohnpolitik unter europäischer Economic Governance: Alternative Strategien für inklusives Wachsum*, edited by Thorsten Schulten, Torsten Müller, and Guy Van Gyes, 9–19. Hamburg: VSA-Verlag.

Verdun, Amy. 1996. "An 'Asymmetrical' Economic and Monetary Union in the EU: Perceptions of Monetary Authorities and Social Partners." *Journal of European Integration* 20, no. 1: 59–81. https://doi.org/10.1080 /07036339608429045.

– 1999. "The Role of the Delors Committee in the Creation of EMU: An Epistemic Community?" *Journal of European Public Policy* 6, no. 2: 308–28. https://doi.org/10.1080/135017699343739.

– 2002. *European Responses to Globalization and Financial Market Integration: Perceptions of Economic and Monetary Union in Britain, France and Germany*. Basingstoke, UK: Palgrave Macmillan.

– 2013. "The Building of Economic Governance in the European Union." *Transfer: European Review of Labour and Research* 19, no. 1: 23–35. https://doi.org/10.1177/1024258912469343.

– 2015. "A Historical Institutionalist Explanation of the EU's Responses to the Euro Area Financial Crisis." *Journal of European Public Policy* 22, no. 2: 219–37. https://doi.org/10.1080/13501763.2014.994023.

– 2018. "Institutional Architecture of the Euro Area." *JCMS: Journal of Common Market Studies* 56, no. S1: 74–84. https://doi.org/10.1111/jcms.12773.

– 2021. "The Greatest of the Small? The Netherlands, the New Hanseatic League and the Frugal Four." *German Politics* 31, no. 2: 302–22. https://doi.org/10.1080/09644008.2021.2003782.

Verdun, Amy, and Jonathan Zeitlin. 2018. "Introduction: The European Semester as a New Architecture of EU Socioeconomic Governance in Theory and Practice." *Journal of European Public Policy*, 25, no. 2: 137–48. https://doi.org/10.1080/13501763.2017.1363807.

Visser, Jelle. 2016. *ICTWSS Database*. Version 5.1. Amsterdam: Amsterdam Institute for Advanced Labour Studies.

– 2019a. "Data Base on Institutional Characteristics of Trade Unions, Wage Setting, State Intervention and Social Pacts, 1960–2017 (ICTWSS)." Amsterdam Institute for Advanced Labour Studies AIAS. https://aias.s3.eu-central-1.amazonaws.com/website/uploads/ICTWSS_v6_codebook_final.pdf.

-. 2019b. "ICTWSS Database." Version 6.0. Amsterdam: Amsterdam Institute for Advanced Labour Studies.

Wallace, Joseph, Patrick Gunnigle, Gerard McMahon, and Michelle O'Sullivan. 2013. *Industrial Relations in Ireland*. Dublin: Gill & Macmillan.

Walsh, Frank. 2015. "Labour Market Measures in Ireland 2008–13: The Crisis and Beyond." International Labour Organisation. https://www.ilo.org/wcmsp5/groups/public/---dgreports/---inst/documents/publication/wcms_449928.pdf.

Walter, Stefanie. 2016. "Crisis Politics in Europe: Why Austerity Is Easier to Implement in Some Countries than in Others." *Comparative Political Studies* 49, no. 7: 841–73. https://doi.org/10.1177/0010414015617967.

Werner Report. 1970. "Report to the Council and the Commission on the Realization by Stages of Economic and Monetary Union in the Community." Luxembourg, 8 October 1970. http://ec.europa.eu/archives/emu_history/documentation/chapter5/19701008en72realisationbystage.pdf.

Whitston, Colin. 2014. "The Reform of Joint Labour Committees – The Re-Commodification of Labour?" *Industrial Relations Journal* 45, no. 5: 409–23. https://doi.org/10.1111/irj.12068.

Wickham, James. 2014. "Nach dem Ende der Party: Irlands Beschäftigungsmodell und das merkwürdige Überleben des Sozialstaats." In *Spaltende Integration: Der Triumph gescheiterter Ideen in Europa - revisited. Zehn Länderstudien*, edited by Stefan Lehndorff, 109–30. Hamburg: VSA-Verlag.

– 2015. "Irish Paradoxes: The Bursting of the Bubbles and the Curious Survival of Social Cohesion." In *Divisive Integration: The Triumph of Failed Ideas in Europe – Revisited*, edited by Stefan Lehndorff, 127–48. Brussels: ETUIS.

Young, Brigitte, and Willi Semmler. 2011. "The European Sovereign Debt Crisis: Is Germany to Blame?" *German Politics and Society* 29, no. 1: 1–24. https://doi.org/10.3167/gps.2011.290101.

Zagermann, Dennis. 2019. "The Role of the ECB during the Euro Crisis: The Case of the OMT Program." In *Europeanisation and Renationalisation: Learning from Crises for Innovation and Development*, edited by Anne Jenichen and Ulrike Liebert, 199–214. Leverkusen: Barbara Budrich.

Zeitlin, Jonathan, and Bart Vanhercke. 2018. "Socializing the European Semester: EU Social and Economic Policy Co-Ordination in Crisis and Beyond." *Journal of European Public Policy* 25, no. 2: 149–74. https://doi.org/10.1080/13501763.2017.1363269.

Index

European Union Studies

Catherine Gegout, *European Foreign and Security Policy: States, Power, Institutions, and American Hegemony*

Frédéric Mérand, Martial Foucault, and Bastien Irondelle, eds., *European Security since the Fall of the Berlin Wall*

Trygve Ugland, *Jean Monnet and Canada: Early Travels and the Idea of European Unity*

Nancy A. Vamvakas, *Europeanizing Greece: The Effects of Ten Years of EU Structural Funds, 1989–1999*

H. Tolga Bolukbasi, *Euro-Austerity and Welfare States: Comparative Political Economy of Reform during the Maastricht Decade*

Dennis Zagermann, *Remaking European Political Economies: Financial Assistance in the Euro Crisis*